35

Metrics

How to Improve Key Business Results

Martin Klubeck

Apress®

Metrics: How to Improve Key Business Results

ISBN-13 (pbk): 978-1-4302-3726-6

ISBN-13 (electronic): 978-1-4302-3727-3

President and Publisher: Paul Manning
Lead Editor: Jeff Olson
Technical Reviewer: Russ Cheesman
Editorial Board: Steve Anglin, Mark Beckner, Ewan Buckingham, Gary Cornell, Morgan Ertel, Jonathan Gennick, Jonathan Hassell, Robert Hutchinson, Michelle Lowman, James Markham, Matthew Moodie, Jeff Olson, Jeffrey Pepper, Douglas Pundick, Ben Renow-Clarke, Dominic Shakeshaft, Gwenan Spearing, Matt Wade, Tom Welsh
Coordinating Editor: Annie Beck
Copy Editor: Kimberly Burton
Compositor: Mary Sudul
Indexer: SPi Global
Artists: Martin Klubeck and Alyssa Klubeck
Cover Designer: Anna Ishchenko

Distributed to the book trade worldwide by Springer Science+Business Media New York, 233 Spring Street, 6th Floor, New York, NY 10013. Phone 1-800-SPRINGER, fax (201) 348-4505, e-mail orders-ny@springer-sbm.com, or visit www.springeronline.com.

For information on translations, please e-mail rights@apress.com, or visit www.apress.com.

Apress and friends of ED books may be purchased in bulk for academic, corporate, or promotional use. eBook versions and licenses are also available for most titles. For more information, reference our Special Bulk Sales–eBook Licensing web page at www.apress.com/bulk-sales.

To all those struggling to improve their organizations, their processes, or themselves. Spend your time chasing your dreams, not data.

To my father: I miss you greatly. My major hope through my writing is to make you proud.

Contents

About the Author ix

About the Technical Reviewer x

Acknowledgments xi

Metrics: The Basics, An Introduction xiii

Chapter 1: Establishing a Common Language: Data, and Measures, and Information, OH MY! 1

Chapter 2: Designing Metrics: The How 25

Chapter 3: Planning a Good Metric: Where to Begin 57

Chapter 4: Using Metrics as Indicators 83

Chapter 5: Using the Answer Key: A Shortcut 97

Chapter 6: Start with Effectiveness 119

Chapter 7: Triangulation: Essential to Creating Effective Metrics 137

Chapter 8: Expectations: How to View Metrics in a Meaningful Way 155

Chapter 9: Creating and Interpreting the Metrics Report Card 171

Chapter 10: Final Product: The Metrics Report Card 211

Chapter 11: Advanced Metrics 243

Chapter 12: Creating the Service Catalog: How to Enhance the Report Card 271

Chapter 13: Establishing Standards and Benchmarks 283

Chapter 14: Respecting the Power of Metrics 293

Chapter 15: Avoiding the Research Trap 309

Chapter 16: Embracing Your Organization's Uniqueness 319

Appendix: Tools and Resources 331

Index 345

About the Author

Martin Klubeck is a strategy and planning consultant at the University of Notre Dame and a recognized expert in the field of practical metrics. He holds a master's degree from Webster University in human resources development and a bachelor's in computer science from Chapman University. He is coauthor of *Why Organizations Struggle So Hard to Improve So Little* and numerous articles on metrics. His passion for simplifying the complex has led to the development of a simple system for developing meaningful metrics. Klubeck is also the founder of the Consortium for the Establishment of Information Technology Performance Standards, a nonprofit organization focused on providing much-needed standards for measures.

About the Technical Reviewer

Russ Cheesman is a senior information technology professional and consultant with experiences in all phases of the System Development Life Cycle. Much of his career had been devoted to enabling IT solutions for business problems and/or opportunities. He has served as an IT manager and practitioner in many industry sectors, including banking/financial, manufacturing, construction, retail, pharmaceutical, telecommunications, and health care. Mr. Cheesman, in recent years, has been practicing business performance measurement and management within several IT and health care organizations through the use of business strategy, balanced scorecards, metrics, key performance indicators, and business analytical systems.

Mr. Cheesman was happy to serve as the senior technical reviewer for this book and related concepts on metrics, and looks forward to its release and subsequent value to all those individuals, groups, and organizations that desire improvement, continuous maturation, and peak performance.

Acknowledgments

The purpose of an acknowledgment, as I understand it, is to let those people who helped make this achievement possible know that I didn't forget their contributions. This chore makes this easily the most stressful part of writing a book.

I don't want to forget any of my friends or colleagues who helped me by reviewing, critiquing, or suggesting edits to the work as it was in progress, especially: Don Padgett, Danita Leese, Leah Lang, Keith (Mac) McIntosh, Marin Stanek, and my brother Irving. Thanks for the short-notice reads. Thanks for the kind words. And thanks for being there.

Of course, Russ Cheesman has to be thanked for his work as my technical reviewer. Although Russ and I disagreed as often as we agreed about metrics and their use, when asked for a recommendation, I immediately thought of Russ for the job. His honest and passionate position, his large knowledge base, and his expertise made him an easy choice. Thanks, Russ, for your hard work, your many suggestions, and your honest appraisals.

I want to give a special thanks to Michael Langthorne. Not only were you my most dependable reviewer, but your early and consistent encouragement to take this journey, on my own, was instrumental to me starting and finishing this work. I appreciate your help, guidance, and gentle but steady shoves very much. Thanks. I truly could not have done this without you.

I also want to thank Jeff Olson, Kimberly Burton, and Annie Beck. Although you made up the Apress editorial team, and were "just doing your jobs," I can't say I saw you that way. I greatly appreciate your help. You were honest, consistent, and fair. You were focused on producing the best product possible for Apress while showing sincere concern for my position as an author. Someday, if the chance ever arrives, I'm buying the first round.

Last, but as the saying goes, not least, I want to thank my family. Especially my wife, Kristine. This time around, you successfully feigned interest in my progress, if not in the work itself. I appreciate the effort and I love you dearly. Alyssa, thanks for your help with the fairy tales and allowing me to use your art work for the book. I look forward to seeing your name on more jacket covers. I love you.

And a final, special thank you to you, whoever you are, reading this book. You are special—you must be because no one reads the acknowledgements unless they think they'll find their name listed. So you must be one of the rare people who read books from cover to cover. That means you may also be the type of reader who will use the material within these pages. You may also be the type of person who will share your thoughts, likes, and dislikes. So, here's to hoping I hear from you and thanks in advance for any feedback you choose to share. I hope this book helps you navigate the sometimes dangerous waters of developing metrics.

Note: While I have worked hard to provide you, the reader, with real examples (real situations, interactions, experiences, measures, and data), I had to temper that effort with protecting the privacy and data owned by others. To this end, I have, where necessary, blended and combined individuals into composites. I have also done the same with data. As you will read, I fully believe that data is "owned" by the provider(s) of that data, so I have protected the identities and data of those whose experiences I used for much of this book.

Metrics: The Basics
An Introduction

Of all the possible organizational-improvement tools, metrics stands out for me as the most requested, misunderstood, feared—and useful. Defining metrics from a high level requires that I give you the What, Why, When, Where, Who, and How.

What

Metrics can be defined in many ways. I spend the beginning of the book offering a common language for defining and using metrics. For me, metrics are a means of telling a complete story for the purpose of improving something. Usually, the idea is to improve an organization. Sometimes, though, you will want to focus on improving a process. In the end, anything you improve should be able to align back to improvements that help the organization.

Metrics are a tool for improvement. By their nature, metrics use different levels of information (data, measures, information, and other metrics) to tell a story. Although I always strive to make this story comprehensive, it's nearly impossible to capture everything. In most cases, I try to capture enough of what's important to help with the improvement.

Metrics affect the improvement effort by helping you determine what was wrong in the first place, how well your efforts have worked (did you improve and did you improve as much as you wanted?), and what the new environment looks like after the change. I say "change" because improvement requires change. It doesn't have to be drastic. It could mean that you do something new, you stop doing something, or you do something differently. But, improvement doesn't come about without some change.

Albert Einstein said, "The definition of insanity is doing the same things, the same way, and expecting a different result."

The following are just a few of the things a metrics program can help you do:

- Improve company "health" in a variety of areas

    - Improve customer satisfaction
    - Improve product/service value
    - Improve employee satisfaction
    - Improve process efficiency
    - Improve strategy, planning, and execution

- Provide a basis for change

    - What to change
    - When to change
    - How to change

- Lay a foundation for understanding your organization by providing insights into

    - strengths
    - problems
    - weaknesses
    - opportunities

Metrics are about change for the purpose of improvement. At least that's how I use them. I offer in the pages to follow a means for developing a metrics program for improving a large area of an organization. I also offer guidance on how to develop individual metrics to improve specific things. I'm an idealist, and you'll see that reflected in my belief that metrics can be a powerful tool for improvement.

Why

Why metrics? To improve. I know I've already stated that. But, why metrics specifically? Why not use any of the other methods du jour (TQM, Six Sigma,

Balanced Scorecard, etc.)? The funny thing is, any of the methods you choose will require you to use metrics—or at least the components of metrics (data, measures, or information). As a foundation, these improvement methods want you to first measure your existing state so that after you implement the methodology for improvement, you will see how well the improvement procedures worked. All of these methods also want you to measure the amount of time, money, and effort that went into the improvement effort. But none of that will actually help you improve the thing you want to improve!

Metrics help you in some basic ways that make it an important tool for improvement on its own accord. Metrics will provide insights into the thing you want to improve—be it a product, service, or process. This insight is valuable to those doing the job—fulfilling the need or providing the service. It helps them see their efforts in a new light, often in a more complete picture. It will help them find ways to improve. It will also help them see the benefits they've reaped. It will provide cherished feedback that the team can use to make continuous improvement a reality (instead of the latest catch-phrase).

Metrics also provides insights for upper management. It allows the team leader to market the improvement effort to those who control the funding. It shines a light on your efforts so you can gain support for the improvement efforts.

It also allows you to share your efforts with your customers in ways they easily understand. They gain insight to how things are changing for the better. Look at any new product release (I especially like Apple's semi-annual announcements) and notice the amount of metrics sprinkled throughout.

Metrics provide insight. They also provide a level of legitimacy to your argument. All other things being equal, data is a tie breaker. If you and another department have competing requests for resources, the one with data wins.

When

Ideally, you'd not undertake a metrics effort of any significant scale until your organization could show that it was not suffering from organizational immaturity—the inability to take on enterprise-wide change. But, that's only a prerequisite for implementing a program organization-wide. If you are in charge of a department or unit and you want to implement a department-wide metrics program, you only have to ensure that your unit is capable of the change. If you provide one or two services or products, you shouldn't have a problem implementing a metrics program. Remember, metrics are only a tool for improvement, so you'll need to implement other improvement tools along with metrics. Metrics can tell you where to focus your efforts. Metrics can tell you how successful your efforts are. But metrics on their own are not a set of solutions.

Chances are very good that you already collect data and measures. You may have automated tools that track, collect, and even spit out reports full of data and measures. You may feed information into an annual report. You may already fulfill requests for specific measures. Depending on your industry, there may be well-worn standards that have been used for years (if not decades). These are not necessarily metrics per my definition, nor are creating such standards the intent of this book. Those data and measures are reported, but not used. They aren't used to improve a process, product, or service.

It may be time for you to start using your information for your own benefit. It may be time for you to develop a metrics program. The major question you have to ask is, are you ready, willing, and able to change? Do you want to improve?

You'll learn in this book that part of the "when" is collecting information on the thing you want to improve *before* you attempt to make it better—just as good researchers do. So, the when is before you start, during, and after your improvement efforts.

Where

The metrics program should reside with the owner of the data. I spend 80 percent of my workday developing metrics for others. I coach my customers through the design, creation, implementation, and maintenance of the metrics. In many cases, I also produce and publish their metrics. But I happily tell anyone who asks that I don't own any of them. I am just helping the owners produce them. They are not mine. My greatest successes are when I can transfer the maintenance and publishing of the metrics to someone on the team who owns the metric. I then transition to a consultant role, helping them use and improve the metrics. This transition takes time—normally because of either a lack of skill or resources. But having the owner of the metric take over the production, maintenance, and publishing of them is always the ultimate goal for me.

So the metrics need to eventually reside in the data owner's domain. That can be on their office walls. It can be on their shared computer drive. It can be on their web site. That's where it belongs. But metrics show up in other places like annual reports, monthly meetings, and public web sites.

The publication of metrics will be up to the owner. The decision of where it will be published should be a careful decision based on the use of the metrics and the need for others to have access to the information. The more mature the organization, the more comfortable it will be sharing the metrics. Many organizations are not mature enough to share metrics with their peers, their customers, and definitely not the public.

Who

I fulfill part of the who question on a daily basis. I am the producer of many of the metrics my organization uses. I am also the lead designer, collector, analyst, and publisher. But as stated in the Where section, I am always looking to transfer as much of this as possible to the metrics owner.

Who are the owners? As I will explain in detail within this book, the owners of the metrics are primarily those who are delivering the product, service, or carrying out the process. But ownership can be spread across the entire organization, depending on how you define the item being measured.

The key here isn't so much who owns the metric but in who doesn't. Don't exclude the frontline worker. Don't think the metric belongs to the CEO or upper management. If the metric is reported at those lofty heights, it doesn't mean they should only reside there. Remember the purpose of metrics. Unless the CEO and top managers are the ones improving their processes (and they rarely directly deliver products or services), then you have to include as owners the people carrying out the work—the ones that will be responsible for making the improvements actual work. How much harm can be done if upper management finds out that a department was using metrics for improvement but hadn't shared them upstream? Some. But now imagine how much trouble can arise if a department finds out that upper management had been reviewing metrics about their processes, services, or products and they didn't even know. Will that significantly harm the organization? I'm willing to bet it will.

If upper management wants metrics on a department, unit, process, service, or product, all of those involved should be included in the distribution of those metrics. They should also be involved in the design, creation, and publication of them.

The simple answer to "who?" is this: everyone in the organization, with the frontline workers being the primary "who."

How

Well, that's what the book is for. I offer you a comprehensive set of guidelines for developing a metrics program or specific metrics for improvement. I call them guidelines because "rules" would mean that I'm offering the only right way. As with most things, there's more than one right way to develop metrics. The language, processes, and tools I offer are a result of more than twenty years of experience. That experience was full of successes and failures. I learned from both and am happy to share the results so you won't have to fall into the same holes I did. And if you're already in one of those holes, my advice is simple: stop digging.

What You'll Find Inside

Having a common language for metrics and its components is an essential foundation for the conversation we'll engage in throughout this book. While putting this book together, and while thinking about all of the tools you can use to make your analysis and publishing of metrics easier, it struck me that there is another important distinction between metrics and other tools for improvement. Besides the definitions of data, measures, information, and metrics, I want to share another view of what I believe metrics are.

First and foremost, for me, metrics are in and of themselves tools for improvement. Even when using metrics to keep track of progress or predict future trends, metrics should be seen as a means for improvement. But that's not enough to distinguish it from a mass of other tools out there. I've used many tools to develop improvement programs or to solve organizational problems. Total Quality Management, the Capability Maturity Model, Lean, and Lean Six Sigma are a few. Each of these improvement methodologies also uses data and measures. Six Sigma uses data throughout its processes, not only to measure improvement but to determine what to improve. There are also measures of success and goal attainment. There are even measures which turn ordinary wishes into SMART (specific, measurable, attainable, realistic, and time-bound) goals.

Many of the tools designed around metrics are for statistical analysis. These powerful tools can be used to determine relationships between different data, causal relationships, and even determine the accuracy of data.

But "metrics," for me, are much more and in some ways a bit less than a statistical analysis tool.

Metrics are not a statistician's dream or an analyst's favorite tool. The school of statistical analysis is much larger and deeper than I plan on digging. A common disclaimer I offer when teaching on metrics is that I am not a statistician, nor will the course include statistics. In these ways, metrics are a bit less.

But metrics are in many ways much more than statistics. They are a means of telling stories, and of providing valuable insights. Metrics are a tool for pointing out the correct direction to take when at a cross-roads—a cross-roads between one improvement effort and another.

Metrics, for me, are the cornerstone of an organizational development program and/or a tool for answering the most important organizational questions.

It is these minor distinctions between metrics and other measurement-based tools for improvement that make this book a necessity. There are courses on statistics (one of my colleagues came to metrics by way of being a statistician), books on various analytical tools, and software tools developed for this purpose (SPSS, MiniTab, and Sigma XL, to name three). But there is little written (well) or taught about the use of metrics. This deficiency has been partially addressed by Kaplan and Norton with their Balanced Scorecard methodology and by Dr. Dean Spitzer's book *Transforming Performance Measurement* (AMACOM, 2007). I intend to take their efforts to their logical and necessary next step—making the design, creation, and use of metrics practical for anyone.

Metrics will make it possible for you to use data, measures, and information to improve your organization and lead to the key business results you need to be a success.

I hope this book helps you to develop metrics that in turn help you improve your organization. Regardless of the size or mission of your organization, metrics can be a powerful tool for improvement, and this book will make metrics as simple as possible.

Establishing A Common Language

Data, and Measures, and Information, OH MY!

It is important to establish a simple, easy-to-understand language so that everyone, regardless of their experience or education, can understand the benefits metrics can provide. I believe a lack of a common language causes more problems in business (and life) than anything else. Developing a shared vocabulary is the first step in ensuring success.

This book presents many concepts that may be new, but I don't see the need to add a new set of words to crowd the already full glossary of organizational development. Instead, I intend to use very common words, plain English as it were, to help make what seems complex into something very simple and straightforward.

Let's start with a story to help get us in the proper frame of mind.

The Three Little Pigs Go Large

There I was, trying to remember a fairy tale so I could get my three-year-old to sleep. She demanded a story, but being on the road without any of her books meant I had to remember one. Well, I have a terrible memory for stories—but an unfailing memory for lessons I've taught. So, like any good father, I improvised. What better way to get her to fall asleep than to tell a story about metrics?

The Story

After effectively dealing with their landlord (Mr. Wolf), the three little pigs settled into a life of luxury and over-indulgence. Three years passed, finding the pigs each living in squalor, dangerously overweight (even for a pig), and in failing health. Each visited his respective doctor. Each doctor came to the same prognosis: this pig was on the fast track to an early barbecue. The pigs did not eat well, sleep enough, exercise, nor did they pay attention to the signs their bodies were giving them. The doctors knew the pigs must change their lifestyles or they would die.

The First Little Pig

Unfortunately for the pigs, the doctors were also very much different. The first little pig's doctor told him that his health was failing and that he would have to change his lifestyle. The little pig needed to get serious about his health. The doctor sent the little pig away with a diet plan, an exercise plan, and an appointment to return in 12 months.

The first little pig was dutifully scared by his doctor's warnings, so he worked hard to change. He stopped eating unhealthy foods. He exercised daily. He even started going to sleep early. After one month, the first little pig felt great. He hadn't felt this good in years! He decided to celebrate. He went out with the lamb twins and partied all night. He had a feast that was followed by an ice cream eating contest (which he won). At about 3 AM he made it home and fell asleep, content on his bed. The next day he forgot to exercise. It was easy to get out of the habit. Eventually, he only exercised on weekends, reasoning that he was too busy during the week. By the end of the next month he was eating poorly again—not as badly as before—but not as good as he should have.

At the end of the year, when the first little pig returned to the doctor, he was shocked to hear that the doctor was disappointed.

> "But Doc, I did what you said," the first little pig pleaded. "I exercise and I eat better. I even go to sleep earlier. I know I'm healthier . . . I feel better than I did last year."

"Yes, but your weight did not improve enough. You may be eating better, but not well enough. You may be sleeping more, but still not enough. Your health is deteriorating overall ... and I fear that you are going to die if you don't change your ways."

The doctor gave the first little pig a new diet and exercise program. He even signed the first little pig up for a spinning class and prescribed medication. The doctor gave the little pig another appointment for the following year and wished him well. The first little pig was dutifully frightened by all of this and swore by his chinny chin chin (which was pretty large) that he'd do better.

This time the first little pig stayed on course. He exercised regularly and ate only healthy foods. When he was hungry he ate carrots, or celery, or nonfat yogurt. He attended the spinning classes every week, like clockwork. Unfortunately, with no way to measure his progress, the first little pig didn't know how well he was doing. After seven months, he felt better, but his anxiety about his health created so much stress that he had a stroke. While he had improved his health, he had not improved it enough to weather the physical needs a stroke put on his system. He died a month later. The first little pig's doctor was sad to learn of his death. He shed a tear as he removed the upcoming appointment from the calendar.

The Second Little Pig

The second little pig's doctor understood the importance of metrics. He was a good doctor who communicated well with his patients. He felt like a father to his patients and sought to help them become healthier. When the doctor looked over the second little pig's charts, he was dismayed. How to help the little pig change course? How could he help him get healthy? He liked metrics and thought the little pig would do well if he had some goals. The doctor designed a plan with three measures: weight, blood pressure, and cholesterol levels. He explained to the little pig that he was at risk for serious health problems. He told the little pig to lower his weight by 100 pounds, get his blood pressure down to recommended levels, and reduce the bad cholesterol levels to acceptable standards. He even gave the little pig a chart to track the three measures. When the little pig asked him for advice on how to achieve these goals, the doctor offered the little pig six pamphlets, two books, and a list of web sites that he could go to for identifying programs for getting healthy. The doctor scheduled follow up appointments every three months for the next year.

The second little pig worked very hard on his program. He posted the chart on his refrigerator. He changed his eating habits, started an exercise program, and tried meditation. He bought a blood pressure monitor, a high-quality scale, and a nifty kit for checking cholesterol levels. He didn't mind the expense—his health was worth it. He measured his blood pressure, weight, and cholesterol when he woke up—and twice more during the day. At his first quarterly checkup, the doctor was happy with his progress. They went over the numbers and decided the second little pig was on the right track. The pig was elated. He decided to step it up a bit. He thought about gastric bypass surgery, but opted instead for eating tofu six days a week. The seventh day, he would eat mixed vegetables. He stepped up his exercise program. He started on a cholesterol-lowering drug he learned about from his spam e-mail. (He loved spam.)

The second little pig's behaviors became more reckless as he neared his second checkup. He went on a water diet three days before and spent the morning of his appointment in a steam bath to shed the water weight. His doctor was amazed. The pig had lost a total of 60 pounds, improved his blood pressure, and lowered his cholesterol levels to within 10 percent of the standard. The doctor applauded his efforts and predicted success by his next appointment, three months hence.

Two months later the second little pig's kidneys failed and he died. The pig hadn't understood the overall goal or how to measure his overall health. He had spent the last eight months chasing a small set of numbers instead of developing "good health." He managed to improve his three areas of measurement, but neglected other areas of his health to do so.

The Third Little Pig

The third little pig's doctor also believed in metrics. He was also good with his patients, but he was different than the second little pig's doctor. He had faith that his patients could deal with the whole truth and that they should know what was behind the metrics. The doctor told the third little pig that his overall health was at risk—mostly due to his lifestyle. The doctor explained how weight, blood pressure, and cholesterol levels are pretty good indicators of health, but can't be used as the only ways to determine true health. A lot would have to depend on the little pig paying attention to his body and communicating with the doctor when things felt "funny." The little pig wondered what metric "feeling funny" was and the doctor explained that it wasn't a metric. It was simply the little pig talking to the doctor.

"So what do I do with the measures?"

"You collect them, track them, and we use them as indicators to see if there's anything we're missing and if you're making progress."

"So, I have to improve these numbers?" the pig asked as he took the chart.

"No. You have to get healthy. Those numbers will just give us an idea if you're on the right track."

The third little pig snorted. "What's the difference?"

"Well, there are many indicators. Blood pressure, weight, and cholesterol levels are just three. I do want you to improve these areas, but not at the cost of other areas, such as how well you sleep, if you get enough exercise, stress tests, memory, nutrition, etc. The goal is to be healthy—not only clinically, but emotionally."

"So, I don't have to improve these numbers?"

"No, you could feasibly get healthier without improving some of those specific measures."

"So, what's the plan?"

"Good question, little pig!" The doctor laid out a simple improvement plan for the little pig. He also showed the third little pig how to take his blood pressure, weight, and cholesterol levels. He had the little pig fill out a daily journal and a weekly online diary. The weekly online diary included the data he collected, a "how I feel today" meter, and a section where he was supposed to log what he had done that week to get healthy. The doctor promised to check the online diary, and if there was anything that seemed out of place, he'd contact the little pig.

"I hope you don't think I'm micro-managing you," the doctor said. "I just want to keep informed on your progress. It's very important to me that you get healthy."

"No, I like it," the third little pig said, knowing that his doctor cared. "But why don't you give me a whole battery of tests every month?"

"That's more than we need. I wouldn't put you through all those tests unless something in the metrics indicates a need for it. That way I don't waste your time or your money."

By the six-month mark, the third little pig was looking better, feeling better, and based on his doctor's evaluation, doing better. By the ninth month, he was doing great. He looked really good. He garnered a lot of compliments from friends and coworkers. He was on his way.

The End

I'm sure my version won't become an accepted sequel to the traditional fable, but it served its purpose. My daughter fell asleep about halfway through.

Data

We'll start with some basic terms that will allow us to communicate more clearly. Data, measures, information, and metrics are distinctly different, but fully intertwined entities. Each builds upon the other. Metrics are made up of other metrics and information. Information is made up of measures, and measures are comprised of data.

Figure 1-1 illustrates disparate entities that many times are mistakenly associated with or thought of as metrics.

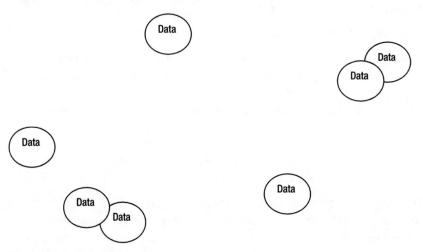

Figure 1-1. Data relationship map

Data is most commonly defined as "individual facts, statistics, or items of information." This definition, however, is overly generous. It implies accuracy. Moreover, it implies a level of usefulness that is not inherently present in data. Data, for our purposes, is the simplest form of information possible and is usually represented by a number or value; for example: six, twenty-two, seventy, true, false, high, or low. By itself, data is essentially useless because it fails to relate any meaningful information. As in Figure 1-1, some data can be "related" as represented by overlapping bubbles, but this is not part of the definition of data.

Data is the simplest form of information possible. It is usually represented by a number or value.

Data can be wildly unrelated (the bubbles far apart) or they can be correlated through a common purpose. When analyzing data, a relationship map can provide a visual representation of the data's relationship to other data. Many times a relationship is mistakenly assumed to exist between data because the data comes from a common source or was gathered with a single purpose in mind. For example, if we looked at "time to respond" and "time to resolve" data, they may seem to be related. The source may be the same—a trouble-ticket tracking system. The type of data (time) may also give the impression it is related more than it is. Frequently sets of data, regardless of the source or purpose, are not related. Assuming there is a relationship among unrelated sets of data causes us to come to incorrect conclusions. Response and resolution times, for example, don't affect one another, and they communicate different things.

Measures

Figure 1-2 illustrates the next level of information: measures and how data is related.

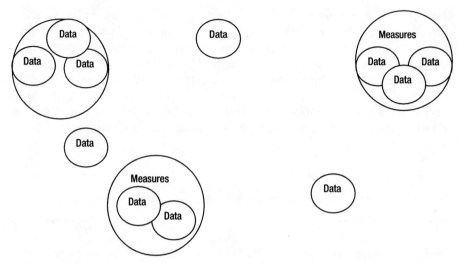

Figure 1-2. Measures and data relationship map

Measures begin to give us a more useful picture by incorporating some level of detail. The detail may include units of measure (in 50%, "percent" is the unit of measure and the data is 50) and information regarding how the data relates to other data. To state "70 percent" is more useful than to simply state "70." Even better, we may have "70 percent of 63 users." Each measure is made up of one or more datum. These measures, like the data, can have different levels of interrelations. One of the bubbles (top left in Figure 1-2) depicts a grouping of data that lacks a parent measure. This data is grouped because it is related, but it doesn't lead to a more meaningful measure. Demographics and height and weight are examples of this—data that may be useful, but doesn't necessarily feed into a larger measure.

Other data are floating independently within the map. These are rogue data (any term that means "no connections" works) that may or may not have a use later.

Measures bring more clarity to the data by grouping them in true relationships and adding a little context. Still, without clear connections to an underlying purpose or root question (more on this later), measures are nothing more than dressed-up data.

Measures bring more clarity to the data by grouping them in true relationships and adding a little context.

Information

Figure 1-3 illustrates the first useful level of information—and that's just what we call it, "information." Information groups measures and data (as well as rogue data) into a meaningful capsule.

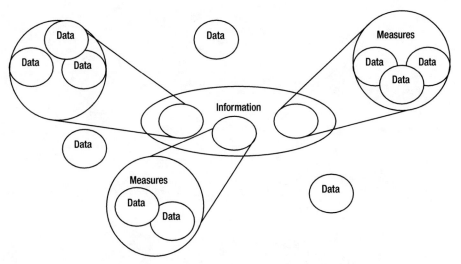

Figure 1-3. Data, measures, and information relationship map

Information takes measures and data and adds context. Notice that some data is not included in the information. Some data, regardless of how well it is collected, no matter how well you plan, may be superfluous. In the end, you may determine that the data does not fit or does not help to answer the root question you are working on. Information pulls in only the data and measures needed.

The context information brings to the data and measures is essential to moving indiscernible numerical points to an understandable state. With measures, we know that we are talking about percentages and that it is related to a number of users. Information adds context in the form of meaning, thus making the measures understandable: "Seventy percent of 63 users prefer the ski machine over the stair stepper."

Information adds context in the form of meaning, thus making the measures understandable.

While information within the right context can be especially useful, a metric may be what is truly needed.

Before we go on to the next piece of the puzzle, it may help to look at an example of how actual information (data and measures) fits into the diagram. Figure 1-4 shows an example using information around Speed to Resolve.

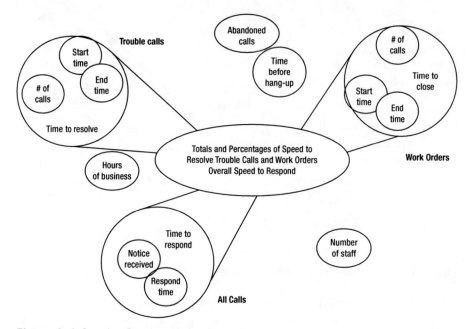

Figure 1-4. Speed to Resolve relationship map

Metrics

Figure 1-5 illustrates a full story, a metric. It's a picture made up of information, measures, and data. It should fulfill the adage, "a picture is worth a thousand words."

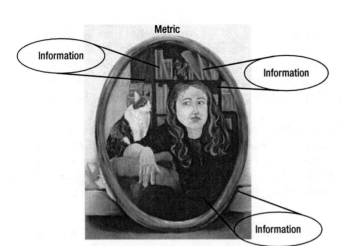

Figure 1-5. Metrics as a picture. Illustration by Alyssa Klubeck.

We finally reach the all-important definition of "metric." A metric is more than simply grouping multiple pieces of information together. Well, not really much more.

A metric, by my definition, is made up of information, measures, and data. Metrics can also include other metrics. The main difference between metrics and information is that a metric tells a complete story, fully answering a root question. And it has to tell the "right" story. If the metric tells the story completely wrong, it's not of much use. Along with the data, measures, and information, the metric includes prose. While a picture may be worth a thousand words, a picture without an explanation is still open to multiple interpretations.

A metric tells a complete story, fully answering a root question.

If you've done a good job with the metric because your charts, graphs, and tables are telling a well-formed story, it will be much harder for misinterpretation. But, it's still possible. Unless you feel confident that those viewing your metrics don't have their own agendas, aren't likely to misinterpret, and are totally open-minded, I highly recommend rounding out the picture with words.

This need for prose is not a new concept. My daughter took an art appreciation class in college. I was not surprised to find that there was a textbook that accompanied the class. Each work of art had pages of text on the artist, some background on why the artist created it, the length of time it took to create it, the medium that was used, and the circumstances behind it becoming relevant. But all this shocked me because when I was in high school, I remember my art teacher explaining how art had no definitive meaning outside the way each viewer interpreted it. This was especially true of modern art (which I still don't understand). Rather than leave the interpretation to the audience, these textbooks had the all-important explanation of the message behind the painting spelled out right there. Each painting, sculpture, and drawing had one. Each etching, carving, and prehistoric wall-painting had one. An explanation of what the artist was trying to "tell" us with his thousand-word image.

If it's useful to explain the meaning behind a work of art, how much more necessary is it to capture the meaning of a metric? And wouldn't it be best to have the meaning explained by the artist herself? This explanation is, of course, an interpretation of the metric. It's true that if you ask five people to interpret a metric, you may get five different answers—but you'll want your interpretation to be the one presented with the picture. If metrics are used properly, your interpretation will not be taken as "truth," but for what it is: one way to view the meaning of the metric.

"Seventy percent of 63 users prefer the ski machine over the stair stepper for the aerobic portion of their exercise program. The wait time for the ski machine is 25 minutes on average. Typically, there is no wait time on the stair steppers. There are 3 ski machines and 12 stair steppers." This is getting close to being a "good" metric. If a picture (chart or graph) is added, it may get even closer. The goal of the metric is to tell a complete (and useful) story, in response to a root question.

The question is actually the driver of a good metric. You can't have a good metric without the root question. When we look at our ski machine vs. stair stepper metric, we don't know the usefulness of the metric because we don't know what the question is. We can jump to conclusions and worse, we can leap to a potentially regrettable decision.

Should we buy more ski machines? Get rid of some of the stair steppers? Should we make the limit for time on the ski machine less? Should we create an exercise class based on the stair stepper? It should be obvious that the proper answer is not obvious. Part of the confusion may be due to the lack of a question. Why did we collect the data? Why did we do the analysis that led us to the metric? It's impossible to tell a complete story without a root question.

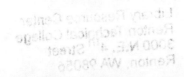

Root Questions

In my book *Why Organizations Struggle So Hard to Improve So Little* (Praeger, 2009), my coauthors, Michael Langthorne and Donald Padgett, and I compare metrics to a tree. In this view, the data are the leaves, the measures are the twigs, the information is the branches, and the metrics are the trunk of the tree. All of these exist only with a good set of roots. These roots represent the root question. This analogy is a great way of showing the relationship between the components of the metric.

Figure 1-6 shows another view of the components that make up a metric. It's fitting that it looks like an organic structure.

Figure 1-6. Metric components

Without a good root question, the answers that you derive may lead you in the wrong direction. Answers are only useful when you know the question. The root question is so integral to the metric that it has to be part of the definition of a metric.

A metric tells a complete story using data, measures, information, and other metrics to answer a root question.

The root question is essentially the most important component of a metric. It is the map we use to help determine our direction. It identifies the goal of our journey. There are instances where you may, with good reason and to good result, collect data without a root question (see Chapter 15), but for the practical use of metrics, this is unacceptable. It would be like taking off on a journey without a destination in mind. No purpose, no plan, and no direction—just get in your car and start driving.

Later you may realize that you forgot your driver's license, your money, and even your shoes. You may realize that you'd already traveled too far to make it back with the amount of fuel remaining in your tank. You may realize that the only logical course of action is to continue on, although you don't know where you will end up. You are more likely to end up where you don't want to be. Since the only right place would be the destination that you forgot to determine, it is much more likely that you will end up someplace other than that right place. And, when you fail to reach the destination (which in the end you may or may not have identified), you will blame the car. It didn't get enough miles to the gallon.

You won't blame the lack of forethought. Even if you get more gas *and* you figure out where you want to go, you'll not go back home for your wallet, license, or shoes. You've invested too much. Instead, you'll continue on and try to reach the destination from where you are, not wanting to admit that everything you'd done to that point was wasted effort.

You need the purpose of the metric, the root question, so that you are as efficient as possible with your resources (the car, fuel, time, and your efforts). Of course, if you have unlimited resources or you make money regardless of how you use the resources (perhaps you have a wealthy passenger who is only concerned with being shuttled around, not caring about the destination, purpose, or how long it takes to get there), then efficiency doesn't matter. But if you're like most of us and need to make the most of what you have, embarking on this meandering journey is more than wasteful. It actually will end up costing much more than the expenses incurred.

The lack of direction will seed a level of despair and resentment in you and your coworkers, your superiors, and subordinates. It can destroy the spirit of your organization.

The root question provides you with focus and direction. You know where you are headed. You know the destination. You know the purpose of the metrics and the question you are trying to answer.

A root question, a correctly worded and fully thought-out question, allows you to determine the right answer(s). Without a root question—*the right question*—the answer you derive will be the result of a meandering journey. This answer will likely do more harm than good.

Even a well-worded root question will fail to lead to good results if the question is not the *right* question.

To put it all together, let's look at a full example. A metric is a complete story told through representation of information. Information in turn, is a compilation of measures, used to convey meaning. Measures are the results built from data, the lowest level of collectable components (values or numbers). The following is a simple example :

- *Data*: 15 and 35
- *Measures*: 15 mpg and 35 mpg
- *Information*: Miles-per-gallon achieved using unleaded gasoline in a compact car: 15 mpg in the city, 35 mpg on the highway
- *Metric*: The metric that would logically follow would be a picture (charts or graphs in most cases) that tells a story. In this case the story may be a comparison between the fuel efficiency of different compact car models (miles per gallon), combined with other indicators used to select the right car for you.
- *Root Question*: What is the best car for me?

The use of data, measures, and information are more relative than hard and fast. I don't mean to dictate inflexible definitions that will keep you from getting to the metric. The goal is to develop metrics—answers—to our questions.

The data could include the miles-per-gallon tag. Measures could include "in the city" and "on the highway." Information could distinguish between the various cars' make and model. The major point to take away is that additional meaning (and context) are provided as we progress from data to measures to information. Also, metrics make a full story of this and much more information.

Let's look at another example, illustrated in Figure 1-7. Using a customer service desk as our model, we can identify each of the components listed.

- *Root Question*: Is the service desk responsive to our customers?
- *Data*:
    - 1,259 per month
    - 59 per month
    - Responses on a 1–5 scale

- *Measures:*
  - The number of trouble calls
  - The number of abandoned calls
  - The length of time before the caller hung up
  - The survey responses

- *Information:*
  - Percentage of total calls that were abandoned, by month
  - Percentage of total calls that were abandoned, by year

- *Metric:*

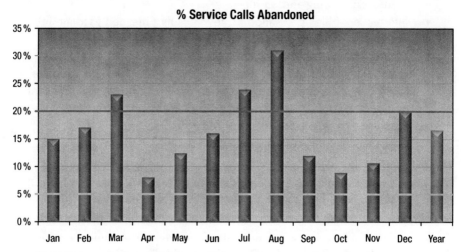

Figure 1-7. Percentage of service calls abandoned, by month and by year

Looking at Figure 1-7, the responsiveness of the service desk for the past year has been well within expectations. During March, July, and August, however, the percentage of calls abandoned were above expectations (more than 20%). These three spikes are worth investigating to determine both the cause and the likelihood that these could be a recurring problem. Also of note is the steady increases leading up to these spikes. April and October were excellent months for responsiveness and should be analyzed to see if the causes are repeatable.

Is this a metric? Yes, this qualifies in our taxonomy as a metric because it tells a story in response to a root question.

Is this a good metric? No, it definitely can be better. It can tell a more complete story. Looking back at the information, we can also incorporate the survey responses on "time to answer" to determine the customers' perceptions of the service desk's responsiveness. Another important component of the metric should be the percentage of abandoned calls under 30 seconds. This standard could vary; it could be under 15 or 45 seconds. It depends on different factors. What is the customer listening to during the time on hold? How long does a person typically stay on the line before he realizes he dialed the wrong number? How short of a wait is considered not to be a lost opportunity? But improving this metric without first addressing the root question is, as a friend recently put it, like putting icing on a rock. It might look good enough to eat, but it's not. We can keep improving this metric so it looks better, but it won't satisfy unless we go back to the root question.

The metric, like its components, are tools that can be used to answer the root question. We will address the proper use of these tools later. For now, it's enough to have a common understanding of what the components are and how they relate to each other.

The Data-Metric Paradox

There is an interesting paradox involving the components of metrics and their relationship to the root question used to derive them.

Data, the easiest to understand, identify, and collect, should be the last item to develop. The most complex and difficult component, the root question, has to come first. As our analogy of the hapless driver on the meandering journey showed, we must first identify our destination and purpose. Rather than start with the simple to build the complex, we must start with the most complex and use it to identify the simple.

The three little pigs also ran into this paradox. The first pig's doctor was happy with data and measures, but ignored the bigger, more important requirement. He lost his patient, but did it with "healthy" numbers. Business can do the same. You can have good data points (sales per customer, profit/sale, or repeat customers) and still go out of business.

We have to start with the complex to uncover the simple—start at the root question and drive unerringly toward data.

Identifying the correct root question is not as simple as it sounds, nor as difficult as we normally make it. We need to be inquisitive. We need to keep digging, until we reach the truth, the question at the root, the need, the requirement. What is the purpose of the metric? What is it that you really want to know? This root need enables us to form a picture of the answer. This picture is the design of the metric.

Once you know the root question, you can draw a picture.

The picture, the design of the metric, can be created without any idea of the actual answers. The metric provides the form for the information. The information tells us what measures we'll need, and the measures identify the data required. This is the best way to create a metric. From the question to the metric to the information to the measures and, finally, to the data.

Unfortunately, most times we attempt it in the opposite direction, starting with the simple (data) trying to expound on it to develop the complex (root question). This process seldom succeeds. But when we start at the complex, forming a picture of what the question is and how the answer will look, it becomes easy to work down to the data.

Data, measures, information, and metrics all serve the same master: the root question. They all have a common goal: to provide answers to the question. Because of this, the question defines the level of answer necessary.

Let's pose the following question: How far is it to Grandma's house? You don't need a metric to provide the answer to this question. You don't even need information. A measure (for example, the number of miles) will suffice. And you will be fully satisfied. For data to be sufficient, you have to ask the question with enough context to make a simple number or value an adequate answer. How many miles is it to Grandma's house? How much longer will it take to get to Grandma's house? In these cases, data is all you need. But data is rarely useful in and of itself.

Let's pose another question: Do we have time to do any sightseeing or shopping along the way and still make it in time for Grandma's turkey dinner? To answer this, we require information. The measures and data might include the following:

- The time Grandma is serving dinner
- The current time
- The number of sightseeing or shopping stops along the way
- The estimated time to sightsee/shop per stop

We still don't need a metric. And we definitely don't need a recurring metric in which we have to collect, analyze, and report the results of building information on a periodic basis.

The problem is, management—anyone above staff level—has been conditioned to almost always start with data. The few that start with metrics already have the answer in mind (not a bad thing per se), but lack the question. This leads to them asking for recurring (weekly, monthly, quarterly, or annual) reports. They'd like to see the metrics in a certain format: trend lines with comparison to a baseline based on best practices, both monthly and with a running annual total. Sounds great, but without knowing the root question, asking for this answer runs the risk of wasting a lot of resources.

Sometimes clients (managers, department heads, organizational leaders, etc.) who know the answer (metric) they want before they know the question, realize that the answers don't really fulfill their needs and try to give a mid-course correction. Like our meandering driver, they refuse to start fresh and go back to the beginning, to ignore the work already accomplished and start over again. When they realize the metric is faulty, they do one of the following:

- Assume the data is wrong
- Decide the analysis is wrong
- Tweak the data (not the metric)

Some really wise managers decide that the metric is incorrect and try again. Unfortunately, they don't realize that the problem is the lack of a root question or that the question they are working from is wrong. Instead of starting over again from the question, they try to redesign the metric.

The bottom line and the solution to this common problem? Pick your cliché, any of them work: We have to start at the top. We have to start at the end. We have to start with the end in mind. You can't dig a hole from the bottom up. We have to identify the correct root question.

The root question will determine the level of the answer. If the question is complex enough and needs answers on a periodic basis, chances are you will need to develop a comprehensive metric. A question along the lines of "How is the health of (a service or little pigs)?" may require a metric to answer it, especially if you want to continue to monitor the health on a regular basis.

The vagueness of the question makes it more complex. Clarity simplifies.

As we design the metric to answer the root question, we realize that we need to have measures of the various components that make up an organization's health. In the case of the three pigs (or humans for that matter), we may want indicators on the respiratory, circulatory, digestive, and endocrine systems. To say nothing of the nervous or excretory systems, bones, or muscles. The point is, we need a lot more information since our question was of wide scope.

If our question had a narrower scope, the answer would be simpler. Take the following question, for example: How is your weight-control going? The answer can be provided by taking periodic measures after stepping on a reliable scale. Unfortunately, rarely is the question this specific. If the first little pig is only asked about his weight, the other indicators of health are missed. Focusing too closely on a specific measure may lead to missing important information. You may be asking the wrong question, like the second little pig's doctor, who only used three indicators and neglected to share the bigger picture with his porcine patient.

Perhaps you know about your blood pressure. Perhaps you had a full checkup and everything is fine—except you need to lose a few pounds. "How is your weight loss coming along?" may be good enough. If it is, then a metric is overkill. A measure will suffice.

When designing a metric, the most important part is getting the right root question. This will let us know what level of information is required to answer it. It will govern the design of the metric down to what data to collect.

Metric Components

Let's recap the components of a metric and their definitions:

- *Data*: Data, for our purposes, is the simplest possible form of information and is usually represented by a number or value; for example, six, twenty-two, seventy, true, false, high, or low.
- *Measures*: Made up of data, measures add the lowest level of context possible to the data. Measures can be made up of other measures.
- *Information*: Information is made up of data and measures. Information can be made up of other information. Information provides additional, more meaningful context.
- *Metrics*: Metrics are made up of data, measures, and information. Metrics can be made up of other metrics. Metrics give full context to the information. Metrics (attempt to) tell a complete story. Metrics (attempt to) answer a root question.

- *Root Question*: The purpose for the metric. Root questions define the requirements of the metric and determine its usefulness.

Recap

This chapter introduced a common language for metrics and their components. It also introduced the Data-Metric Paradox, in which we learned that we have to start with the most complex to drive to the simple. We have to start with the root question to get us safely to the proper level of information necessary to answer the question. It's possible the question may not require a metric, or even information. When tasked by management to create a metric (or a metric program) we have to slow down and ask what the root questions are. We have to be willing and able to accept that the answer may not lie in creating a metric at all.

Bonus Material

I fear I may have misled you. By presenting this chapter in the manner I did, you might wonder if I'm leading you down the wrong track. But there was a logical reason for it. I considered presenting the definitions from the top-down order that I'd like you to address them: root question to metric to information to measures and, finally, to data. But I worried that readers would rebel. This is not the normal order in which we come to metrics. Unfortunately, our normal journey to metrics starts with requests for data.

Figure 1-8 depicts the hierarchy between the components, from the bottom up.

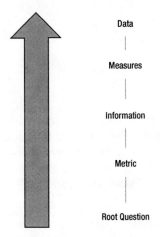

Data

Measures

Information

Metric

Root Question

Figure 1-8. Hierarchy of metrics components

I've worked with many managers who have been tasked to present meaningful information (metrics) on how their departments or units were doing. The first step they all take is to ask, what data do we have? This tack is taken in an innocent attempt to keep from creating more work for the staff. The hope is to fill the "box" with existing data and placate the organization's leadership. But, because we don't take the demand for metrics as an opportunity to develop something useful for all levels of the organization, we do as little as possible to satisfy the request. The next question is (if the existing data doesn't seem to be enough), what data can we get? So, rather than introduce them in the order that I insist is right, I presented them to you in the order I thought you would find familiar. Now, I hope you'll take the leap of faith to trust me—and start with the big picture first.

So, please accept my apology and now allow me to ensure that you have a proper foundation for the rest of this book.

Misconception 1. Data is not useful.

I may have given you the impression that data is not useful. Or that measures and information, without being part of a larger metric, lack applicability to improving your organization. The Data-Metric Paradox addressed this, but it's worth pointing out again. Data can be very useful, if your question is extremely specific and requires only a numeric/value answer like, what time is it? If data is all that is required, it is likely that you won't need a metric or any of the detailed information that accompanies it.

Misconception 2. Start with data and then build toward metrics.

Most of the time, this misconception is born of the misguided belief that you need data, you need answers. The other catalyst for this misconception is the abundance of data available, thanks to technology. You may believe that you should collect data, try to group them into measures, then take the measures and compile them into meaningful pieces of information, and finally, take these components and build a metric to give it all meaning and clarity.

The truth is just the opposite. There are so many possible data that you can collect, that beginning at the data level will almost assure that you fail to create a useable metric. As you will see, it is important to start with the end in mind; the metric is the end (if the question warrants it) and, therefore, also our beginning.

Misconception 3. You have to have a root question before you gather data, measures, or information.

While I wish this were true, you'll find many times that you are required to gather data, analyze measures, and create informative reports with no idea of the reason why. Like most good soldiers, you may very well have to do what is short of "right." I highly suggest that you do your best to identify the root question before you start, but if you can't, of course you can gather information without it. If this happens, I recommend you try to get to the root question as soon as possible within the process.

When you get the "I'll know it when I see it" argument from a higher-up, stay strong. The best way to help customers identify what they really want is to help them identify their root question. In Douglas Hubbard's excellent book, *How to Measure Anything: Finding the Value of Intangibles in Business* (Wiley, 2010), the author introduces his methodology for identifying what people really want to know.

Hubbard uses what he calls a "clarification chain," which allows you to keep digging deeper into what matters to the client. He asks simply, "What do you mean by x?" In his example of working with the Department of Veterans Affairs, he ended up holding multiple workshops just to get to the root question. Hubbard doesn't require a root question per se, he stops well short. But his book is about measures, not metrics (in our definition). The good news is that he is totally correct about being able to measure anything. I've used his book numerous times. Sometimes when I work with a client, we run into a roadblock after we've identified the question, designed a plausible metric, and determined the information we need. Often, the client doesn't want to get past the picture because she doesn't believe we can measure what we need to compile the information. I pull out Douglas Hubbard's book from the shelf and assure her that we can really measure anything. This is even easier because with the root question, metric, and information requirements in hand, identifying the measures become very simple.

So, it's not impossible to start at the bottom, it's just not the wise choice.

Designing Metrics

The How

Now that we have a common language to communicate with, the next step is to discuss how to proceed. I've read numerous books, articles, and blog posts on Balanced Scorecards, Performance Measures, and Metrics for Improvement. Each pushes the reader to use the author's methods and tools. But, I haven't found one yet that puts "how to develop a metric from scratch" into plain English. It's about time someone did.

In this chapter we'll cover the following:

- How to form a root question—the right root question
- How to develop a metric by drawing a picture
- How to flesh out the information, measures, and data needed to make the picture
- How to collect data, measures, and information

This will seem like a lot of work (and it is), but I guarantee you that if you follow this method you will save an enormous amount of time and effort in the long run. Most of your savings will come from less rework, less frustration, and less dissatisfaction with the metrics you develop.

Think of it this way: You can build a house by first creating a blueprint to ensure you get the house that you want. Or you can just order a lot of lumber and supplies and make it up as you go along. This process doesn't work when building a house or developing software. It requires discipline to do the groundwork first. It will be well worth it. I've never seen anyone disappointed because they had a well thought-out plan, but I've helped many programmers try to unravel the spaghetti code they ended up with because they started programming before they knew what the requirements were.

While programmers have improved at upfront planning, and builders would never think to just start hammering away, sadly those seeking to use metrics still want to skip the requirements phase.

So let's start working on that blueprint.

Getting to the Root Question

Before you can design a metric, you have to first identify the root question: What is the real driving need? In the service desk example in the last chapter, the director asked, "Is the service desk responsive to our customers?" The analyst took that question and developed a decent metric with it—percentage of service calls abandoned. He didn't do a great job, however, because he didn't make a picture (metric) first. Instead, he went straight to collecting data and measures. He also didn't determine if the question was a root question or the *right* question.

The discussion I've had many times with clients often goes like the following dialog (in which I'm the metrics designer):

> *Director: "I'd like to know if our service desk is responsive to our customers."*

The first clue that the metrics designer has to dig deeper for the real root question is that the answer to the given question could be yes or no.

> *Metrics Designer: "What do you mean by responsive?"*
>
> *Director: "Are we answering calls in a timely manner?"*
>
> *Metrics Designer: "What exactly is a 'timely manner'? Do you mean how many seconds it takes or how many times the phone rings?"*
>
> *Director: "I guess within the first three rings?"*

The designer made a note—that the director guessed calls should be answered within three rings, but that end users had to provide the actual answer.

> *Metrics Designer: "Okay. Why do we need to know this? What's driving the curiosity?"*

Director: "I've had some complaints that we aren't picking up the phone quickly enough. Customers say they can't reach us or they have to wait too long to get to speak to a person."

Metrics Designer: "What constitutes 'not quick enough'? Or, what is a wait that is 'too long'?"

Director: "I don't know."

The designer made some more notes. The director was willing to admit that he didn't know what the customer meant by "quick enough" and that he didn't know what would please the customer. This admission was helpful.

Metrics Designer: "I suggest we ask some of your customers to determine these parameters. This will help us determine expectations and acceptable ranges. But we also need to know what you want to know. Why do you want to know how responsive the service desk is?"

Director: "Well, the service desk is the face of our organization—when most customers say 'Emerald City Services' they think of the service desk."

Metrics Designer: "So, what do you want to know about the face of your organization?"

Director: "How well it's received by our customers. I want to know if it's putting forth a good image."

This is a much better starting point for our metric design. With the root question (How well is the service desk representing Emerald Services?) we can decide on a more meaningful picture—a picture that encompasses everything that goes into answering the question.

There are other possible results of our inquisition. Of course, we shouldn't think of it as an interrogation. That would not only give the director the wrong impression and it would also lead us to ask the wrong questions. No, our job is to reach the root question. We have to help our clients determine what their real underlying needs are and what they need or want to know. One tool for doing so is the Five Whys.

The Five Whys is simple in its concept. You ask "why" five times, until the client can no longer answer with a deeper need. Of course, you can't ask "why" repeatedly like a child being told they can't play in the rain. You have to ask it in a mature manner. Many times you don't actually use the word, "why." As in the earlier example, sometimes you ask using other terms—like "what" and "how" and "what if?"

The process isn't so predicated on the use of the word "why" as it is grounded in attempting to reach the root purpose or need. Perhaps the worst error is to jump happily at the first "why" in which you feel some confidence that you could answer. We are all problem solvers by nature, and the possibility of latching onto a question with which we can easily provide an answer is very tempting.

Let's look at another example, this one illustrating how the Five Whys can help us get to the root question.

Director: "I'd like to know if our service desk is responsive to our customers."

Metrics Designer: "What do you mean by responsive?"

Director: "Are we answering calls in a timely manner?"

Metrics Designer: "Why do we need to know this? What's driving the curiosity?"

Director: "My boss is demanding metrics, and I understand from the service desk that this information is readily available from our Trouble Call System."

Metrics Designer: "Yes, it is. But, we might give the wrong impression of what you think is important if we choose this metric. Perhaps we can see if something meaningful to you could also be provided without additional work to the staff. If we can identify different measures that are easy to collect and give you a better picture of the department, would you be willing to use them instead?"

Director: "Sure."

Metrics Designer: "Excellent. Usually we form metrics around goals you are trying to achieve, processes you want to improve, or problems you're trying to solve."

Director: "But leadership wants service desk metrics."

Metrics Designer: "Okay. Why do they want service desk metrics?"

Director: "I think they're asking managers to demonstrate progress on their strategic plans."

Metrics Designer: "Do you have a strategic plan for the service desk?"

Director: "Yes, of course."

Metrics Designer: "So, perhaps we should look at the goals within the plan…"

To get to a root question, ask "why" five times—digging until you reach a root need or question.

I was able to narrow the need down to metrics around a set of goals. Not a perfect root question, but much better than what we started with.

The problem is that you may not even be close to a root question. You may be driven by decrees from above, like the director in the scenario. You may be filling a box on a checklist.

When I run into this problem, I seriously consider walking away. I just let them know that although they believe they want a metric, I don't believe they actually *need* one. If they want to look at a couple of measures or provide some data points to someone asking for them—I or someone else can provide them, but again, they don't need a full-blown metric. If I'm consulting (and not an employee at the organization who feels he must obey), I run away.

Most root questions come from goals, improvement opportunities, or problems you want to solve.

If you don't have a list of goals for your unit, you can add value by first developing them. This may seem to be outside of the process for designing metrics, but since you must have a good root question to move forward, you don't have much choice.

If you have a set of goals, then your task becomes much easier. But be careful; the existence of a documented strategic plan does not mean you have usable goals. Unless you have a living strategic plan, one that you are actually following, the strategic plan you have is probably more of an ornament for your shelf than a usable plan. But, let's start with the assumption that you'll have to identify your goals, improvement opportunities, and/or problems.

The best way I've found to get to the root questions when starting from a blank slate is to hold a working session with a trained facilitator, your team, and yourself. This shouldn't take longer than two or three one-hour sessions.

To start, I usually break out the large Post-it® pads and markers and we brainstorm goals for the unit. I've also done this one-on-one with managers or with their teams. Even when I start with the manager, by the second meeting we end up pulling in key team members. If I'm one-on-one with a client, I have to encourage them, coach them, and keep them motivated since there is no one else for them to feed off of.

When I'm working with a team, I have to focus them early. I work hard to keep them on target, avoiding trips down any rabbit holes. This requires that the team be fully present. No phones, laptops, or side conversations. This may seem a bit "controlling," but they thank me later—and I get the job done much faster.

You may need to elicit the root need through one or more facilitated sessions.

The itinerary runs as follows:

- *Five minutes of brainstorming.* Five minutes is more than enough if I keep everyone focused and avoid any discussion, critiques, or explanations of what I capture on paper. This is of course harder in a group, but since the facilitator is in charge—she can force the team to truly brainstorm. I find it helpful to remind everyone they'll have time to explain, modify, delete, add, and/or critique later.
- *Five to ten minutes of clarifications.* Again, you need a facilitator. I end up doing both roles—facilitator and metric designer, and I like it that way. But if you're doing this on your own, you'll probably need to enlist a facilitator to help you. Once the team runs out of inputs—it could be in less than five minutes or a little more—I hit each item and ensure the meaning is clear. I allow the client(s) to delete items that they feel are "wrong," add more, and/or modify them for clarity. I *don't* allow them to delete or change anything because they don't think it's possible to achieve (goals) or to measure (root questions).
- *Five minutes grouping or categorizing the results.* This step is optional. If you have identified more than ten "goals," then there may be a benefit in organizing the items around themes. Again, a trained facilitator will be able to think on her feet here. Sometimes I simply ask

the team if they see any logical groupings, rather than try to find them myself.

Five minutes classifying each item as a Goal/Objective, Task, Motto/Slogan, or Measure of Success. Although the purpose was to brainstorm goals—one of the benefits of brainstorming is the identification of other related items. Goals and objectives are "achievable" items on the list you've captured. It is very unlikely that you'll have strategic (long range) goals, but you may find that some are objectives needed for achieving others. I group them together and identify their classification. You'll also find some tasks. These should be rather obvious as things that the team or you want to do. They may be process steps or just material for a "to do" list. If they fall under a goal or objective, group them accordingly. If the tasks don't have a goal, I help them determine if there is a missing goal or if they are simply job tasks. This is not necessary for identifying root questions, but having a well-developed set of goals is useful. Some of the items will be measures of success (MoS). Basically, they are "how" you know you've succeeded at achieving the goal or completing the task. These measures may satisfy your desire for metrics—but they won't be "metrics." More on these later. Just remember that the root question may not need a metric as the answer—sometimes MoS are enough.

- *Five minutes per goal.* So far you've invested about a half hour on identifying goals (and other items)—the rest of the effort may have to span across more than one meeting. Once we have goals identified, we'll be able to identify MoS for each (some may have already been identified). These will be new items. If all you need is to track progress to the goal or to know when you've succeeded at achieving the goal—you can stop. You can also skip down to "how to create and collect measures" instead of developing a metric. If you have larger questions (or larger goals) a metric may be appropriate. Remember, metrics tell a complete story, using information, measures, and data. So, if you have simple, tactical goals, the need may be for measures rather than a metric. If the goal is strategic and "large" the questions will also be bigger, and likely lead to a metric. Many times the goal will generate questions, other than if the team will achieve the goal. How to achieve the goal is one possibility. Another is to determine the "why" for the goal—the reason for it. Many times these also lead to a metric.

Remember, the result of getting to the root need may not be a metric.

We've discussed using five "whys" to get to a root need and using or developing a strategic plan (simplified version) for getting to the root need. However, any method for eliciting requirements should work. The important thing is to get to the underlying need. The root question should address what needs to be achieved, improved, or resolved.

What is important is to remember that you can work from wherever you start back to a root question and then forward again to the metric (if necessary). I told a colleague that I wanted to write a book on metrics.

"Why? Don't you have enough to do?" She knew I was perpetually busy.

"Yes, but every time I turn around, I run into people who need help with metrics," I answered.

"Why a book?" She was good at The Five Whys.

"It gives me a tool to help teach others. I can tell them to read the book and I'll be able to reference it."

"So, you want to help others with designing metrics. That's admirable. What else will you need to do?"

And that started me on a brainstorming journey. I captured ideas from presenting speeches, teaching seminars and webinars, to writing articles and proposing curriculum for colleges. I ended up with a larger list of things to accomplish than just a book. I also got to the root need and that helped me focus on why I wanted to write the book. That helps a lot when I feel a little burned out or exhausted. It helps me to persevere when things aren't going smoothly. It helps me think about measuring success, not based on finishing the book (although that's a sub-measure I plan on celebrating) but on the overall goal of helping others develop solid and useful metrics programs.

Once you think you have the root question, chances are you'll need to edit it a little. I'm not suggesting that you spend hours making it "sound" right. It's not going to be framed and put over the entrance. No, I mean that you have to edit it for clarity. It has to be exact. The meaning has to be clear. As you'll see shortly, you'll test the question to ensure it is a root—but beforehand it will help immensely if you've defined every component of the question to ensure clarity.

Define the terms—even the ones that are obvious. Clarity is paramount.

Keep in mind, most root questions are very short, so it shouldn't take too much effort to clearly define each word in the question.

As with many things, an example may be simpler. Based on the conversation on why I wanted to write this book, let's assume a possible root question is: How effective is this book at helping readers design metrics? You can ensure clarity by defining the words in the question.

1. **How effective** is this book at helping readers design metrics?

   a. What do we mean by effective? In this case, since it's my goal, I'll do the definitions. How well does it work? Does it really help readers?

   b. What do I mean by "how effective?" The how portion means which parts of the book are helpful? Which parts aren't? Also, does it enable someone to develop high-quality metrics? After all, my goal is to make this book a practical tool and guide for developing a metrics program.

2. How effective **is this book** at helping readers design metrics?

   a. This may seem obvious, and in this case it is. But, you should still check. There may be a greater need for a definition if I had instead asked, "How effective is my system for designing metrics?"

   b. Even obvious definitions, like this one—may lead you to modify the question. If asked, "What do you mean by this book?" I might very well answer, "Oh, actually I want to know if the system is effective, of which the book is the vehicle for sharing." This would lead us to realize that I really wanted to know if my system worked for others—more so than if this form of communication was effective.

3. How effective is this book **at helping readers** design metrics?

   a. Does it *help*? I have to define if "*help*" means

      i. Can the reader develop metrics after reading it?

      ii. Is the reader better at developing metrics after reading it?

      iii. Does the reader avoid the mistakes I preach against?

   b. *Readers* are another obvious component—but we could do some more clarification.

      i. Does "reader" mean someone who reads the "whole" book or someone who reads any part of the book?

      ii. Is the reader based on the target audience?

4. How effective is this book at helping readers **design metrics**?

   a. What do I mean by "design"? As you have read, for me designing a metric involves a lot more than the final metric. It includes identifying the root need and then ensuring a metric is the proper way to answer it. So, while "design" may mean development, it has to be taken in the context of the definition of a metric.

   b. What do I mean by metric? Do I mean the metric part of the equation or does it include the whole thing—root question, metric, information, measures, and data? If you'd read the book already, you'd know the answer to this question. The metric cannot be done properly without the root question, and is made up of information, measures, data, and other metrics. Even with that—what I mean in the root question may be a little different than this because the outcome of following the process may be to not create a metric. In that case, using the root question to provide an answer would be a success—although no metric was designed.

Based on this exercise, if I chose to keep the root question the same, I'd now know much better how to draw the picture. Chances are though, after analyzing each word in the question, I would rewrite the question. The purpose behind my question was to determine if the book was successful. And since success could result in not designing metrics, I would rewrite my question to be more in tune with what I actually deem success—the effective use of my system. The new root question might be: How effective is my system in helping people who want or need to design metrics?

Testing the Root Question

If you think you've got the root question identified, you're ready to proceed. Of course, it may be worthwhile to test the question to see if you've actually succeeded.

Test 1. Is the "root" question actually asking for information, measures, or data? "I'd like to know the availability of system X." This request begs us to ask, "Why?" There is an underlying need or requirement behind this seemingly straightforward question. When you dig deep enough, you'll get to the real need, which is simply a request for data. The root question should *not* be a direct request for data. The following are examples of requests for data: Do we have enough gas to reach our destination? Is the system reliable or do we need a backup? How long will it take to complete the project?

Test 2. Is the answer to the question going to be simple? Is it going to be a measure? Data? If the answers are either "yes" or "no," chances are you're not there yet or the question doesn't require a metric to provide an answer. It may seem too easy—that you wouldn't get questions after all this work that could be answered with a yes or no. But, it happens. It may mean only a little rework on the question, but that rework is still necessary. Is our new mobile app going to be a best seller? Should we outsource our IT department? Are our employees satisfied? These may seem like good root questions, but, they can all be answered with a simple yes or no.

Test 3. How will the answer be used? If you've identified a valid root question, you will have strong feelings, or a clear idea of how you will use the answer. The answer should provide discernable benefits. Let's take my question about the effectiveness of this book at helping readers develop metrics. If I learn that it's highly effective at helping readers, what will I do? I may use the information to gain opportunities for speaking engagements based on the book. I may submit the book to be considered for a literary award. I may have to hold a celebration. If the answer is that the book is ineffective, then I may investigate possible means of correcting the situation. I may have to offer handbooks/guidelines on how to use the book. I may have to offer more information via a web site. If the feedback is more neutral, I may look at ways to improve in a later edition.

The key is to have predefined expectations of what you will do with the answers you'll receive. When I ask a client how they'll use the answer, if I get a confused stare or their eyes gloss over, I know we're not there yet.

Test 4. Who will the answer be shared with? Who will see the metric? If the answer is only upper management, then chances are good that you need to go back to the drawing board. If you've reached the root question, many more people should benefit from seeing the answer. One key recipient of the answer should be the team that helped you develop it. If it's only going to be used to appease upper management—chances are you haven't gotten to the root *or* the answer won't require a metric.

Test 5. Can you draw a picture using it? When you design the metric, you will do it much more as an art than a science. There are lots of courses you can take on statistical analysis. You can perform exciting and fun analysis using complex mathematical tools. But, I'm not covering that here. We're talking about how to develop a useable metrics program—a tool for improvement. If you can't draw a picture as the answer for the question, it may not be a root question.

Not all root questions will pass these tests.

I'm not saying that all root questions *must* pass these tests. But, all root questions that require a "metric" to answer them must. If your question doesn't pass these tests, you have some choices.

1. Develop the answer without using data, measures, information, or metrics. Sometimes the answer is a process change. Sometimes the answer is to stop doing something, do it differently, or start doing something new. It doesn't have to result in measuring at all.

2. Develop the answer using measures (or even just data). This may be a one-time measure. You may not need to collect or report the data more than once.

3. Work on the question until it passes the five tests—so you can then develop a metric. Why would you want to rework your question simply to get to a metric? You shouldn't. If you feel confident about the result, stop. If the client says you've hit upon the root question, stop. If the question resonates fully, stop. Wherever you are, that's where you'll be. Work from there. *Don't force a metric if it's not required.*

Your task is *not* to develop a metric—it's to determine the root question and provide an answer.

Developing a Metric

It's an interesting argument: is the process of designing metrics a science or an art? If you read statistics textbooks, you might take the side of science. If you read *Transforming Performance Measurement: Rethinking the Way We Measure and Drive Organizational Success* by Dean Spitzer (AMACON, 2007), or *How To Measure Anything* by Douglas Hubbard (Wiley, 2010), you might argue that it's an art. I propose, like most things in real life (vs. theory), it's a mixture of both.

One place it's more art than science is in the *design* of a metric. I can say this without reservation because to design our metric, you want to actually draw a picture. It's not fine art. It's more like the party game where you're given a word or phrase and you have to draw a picture so your teammates are able to guess what the clue is.

At the first seminar I taught on designing metrics, "Do-It-Yourself Metrics", I broke the students into groups of four or five. After stepping through the exercise for identifying root questions, I told them to draw a picture to provide an answer to a question. The question was, "How do we divide our team's workload to be the most productive?" Figure 2-1 shows the best of the students' answers.

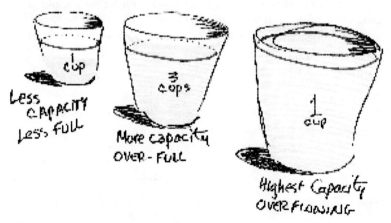

Figure 2-1. Workload division metric

This picture shows how each person (represented by a different cup) has different levels of work. The level of the liquid represents the amount of work "in each person's cup." The line near the top is the highest level the liquid should be poured to, because the froth will cause it to overflow. This line represents the most each person can actually handle, leaving room at the top for the "extra"—like illness, lunch, vacation, etc. By looking at the picture, the manager gets an easy-to-understand story of who has too much work, who can take on more, who is more productive, and who needs to improve their skill sets so that they can eventually have a larger cup.

A useful part of drawing the picture was clarity around the question. To ensure that we drew it right, we needed to also define the terms we were using in the picture: productivity, workload, and team.

Define the terms—even the ones that are obvious. Here too, clarity is paramount.

We found out that workers A, B, and C made up the team—they did the same type of work in a small unit of the organization. We also learned that the word "team" didn't mean that the group normally worked together. On the contrary, this "team" worked independently on different tasks. This simple realization gave the manager more ideas.

Workload was defined as the tasks given to the workers by the manager. It excluded many other tasks the workers accomplished for other people in the organization, customers, and each other. The only tasks that counted in this picture were the ones with deadlines and accountability to the management chain.

Productivity was defined as how many tasks were completed on time (or by the deadline).

These definitions are essential to developing the "right" metric. We could have drawn a good picture and designed a metric without these clarifications, but we would have risked measuring the wrong things.

Don't assume the terms used in the question are understood.

The metric would also be useful later, when the manager provided training opportunities for the staff. If the training did what was expected, the cups would increase in size—perhaps from a 32-ounce to a 44-ounce super size.

Does this seem strange? Does it seem too simple?

While I can't argue against things being "strange," very few things are ever "too simple." Einstein once said, "Make it as simple as possible, but no simpler." This is not too simple—like Goldilocks was fond of saying, "it's just right."

Once we have clear definitions for the terms that make up the root question, we will have a much better picture! Remember the importance of a common language? It is equally important that everyone fully understands the language used to create the root question.

I work with clients to modify these drawings until it provides the full answer to their question. This technique has excellent benefits. By using a picture:

- It's easier to avoid jumping to data. This is a common problem. Remember the natural tendency to go directly to data.
- It's easier to think abstractly and avoid being put in a box. Telling someone to "think outside the box" is not always an effective way to get them to do so.
- We avoid fears, uncertainty, or doubt about the ability to collect, analyze, and report the necessary information. These common emotions toward metrics restrict your ability to think creatively and thoroughly. They tend to "settle" for less than the ideal answer.
- We have a non-threatening tool for capturing the needs. No names, no data or measures. No information that would worry the client. No data at all. Just a picture. Of course this picture may change drastically by the time you finalize the metric. This is essentially a tool for creatively thinking without being restricted by preconceptions of what a metric (or what a particular answer) should be.

One key piece of advice is not to design your metric in isolation. Even if you are your own metric customer, involve others. I am not advocating the use of a consultant. I am advocating the use of someone—anyone—else. You need someone to help you generate ideas and to bounce your ideas off of. You need someone to help you ask "why." You need someone to discuss your picture with (and perhaps to draw it). This is a creative, inquisitive process—and for most of us, it is immensely easier to do this with others. Feel free to use your whole team. But don't do it alone.

A good root question will make the drawing easier.

Having a complete picture drawn (I don't mean a Picasso) makes the identification of information, measures, and data not only easy, but ensures you have a good chance of getting the right components.

The picture has to be "complete." After I have something on paper (even if it's stick figures), I ask the client, "what's missing?" "Does this fully answer your question?" Chances are, it won't. When I did the conference seminar, the team members had cups—but they were all the same size and there was no "fill-to-here line." After some discussion and questioning, the group modified the drawing to show the full story.

It's actually fun to keep modifying the picture, playing with it until you feel it is complete. People involved start thinking about what they want and need instead of what they think is possible. This is the real power of drawing the metric.

Identifying the Information, Measures, and Data Needed

Only after you have a complete picture do you address the components. This picture is an abstract representation of the answer(s) to our root question. It's like an artist's rendition for the design of a cathedral—the kind used in marketing the idea to financial backers. When you present the idea to potential donors, you don't need to provide them with blueprints, you need to pitch the concept.

Next are the specific design elements to ensure the building will be feasible. As the architect, you can provide the artist's conception and do so while knowing from experience whether the concept is sound. Your next step is to determine what will go into the specific design—the types of structures, wiring, plumbing, and load-bearing walls. Then you will have to determine the materials you need to make it a reality—what do we need to fill in the metric?

Let's look at the workload example. How do we divide our team's workload to be the most productive? Remember, the picture is of drink cups—various sizes from 20-ounce, to 32-ounce, to a super-sized 44-ounce. Each cup has a mark that designates the "fill" level—and if we fill above this line, the froth will overflow the cup. Using the picture, we need to determine the following:

- How do we measure our team's level of productivity?
- How do we currently allocate (divide) the work?
- What are other ways to allocate the work?

Of the three pieces of information listed, only the first seems to need measures. The other two are process definitions. Since our question is driven by a goal (to improve the team's productivity), the process for designing the metric will produce other useful elements toward the goal's achievement.

Information can be made up of other information, measures, and data. It isn't important to delineate each component—what's important is to work from the complex to the simple without rushing. Don't jump to the data!

An example of how you can move from a question to measures and then to data follows.

- How do we measure our team's level of productivity?
  - How much can each worker do?
    - Worker A?
    - Worker B?
    - Worker C?
  - How much does each worker do?
    - By worker (same breakout as the previous measure)
  - How much does each worker have in his or her cup?
    - By worker
  - How long does it take to perform a task?
    - By worker
    - By type of task
    - By task

I logged a sub-bullet for each worker to stress what seems to be anti-intuitive to many people—most times there is no "standard" for everyone. When developing measures, I find it fascinating how many clients want to set a number that they think will work for everyone.

Machinery, even manufactured to painstakingly precise standards, doesn't function identically. Why do we think that humans—the most complex living organism known, and with beautiful variety—would fit a standardized behavior pattern?

Of course it would be easier if we had a standard—as in the amount of work that can be done by a programmer and the amount of work each programmer does. But this is unlikely.

You may also be curious why we have the first and second measures—how much a worker can do and how much he accomplishes. But since the goal is to increase the productivity of the team, the answer may not be in reallocating the load—it may be finding ways to get people to work to their potential. A simpler reason is that we don't know if each worker is being given as much as they can do—or too much.

Looking back at Figure 2-1, we may need to decide if the flavor of drink matters. Do we need to know the type of work each worker has to do? Does the complexity of the work matter? Does the customer matter? Does the purpose of the work matter? Does the quality of the work matter? Should we only be measuring around the manager's assigned work? If we exclude other work, do we run the risk of improving productivity in one area at the cost of others?

These questions are being asked at the right time—compared with if we started with the data. If we started with a vague idea (instead of a root question) and jumped to the data—we'd be asking these questions after collecting reams of data, perhaps analyzing them and creating charts and graphs. Only when we showed the fruits of our labor to the client would we find out if we were on the right track.

I want to help you avoid wasting your time and resources. I want to convince you to build your metrics from a position of knowledge.

Collecting Measures and Data

Now that we've identified the information needed (and measures that make up that information) we need to collect the data. This is a lot easier with the question, metric picture (answer), and information already designed. The trick here is not to leave out details.

It's easy to skip over things or leave parts out because we assume it's obvious. Building on the workload example, let's look at some of the data we'd identify.

First we'll need task breakdowns so we know what the "work" entails. What comprises the tasks—so we can measure what tasks each worker "can" do. With this breakdown, we also need classifications for the types of tasks/work. When trying to explain concepts, I find it helpful to use concrete examples. The more abstract the concept, the more concrete the example should be.

Task 1: Provide second-level support

Task 1a: Analyze issue for cause

Task 1b: Determine solution set

Task 1c: Select best solution

This example would be categorized as "support." Other categories of a task may include innovation, process improvement, project development, or maintenance.

We'll also need a measure of how long it takes each worker to perform each task, as seen in Table 2-1.

If we have measures for the work components, we should be able to roll this data "up" to determine how long it takes to do larger units of work.

Table 2-1. Amount of Time Workers Perform Tasks

Worker	Task 1	Task 2
A	1 hr average	15 minutes average
B	1.5 hrs average	30 minutes average
C	1.6 hrs average	28 minutes average

Next, we'll need measures of what is assigned currently to each worker.

Worker A is working on support while workers B and C are working on mainte-nance.

Since we need to know what each worker is capable of ("can do") we will need to know the skill set of each worker. With specific identification of what they "can't" do. Many times we find the measure of X can be de-termined in part (or fully) by the measure of the inverse value $1/x$.

Worker A is not capable of doing maintenance work. That's why he isn't assigned to maintenance and does the support-level work instead.

Again, it's a lot easier once we work from the top down. Depending on the answers we would perform investigations to ensure the assumptions we come to are correct. Then we can make changes (improvements) based on these results.

Worker A wants to do more maintenance-type tasks, but doesn't feel confident in her abilities to do so. The manager chose to develop a comprehensive training program for Worker A.

Workers B and C showed they had the skills necessary to provide support, and were willing to do so. The manager divided the support work more evenly between the team.

These types of adjustments (and new solutions) could be made throughout, depending on the answers derived from the metrics.

It was not necessary to be "perfect" in the identification of all measures and data. If you are missing something, that should become evident when trying to build the information and, finally, the metric. If you're missing something, it will stand out. If you have data or measures that you don't need, this, too, will become quickly evident when you put it all together for the metric.

You're not trying to be perfect out of the gate, but you definitely want to be as effective as possible. You'd like to be proactive and work from a strong plan. This happens when you use the root question and metric as your starting point.

It is truly amazing to see how a picture—not charts and graphs, but a creative drawing depicting the answer—works. It helps focus your efforts and keeps you from chasing data.

The metric "picture" provides focus, direction, and helps us avoid chasing data.

How to Collect Data

Once we've designed what the metric will look like, and have an idea of what information, measures, and data we'll need to fill it out, we need to discuss how to gather the needed parts. I'm not going to give you definitive steps as much as provide guidelines for collecting data. These "rules of thumb" will help you gather the data in as accurate a manner as possible.

Later, we'll expand on some of the factors that make the accuracy of the data uncertain. This is less a result of the mechanisms used and more a consequence of the amount of trust that the data providers have with you and management.

Use Automated Data When Possible

When I see a "Keep Out, No Trespassing" sign, I think of metrics. A no-trespassing sign is designed to keep people out of places that they don't belong. Many times it's related to safety. In the case of collecting data, you want to keep people out.

Why? The less human interaction with the data, the better. The less interaction, the more accurate the data will be, and the higher level of confidence everyone can have in its accuracy. Whenever I can collect the data through automated means, I do so. For example, to go back to the example in Chapter 1, rather than have someone count the number of ski machine or stair stepper users, I'd prefer to have some automated means of gathering this data. If each user has to log in information on the machine (weight, age, etc.) to use the programming features, the machine itself may be able to provide user data.

The biggest risk with using automated data may be the abundance and variety. If you find the exercise machines can provide the data you are looking for (because you worked from the question to the metric, down to the information and finally measures/data), great! But normally you also find a lot of other data not related to the metric. Any automated system that provides your data will invariably also provide a lot of data you aren't looking for.

For example, you'll have data on the demographics I already listed (age and weight). You'll also have data on the length of time users are on the machines, as well as the exercise program(s) selected; the users' average speed; and the total "distance" covered in the workout. The machine may also give information on average pulse rate. But, if none of this data serves the purpose of answering your root question, none of it is useful.

In our workload example, it will be difficult to gather data about the work without having human interaction. Most work accounting systems are heavily dependent on the workers capturing their effort, by task and category of work.

Beware!

So what happens when your client finds out about all of this untapped data?

He'll want to find a use for it! It's human nature to want to get your money's worth. And since you are already providing a metric, the client may also want you to find a place for some of this "interesting" data in the metric you're building. This risk is manageable and may be worth the benefit of having highly accurate data.

The risk of using automated data is that management will want to use data that has no relation to your root question, just because this extra data is available.

You should also be careful of over-trusting automated data. Sometimes the data only seems to be devoid of human intervention. What if the client wants to use the weight and age data collected in the ski machine? Well, the weight may have been taken by the machine and be devoid of human interaction (besides humans standing on the machine), but age is human-provided data, since the user of the machine has to input this data.

Employ Software and Hardware

Collecting data using software or hardware are the most common forms of automated data collection. I don't necessarily mean software or hardware developed for the purpose of collecting data (like a vehicle traffic counter). I mean something more like the ski-machine, equipment designed to provide a service with the added benefit of providing data on the system. Data collected automatically provides a higher level of accuracy, but runs the risk of offering too much data to choose from. Much of the data I use on a daily basis comes from software and hardware—including data on usage and speed.

Conduct Surveys

Surveys are probably the most common data-gathering tool. They are used in research (Gallup Polls), predictive analysis (exit polls during elections), feedback gathering (customer satisfaction surveys), marketing analysis (like the surveyers walking in shopping malls, asking for a few minutes of your time) and demographic data gathering (the US census). Surveys are used whenever you want to gather a lot of data from a lot of people—people being a key component. Surveys, by nature, involve people.

The best use of surveys is when you are seeking the opinions of the respondents. Any time you collect data by "asking" someone for information, the answer will lack objectivity. In contrast to using automated tools for collecting (high/total objectivity), surveys by nature are highly/totally subjective. So, the best use of the survey is when you purposefully want subjectivity.

Customer satisfaction surveys are a good example of this. Another is marketing analysis. If you want to know if someone likes one type of drink over another, a great way to find out is to ask. Surveys, in one way or another, collect your opinion. I lump all such data gathering under surveys—even if you don't use a "survey tool" to gather them. So, focus groups, and interviews fit under surveys. We'll cover the theories behind the types of surveys and survey methods later.

Use People

So far I've recommended avoiding human provision of data when accuracy is essential. I've also said that when you want an opinion, you want (have) to use humans. But, how about when you decide to use people for gathering data other than opinions? What happens when you use people because you can't afford an automated solution or an automated solution doesn't exist?

I try to stay fit and get to the gym on a regular basis. I've noticed that a gym staff member often walks around the facility with a log sheet on a clipboard. He'll visually count the number of people on the basketball courts. He'll then take a count of those using the aerobic machines. Next, the free weights, the weight machines, and finally the elevated track. He'll also check the locker room, and a female coworker will check the women's locker room.

How much human error gets injected into this process? Besides simply miscounting, it is easy to imagine how the counter can miss or double-count people. During his transition between rooms, areas, and floors of the facility, the staff member is likely to miss patrons and/or count someone more than once (for example, Gym-User A is counted while on the basketball court, and by the time the staffer gets to the locker room, Gym-User A is in the locker room, where he is counted again). Yet, it's not economically feasible to utilize automated equipment to count the facility's usage by area.

We readily accept the inherent inaccuracy in the human-gathered form of data collection. Thus we must ask the following:

- How critical is it to have a high degree of accuracy in our data?
- Is high accuracy worth the high cost?
- How important is it to have the data at all? If it's acceptable to simply have some insight into usage of the areas, a rough estimate may be more than enough

Many times you collect data using humans because we need human interaction to deal with the situation that generates the data. A good example is the IT help desk. Since you choose to have a human answer the trouble call (vs. an automated system), much of the data collected (and later used to analyze trends and predict problem areas) is done by the person answering the phone. Even an "automated" survey tool (e-mails generated and sent to callers) is dependent on the technician correctly capturing each phone caller's information.

Another Example

I want to provide you another example of how to develop a metric. This one is from a work experience.

I once worked with a web and teleconferencing technician. His boss wanted to know the answer to the following question: "Is the service worthwhile to maintain?" The technician's service cost the amount of a full-salaried employee, plus expensive equipment, a dedicated room, and monthly fees. The boss wanted to know if the costs were worth the benefits.

By now you're probably demanding that I define "the service," "worthwhile," and "maintain." You should be! The service could be all forms of conferencing, *or* it could be only web conferencing that requires the technician's time and has a recurring fee. If the teleconference method is a sunk cost and doesn't require intervention by the technician, this may not be a factor.

When we ask if something is "worthwhile"—what exactly do we mean? Is it simply a question of monetary return on investment? Does goodwill count? Do employee productivity, effectiveness, and efficiency matter? And finally, what do we mean by maintain? To have it at all? To pay the salary of the technician? To have our own facility vs. using a contracted or hosted solution? Does "maintain" include hardware maintenance? Does it include upgrades to software? How about repairs and replacements?

Once we have clear definitions for the terms that make up the root question, we will have a much better picture! Remember the importance of a common language. It is equally important that everyone fully understands the language used to create the root question.

Figure 2-2 shows the picture the technician and I drew of his service metric.

Figure 2-2. Web/teleconferencing value

The picture we drew depicts the value gained (costs avoided) by using the web-conferencing system. We anticipated showing information on money savings (travel and hotel costs), time savings (the time to travel), environmental savings (fuel consumption and CO_2 emissions), and the happiness of the clients who were able to more easily meet "face-to-face" with others. These factors would be compared to the actual costs incurred.

This is not a perfect metric. There is no such thing in my experience. You can't prove that the costs would have been incurred without the system. It's like assuming that if we didn't have telephones, we'd write or visit family more often. While we can't categorically say this would happen, for the purposes of determining the avoided costs, or the value of the service, we have to make these assumptions.

Information

We asked a lot of clarifying questions—seeking definitions for all of the parts of the root question. The definitions led us to the following information decision (we only wanted to answer one aspect of the root question): How much do we save? How much money, jet fuel, CO_2 emissions, and time do we potentially save by maintaining the conferencing center? This clarification made the next phase purposeful. Rather than chase all manner of data, we could focus our efforts only on the measures and data we needed.

Measures

We designed measures that would reveal the following:

- The amount of time saved for each conference
- The amount of money saved for each conference
    - Travel funds saved (plane fare and taxis)
    - Hotel funds (when the distance dictates an overnight stay)
- The amount of CO_2 emissions saved for each conference

Data

To build the measures, we needed data like the following:

- Locations participating in the web/teleconference
- Number of participants at each location
- Distance from each location to the "host" location. For purposes of the metric, we had to determine a "host" location that participants would travel to. If our location were the host, we wouldn't gain the savings—but our colleagues could claim them
    - If the meeting is held at location X (because of protocol, for example) the distance from each participating starting point.
    - If protocol doesn't dictate a specific meeting location—then which location has the most participants
- Plane fare amounts to and from the host location
- The CO_2 emissions from airplanes for these flights
- If the location is not at an airport:
    - The distance to the location from/to the airport
    - The cost for ground travel from/to airport
- The average nightly cost of a hotel room at the host site
    - At international locations
    - At domestic locations
- The cost for the web/teleconference
    - A system with recurring fees
    - A system with annual fees
    - The salary of the technician

- The amount of time the technician spends on each conference
- The total number of web/teleconferences

This metric is a good example of how to build from a root question to an abstract picture and finally to the data, measures, and information needed to tell the story. The best part of this example, though, is that it was created to satisfy the request of the service provider. Our webconferencing technician requested the metric to answer the question his boss had been asking him. I warned him that if the answer came back, "No, get rid of the service," that I wasn't going to hide the results. He agreed. Partly because he is a loyal employee—and if the data accurately showed that it was not worth the cost, he'd be the first to advocate dropping the service. And partly because he "knew" that the service *was* a worthwhile one. He knew the worth of it since he worked with it every day.

The service provider usually already knows the answers that you'll build metrics to validate.

This metric is published quarterly to show the benefits of web/teleconferencing for the organization.

Recap

In this chapter, we covered the following:

- *Getting to the root question:* It is imperative to get to the root question *before* you start even "thinking about" data. The root question will help you avoid waste. To get to the real root, I discussed using Five Whys, facilitating group interventions, and being willing to accept that the answer may not include metrics. Make sure you define every facet of the question so you are perfectly clear about what you want.
- *Testing the root question:* I provided some suggestions on how you can test if the question you've settled upon is a true root question. Even with the tests, it's important to realize that you may not have reached it when you draw your picture. You may have to do a little rework.

- *Developing a metric:* This is more about what you shouldn't do than what you should. You shouldn't think about data. You shouldn't design charts and graphs. You shouldn't jump to what measures you want. Stay abstract.
- *Being an artist:* The best way I've found to stay abstract is to be creative. The best way to be creative is to avoid the details and focus on the big picture. One helps feed the other. Draw a picture—it doesn't have to be a work of art.
- *Identifying the information, measures, and data needed:* Once you have a clear picture (literally and figuratively) it's time to think about information, measures and data. Think of it like a paint-by-numbers picture. What information is required to fill the picture in? What color paints will you need? And make sure you don't leave out any essential components.
- *Collecting measures and data:* Now that you know what you need, how do you collect it?
- *How to collect data:* I presented four major methods for collecting data: Using *automated sources, employing software and hardware, conducting surveys, and using people.*

Conclusion

This chapter covered how to create a root question and, based on that, how to design a metric. I also covered how to identify and collect the information, measures, and data needed to turn the metric picture into a usable metric.

Bonus Material

A different way of thinking about metrics. A different way of approaching metrics. These are part of what I'm trying to share with you.

The school my six-year-old attends uses fundraisers to supplement its funding. Recently, the school was selling coupon books for local fast-food restaurants at the low cost of five dollars. Not a bad deal—I easily got back my investment by using just one coupon.

I like this fundraiser. In my opinion, it gives a more-than-fair value for the price and the school gets a generous share of the funds. The principal liked it, too, but wanted confirmation of how well the program worked—

ostensibly so he could decide whether to keep doing this fundraiser or investigate a replacement.

After I dropped my daughter off at class one day, the principal approached me. "Marty, we collected some data..." He knew I was a metrics expert. The fact that he was already "collecting data," and that he led with that, gave me pause.

"Really?" I tried to stay non-committal. I love talking metrics, and like most people I also like talking about my profession. But, I can't remember anyone who has ever been happy with the answers I give to their questions. Most people don't have a root question. Most don't want to be creative. Most simply want data to prove them right and that's "simpler than possible."

"Yes. We collected data on how successful the coupon book program was this year."

"Uh huh." I bit my tongue.

"I wanted to know if it was successful, so we counted how many books we sold."

Without defining "success" and without looking for the root question, he did a couple of things he could have avoided. The good news was that I knew that it didn't take much effort to collect the data—he just had to count how many books were left at the end of the year compared to how many the school had purchased.

He even built a nice chart showing the percentage of the total sold by week and overall.

"Nice graph," I said.

"As you can see, we sold all of our coupon books a week before the planned deadline. So, I'm doubling our order for next year."

"Really?"

"Sure, it was a tremendous success!"

"O-kay..." I couldn't hold back a small frown.

In the short pause that followed, I actually imagined that I was going to escape with no further discussion.

"I know you well enough to know that you think I did something wrong. Come on, tell me."

If this were a seminar instead of a book, I'd give you a test at this point. I'd ask you, "What did the principal miss? What should he have done? How might his conclusions be wrong? How might those errors be a problem?"

If this were a seminar, I'd give you five minutes to capture the answers. Since this is a book, if you want to try and figure it out, close the book now and take a shot.

I took the time to explain, as kindly as I could where he went wrong.

"John, it's not that you did something wrong, but you might have missed some-thing. I'd at least ask you not to make a decision before you investigate fur-ther. The first thing I would do before going further is to define what you mean by "success." Is it simply selling a lot of coupon books?"

"Sure. Isn't it?"

"I truly don't know. Why are you selling the books? What's your purpose?" He nearly rolled his eyes. He felt I was making him state the obvious.

"To raise funds."

"Ok. And you succeeded at that, right?"

"Yes."

"And is that all you wanted to know?"

"Sure."

"Really? Then why are you deciding to double your order next year? It seems that you actually wanted to know how many books you should order next year..."

"Well, yeah. If it was a success, I figured we'd increase our order."

"And what would you have done if you didn't sell them all? What if you sold only half as many as you ordered?"

"I don't know. Probably order only three-quarters next year and try harder to sell them. Or maybe find a different fundraiser?"

"John, one of the things I encourage clients to do is determine how they will use the answers to their questions before they collect any data. So, I would have asked you—what will you do if the answer is 'very successful?'"

"Tremendously successful!" He said with a smile.

"Tremendously successful. The point is, if you told me that you'd double your order I would help you get to your real question—which sounds like it's 'How many cou-pon books should I buy next year' with the possible answer being anything from none—drop the program—to doubling the order."

"What's the difference?"

"Well, if we go with the new question, you'd look at your data differently, and you'd also collect some other data, like:

- Who made your sales?
- Who bought the coupons?
- Why did you sell out?
- How many requests did you have that you couldn't satisfy?
- How did you market the program?

"I hear what you're saying, but I don't see how any of that would make a difference."

"I'll give you a simple scenario. What if I told you that you sold half of your tickets in one day? A week before your deadline, you sold all the tickets you had left, all in one day."

He stopped and thought a bit.

"Half?"

"Yes."

"Hmm. I might have to know why we sold so many in such a short span of time."

"Good. And if I told you that they were all sold by one person?"

"Wow! I'd have to give that person a big thank-you card. Perhaps we could give them an award?"

I gave him a look that only a parent or principal could understand.

"I'm jumping to conclusions again?" he offered.

I nodded.

"I guess I'd want to know how that happened."

"Good. Let's say you find out that someone, an anonymous donor knew that you had only sold half of your goal after two-and-a-half months into your program. Let's say that the donor decided to help you out by buying all of your remaining coupon books."

"What did they do with all of them? That's a lot of books! Wait, I should care, right? I mean that's important, isn't it?"

"Actually, I'm glad you want to know. That means you're not jumping to conclusions and you're starting to think of the measures properly. They should be something that you use to help you think. Good job."

He smiled.

"The donor gave them away to people like a secret Santa. He just gave them out like candy. Now, what's more important though is—what if you double your order next year?"

"Well...I guess if the donor doesn't decide to bail us out, especially since we could have three times as many coupon books left at the same time in the program... Oww. It could be a catastrophe."

Now I smiled. "So, let's talk about your real information needs, what you really want to know, and we can build a metric if need be."

Designing metrics, like almost every organizational development activity involves much more than the actual task. You get a lot more out of the effort to design a metric then just the metric. And sometimes you don't end up with the expected result (a metric) at all, but you always end up with something useful.

Planning a Good Metric

Where to Begin

In *Why Organizations Struggle So Hard to Improve So Little,* my coauthors and I addressed the need for structure and rigor in documenting work with metrics. More than any other organizational development effort, metrics require meticulous care. Excellent attention to detail is needed—not only in the information you use within the metric (remember the risks of human involvement), but also with the process involved.

In this chapter, we'll cover identifying the many possible components of a metric development plan and documenting the metric development plan so that it becomes a tool for not only the creation of the metric, but a tool for using it effectively.

The Metric Development Plan

We already discussed the building blocks of the metric. If we envision metrics as a house, the root question can logically signify the foundation of the structure. Without a solid foundation, the house may not last (ask the Three Pigs). Of course, if the structure isn't intended to be a long-term home, then the foundation becomes much less important. We also discussed the load-bearing wall (metric), the two-by-fours (information), the drywall (measures), and the nails (data). We haven't yet discussed the various other items that go into building a house or the components that go into turning a structure into a home.

While a metric is designed to answer a root question, and uses information, measures, and data to give it substance, metrics also require other components to make it a useful tool. These components are included in a metric development plan.

The Components of a Metric Development Plan

A metric development plan captures all of the components of the metric— data, measures, information, pictures, and of course, the root question. The plan also documents how these components are collected, analyzed, and reported. The development plan includes timetables, information on who owns the data, and how the information will be stored and shared. Like most plans, it gives guidance from the beginning (designing and creating the metric) to the end (reporting and using the metric). The plan may also include when the metric will no longer be necessary.

The metric development plan provides a game plan for making metrics well-defined, useful, and manageable. At a minimum, it should include the following:

- A purpose statement
- An explanation of how it will be used
- An explanation of how it won't be used
- A list of the customers of the metrics
- Schedules
- Analysis
- Visuals or "a picture for the rest of us"
- A narrative

The plan not only helps in the creation of the metric, but it also provides guidance for the maintenance and final disposition.

If it's worth doing, it's worth planning to do it right.

The Purpose Statement

Is the purpose statement the same as your root question? The answer is, "maybe." You will document the purpose statement in your Development Plan when you identify the root question as shown in Figure 3-1.

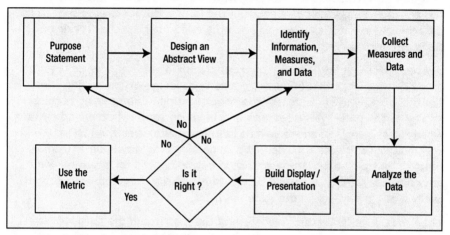

Figure 3-1. Purpose Statement

If you have a well-formed root question and you have dug as deep as you can, your root question may very well contain the purpose statement. Consider the following example:

> Root Question: *"How well are we providing customer support using on-line chat?"*

> Purpose Statement: *"To ensure that we are providing world-class customer support using online chat."*

Not much of a distinction between the two. It does provide a clearer requirement. It gives the underlying reasons for the question, and therefore the metric. The purpose of the metric is usually larger than providing insights or an answer to your root question. There is usually a central purpose to the question being asked. This purpose allows you to pull more than one metric together under an overarching requirement.

Let's take my example of customer support through chat. If we kept asking "why," we may find that there is an underlying need to improve overall customer service/support to the point that the customer support team is a key component to the overall organization's success. The requirement is to make the customer support a selling point to customers. It should be one of the reasons the customer becomes a loyal, repeat promoter of the organization.

This underlying purpose will give us a much clearer guide for the metric. It will also allow us to identify other metrics needed, if you are ready to do so. You may have to settle for working with the question you currently have and get to the bigger-picture needs in the future. But it's always best to have the big picture—it allows you to keep the end in mind while working on parts of the picture.

I've been working lately with numerous clients in another area of organizational development that I find extremely rewarding—vision setting. Much like the work we did to identify the root question, vision setting requires getting to the underlying need or want. In vision setting, I do *not* advocate a wordy statement. When we write a statement, we often tend to use flowery, multi-syllabic words to describe something that should be extremely simple. Your purpose statement should not be crafted for beauty—you're not going to frame it. It should be edited for clarity. Remember to define every word and clause in the statement.

Your root question is the foundation of the metric *and* the purpose statement. If you've identified a good root question, the question and your purpose may be one and the same.

When documenting the metric development plan, I make a point to capture both the root question and the purpose. If they are synonymous, no harm is done. If they are not, then I gain more insight into what the metric is really all about.

Allow me to give you an actual example. The executive director of a center for women and I were working on a possible metric and our conversation went as follows:

> *"I want to know how many women come through the door each day,"* she said. This seemed a valid question, but not a fully vetted one.

> *"Why? What will you do with the number?"*

> *"I need to show our board of directors our worth."*

> I asked, *"Will they know your worth based on the number of people who come through your door?"*

> She thought for a moment, seeing my point. *"No. Our worth is based on the number of women we help."*

I said, "There may be other ways to measure your worth, so before we go into actual measures, let's look deeper at your question. Why do you want to prove your worth to your board?"

"They don't think I'm doing a good job."

"How do you know that they think that?" I asked. "Have they told you so?"

"No, of course not. But they are asking me for ways to measure my performance."

"Is evaluating your performance part of their mandate?"

She said, "Well, yes. I guess so."

"OK, then. Let's assume that they are only asking for input from you so that they can carry out their responsibilities. Perhaps a good question to start with is 'How well is the executive director performing her duties?'"

"Yes, that sounds OK."

"So, what are your job responsibilities, exactly?"

From this starting point, I was able to determine what the position of executive director meant. We could have rolled it all up into a pretty purpose statement like, "To ensure the care center's day-to-day operations are executed in a timely, efficient, and effective manner." This would be plaque worthy, but not useful for defining the metric in answer to the question of how well the director was performing. No, I needed a breakdown of the tasks and responsibilities that made up the executive director's position.

With a direct question like "what are your job responsibilities?" you can identify the proper measures to provide a meaningful answer. As with any requirements-gathering exercise, you have to get the real need, the root need.

When I've worked with clients who need to answer questions from above (in their organizational chain of command, not heaven), many times we don't get to a "good" root question—we're just not afforded the luxury due to the time involved or the ways in which we're asked to produce data. Even in that case, I cannot overstress the importance of trying. Push the envelope as far as you feel comfortable. Ask for the "why." You will do a much better job of designing the metric, collecting, and analyzing the data if you understand "why."

Figure 3-2 shows the three major things to capture during the collection of data, measures and information.

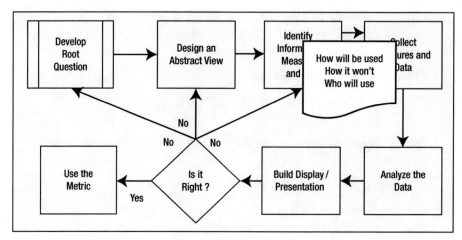

Figure 3-2. The "How" and "Who"

How Information Will Be Used

Along with the root question and purpose, you should articulate clearly *how the metric will be used*. This part of the metric development plan provides a key tool in helping overcome the fear people have of providing data. It will also help with the fear, uncertainty, and doubt people have toward the way the data will be used. Again, if you have a well-formed, clear, and foundational root question and purpose statement, this should be easy. While it may be easy to define how the metric will be used, that doesn't make the definition obvious. You need to ask the question directly: "How will you use the metric?" Your goal is to try and get the most direct answer. The more direct the question, the higher likelihood that you'll get a direct answer.

- *Vague answer: "To improve our processes."*
- *Direct answer: "To measure how the changes we implemented affect the process."*
- *More specific answer: "To measure how the changes we implemented affect the process and allow for course corrections."*

If public speaking is one of the greatest fears, the use of personal data might be a close second. Not just *any* numbers and values—but data that can be used to hurt an individual or create negative public perception of our organization. We imagine the worst, it's in our nature. So when we are asked to provide data, especially data that we believe reflects in any way upon ourselves or our departments, tremendous fear is created.

When we don't know the reason, we imagine the worst possible scenarios. It's our nature.

The greatest basis for fear is found in data that people believe addresses them at a personal level. This is why I recommend starting metrics programs at the effectiveness level.

When the data you are collecting (and later analyzing and reporting on) can be indicators about an individual, the fear factor becomes exponentially greater. It doesn't even matter if you plan to use the data at an aggregate level, never looking at the individual. If the data *could* be used at the individual level, the fear is warranted.

Time to Resolve can be a good effectiveness measure, used to improve overall customer service. The purpose may be simply to achieve better customer service and, therefore, satisfaction. But if you fail to communicate this purpose, the root question, and how you will use the answers—the individuals providing the data will imagine the worst.

Be forewarned. Even if you have an automated system to collect the data (for example, the day and time the incident was opened and closed), the ones opening and closing the case in that system are still providing the data.

If the staff learns that you are gathering data on resolution speeds, they will "hear" that you are collecting data on how long it takes them to resolve the case. Not how long it takes the team or the organization to resolve most cases, but instead how long it takes each of them individually to do the work. And, if you are collecting data on an individual's performance, the individual in question will imagine all of the worst possible scenarios for how you will use that data.

So your innocent and proper Time to Resolve measure, if unexplained, could create morale problems due to fear, uncertainty, and doubt.

If fear is born of ignorance, then asking for data without sharing the purpose makes you the midwife.

The boss says: *"I only want the data so I know what's going on."*

The worker hears: *"I want data so I can see where you're screwing up."*

The boss says: *"I need the data so I can make better decisions."*

> *The worker hears: "I need data so I can decide who to fire, cut work hours from, or penalize."*
>
> *The boss asks: "What's the problem with reporting on your performance? I should know about it, shouldn't I?"*
>
> *The worker wonders: "Yes, so why don't you know about it? Why ask me for data about it? Why not just ask me? Why not spend some time with me?"*

If you have spent any considerable amount of time in an organization with multiple layers of management, the preceding conversation may sound extremely familiar. Unfortunately, this conversation is not a unique one. I believe it (or something close to it) occurs in every workplace, every work day of the year.

We need to combat this common problem. To create a useful metric, you have to know, in advance of collecting the data, how the results (answers) will be used. It is essential for designing the metric properly and identifying the correct information, measures, and data. It is also essential if you want accurate data wherever human-provisioning is involved.

There is a simple enough test you can perform. Ask your friend, relative, coworker, or boss a simple, personal question. Better yet, ask your significant other a simple question like, "How much do you weigh?" Don't do it yet. First read about the expected outcomes—before you get injured.

When you ask someone a personal question without offering any explanation as to the reason, one of the following five reactions will likely occur:

1. You are physically accosted. At least that's what happened to me in the case when I asked my wife the same question.

2. You get data that accurately reflects what the data provider *believes* you want to hear.

3. You get data that accurately reflects what the data provider *wants* you to hear.

4. You get accurate data.

5. You get a question in return: "Why do you want to know?"

Most likely people will in turn ask you, "Why do you want to know?" It's a natural reaction. Along with the expected response, you may also notice respondents becoming defensive. Watch their body language. They may not provide your answers, but if they do, they probably won't do so happily or willingly.

Part two of this experiment would be for you to provide a seemingly valid purpose for your question, which would not be, "Oh, I'm just curious," or "I just want to gain some insight into your weight." Though, many times when we ask management why they want certain data, we get an equally ambiguous answer: "Oh, I just want to know what's going on," or "I just need insight into how *we're* doing." A lack of clarity will create inaccuracy in the data. In software programming, we use the term GIGO—garbage in, garbage out. This is true for dealing with emotionally-charged discussions with others. Don't be fooled. Asking for data will create emotional tension. If you provide garbage reasons for asking a question, you'll get garbage answers.

It won't help to simply assure the people that you're interviewing that everyone is being asked the same questions. But, for example, if you first tell them that you're doing a study for school and you need to gather the weight of ten random people, they may answer your question.

Instead of an immediate answer, you may get one or more of the following responses:

- *"Will you use my name?"*
- *"Who will see it?"*
- *"What are you going to do with it?"*

All of these questions are trying to get at the same thing: how are you going to use the answer that I give you? Until you answer this question to the satisfaction of the respondent, any answer you receive will be highly suspect.

Even if you explain fully how you will use it, depending on how the respondent feels personally about the information, the accuracy will be suspect. This may seem logical to you. I've heard the arguments before. You may argue that you aren't looking for personal information about your workers, you're trying to develop metrics around staffing so you can justify another position!

Back to our experiment. Ask someone, "How much do you weigh?"

If by some small chance you get an answer to this question, write it down. Also write down the level of confidence you have in the accuracy of the answer. Are you 90 percent confident that it's accurate?

If you didn't get an answer at first, then explain the purpose of your question (for example, that you are collecting data for a class project). If you get an answer, write it down. What's your confidence in its accuracy now?

As a third attempt, share how you intend to use the answer. It doesn't really matter what you say. You can go with, "I'll aggregate the data and show the average weight of the ten people I ask. Then we'll discuss if that weight is a healthy norm for people." See if you get an answer yet.

Don't forget to observe body language the whole time. See if the respondent is less defensive as you provide more information. Check your level of confidence in the answer.

The explanation of how the metric and its components will be used should be documented in the metric development plan. Don't get hung up on the need to document everything or to make it pretty. The value of the development plan lies in the clarity of its purpose. Of course, plans also provide consistency, prolonged guidance, and direction for others who may use it. By creating the development plan, you will have thoroughly thought out the metric and will be able to communicate its worth to any who ask.

We've seen that the questions we ask can result in a lack of answers or inaccurate answers unless we clearly define our intentions for the information gathered. Another key to getting better answers (or one at all if the respondent is still reluctant), is to communicate how the results *won't* be used.

Explain How Information *Won't* Be Used

When you're questioning a person about his weight, tell him how you *won't* use the information. Sincerely assure him that no matter what, you will not use his information in a way that he'd find offensive. This could include using it in a published study or as a case study for a class. You may not know what his particular fears are. By explaining how you won't use the information, you provide an opportunity for him to share what he would find inappropriate (threatening or fearful). If you want accurate data, you have to be able to assure the people involved in providing the data how you will and how you won't use the data. And how you *won't* use it may be more important to the person providing the data to you than how you *will* use it.

This promise takes some diligence on your part. You have to remember your promises—which can be tricky when you get a very innocent request for information. You have to make sure it's within the agreement you made with the data provider.

The most common and simple agreement I make is to not provide data to others without the source's permission. If you provide the data, it's your data. You should get to decide who sees it.

This should be captured in the development plan under "How it won't be used." Probably the major reason to put the plan in writing is that documented agreements allow you to keep your word with less difficulty.

Defining how the metrics won't be used helps prevent fear, uncertainty, and doubt.

Identify Who Will Want to Use the Metrics

While you may believe you are the only customer who wants to view or use the metric, chances are there are many customers of your metrics. A simple test is to list all of the people you plan on sharing your information with. This list will probably include your boss, your workers, and those who use your service.

Anyone who will use your metric is a customer of it. You should only show it to customers.

Everyone that you plan to share your metrics with becomes a customer of that metric. If they are not customers, then there is no reason to share the information with them. You may be a proponent of openness and want to post your metrics on a public web site, but the information doesn't belong to you. It is the property of those providing the data. It is not public information; it was designed to help the organization answer a root question. Why share it with the world? And today we know that if you share it publicly, it's in the public domain forever.

The provider of the data should be the primary metric customer.

The possible customers are as follows:

- Those who provide the data that goes into creating the metric.
- Those who you choose to share your metrics with.
- Those who ask you for the metric *and* can clearly explain how they will use the metric.

It is important to clearly identify the customers of your metrics because they will have a say in how you present the metric, its validity, and how it will be used. If you are to keep to the promise of how it will and won't be used, you have to know who will use it and who won't.

These customers should be documented in your development plan, with a note on the type of customer they are. Are they providing the data? Are they the front-line supervisors? Are they executive management? The type of customer will help define what level of information they receive and the communications necessary around the metric's use.

Who will and won't use the metric is as important as how it will and won't be used.

Before I go to the next component, let's take a sanity check. I know quite well that sometimes you can't tell your boss "no." I know that your boss may be demanding data, measures, or information and may not be sympathetic to your need for assurances that he won't misuse or abuse the information you provide. If I believe the accounts of numerous authors, coworkers, and friends—bad managers far outnumber good ones.

I am not advocating that you fall on your sword over an innocuous information request. I am promoting that, depending on your position in the organization, that if you are put in the unenviable position as a middle person between a "bad" manager and the workers—do *everything* you can within your power to ensure that the information you provide is not misused.

Schedule for Reporting, Analyzing, and Collecting

The gathering of the data, measures, and information you will use to build the metric requires a plan. Figure 3-3 shows the timing for developing this part of the plan.

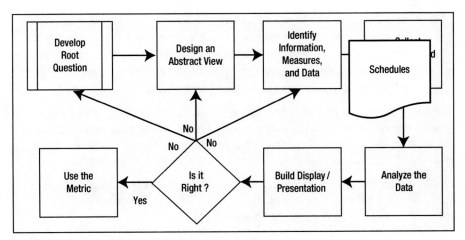

Figure 3-3. Schedules

Most metrics are time-based. You'll be looking at annual, monthly, or weekly reports of most metrics. Some are event-driven and require that you report them periodically. As part of your metric development plan, you will have to schedule at least three of the following facets of your metric:

- *Schedule for reporting.* Look at the schedule from the end backward to the beginning. Start with what you need. Take into account the customers that you've identified to help determine when you will need the metrics. Based on how the metrics will be used will also determine when you'll need to report it.

- *Schedule for analysis.* Based on the need, you can work backward to determine when you'll need to analyze the information to finalize the metric. This is the simplest part of the scheduling trifecta, since it is purely dependent upon how long it will take you to get the job done. Of course, the other variable is the amount of data and the complexity of the analysis. But, ultimately, you'll schedule the analysis far enough in advance to get it done and review your results. I highly recommend you have at least one other pair of eyes review your analysis. Depending on the complexity of your data, you may need a quality check of the raw data used in the analysis also.

- *Schedule for collection.* When will you collect the data? Based on when you will have to report the data, determine when you will need to analyze it. Then, based on that, figure out when you will need to collect it. Often, the schedule for collecting the data will be dependent on how you collect it. If it's automated, you may be able to gather it whenever you want. If it's dependent on human input, you may have to wait for periodic updates. If your data is survey-based, you'll have to wait until you administer the surveys and the additional time for people to complete them.

Since you started at the end, you know when you need the data and can work backwards to the date that you need to have the data in hand. Depending on the collection method you've chosen, you can plan out when you need to start the collection process and schedule accordingly.

Nothing new here—if you want to achieve success, you must plan to succeed. Don't do it when you "get the chance." Plan it. Schedule it. If it's worth doing, it's worth planning to do it right.

And if it's worth doing right, it's worth making sure you can do it right more than once. But remember, the development plan isn't just about repeatability, it's about getting it right the first time by forcing yourself to think it all out.

Analysis

Documenting analysis happens when you think it does…during the analysis phase.

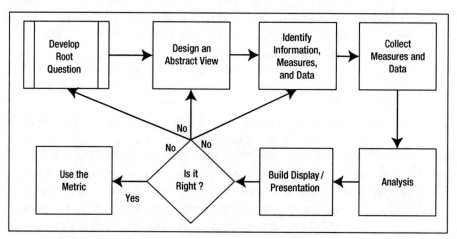

Figure 3-4. Analysis

This may be the most obvious section of the metric development plan so far. After data collecting, the next thing most people think of when I mention metrics is analysis. All of the statistics classes I've taken lead to the same end: how to analyze the data you've carefully gathered. This analysis documentation in the plan must include all metric data rules, edits, formulas, and algorithms; each should be clearly spelled out for future reference.

What may be in contention is the infallibility of the analysis tools. There are those that believe if you have accurate data (a few don't even care if it's accurate), you can predict, explain, or improve anything through statistical analysis. I'm not of that camp.

I have great respect for the benefits of analysis and, of course, I rely on it to determine the answers my metrics provide. For me, the design of the metric—from the root question, to the abstract picture, to the complete story—is more important than the analysis of the data. That may seem odd. If we fail to analyze properly, we will probably end up with the wrong conclusions and, thereby, the wrong answers. But, if we haven't designed the metric properly to begin with, we'll have no chance of the right answers—regardless of the quality of our analysis.

And if we have a good foundation (the right components), we should end up with a useful metric. If the analysis is off center, chances are we'll notice this in the reporting and review of the metric.

Without a strong foundation, the quality of the analysis is irrelevant.

While the analysis is secondary to the foundation, it is important to capture your analysis. The analysis techniques (formulas and processes) are the second-most volatile part of the metric (the first is the graphical representation). When the metric is reported and used, I expect it to be changed. If I've laid a strong foundation through my design, the final product will still need to be tweaked.

Consider it part of the negotiations with management. If you've worked with the leadership to determine the root questions—and you managed not to wear out your welcome—when you deliver your metric, you are fulfilling your part of the bargain. You are going to give the leader what she wants— useful answers to help inform her decisions. Although the question is hers, she may have the need to tweak the answer. It is rare that a manager accepts a metric as is. They almost always feel the need to modify the final picture.

Whether this is because of their bigger-picture view of the organization or simply the need to feel that they contributed, I don't know and it doesn't matter. You should be open to recommendations for changing the graphical representation.

If the graphical presentation changes, you may very well have to also tweak the analysis that fed the metric. If the leader wants to see the percentage of customers who were satisfied instead of the average customer satisfaction rating, you will have to change your analysis.

The raw data (the number of respondents, ratings from each, the date of the response, and what each rating means) is still good, but the way you are presenting the analysis and the analysis itself needs to change.

It helps to have the analysis documented in the development plan—again to help you think it through, but also for replication. Of all the parts of the plan, this component needs to be documented to allow repeatability. You have to ensure that you analyze the data the same way each time and that any changes are captured since this directly affects the final metric displayed.

A Picture for the Rest of Us

You've drawn a picture of your metric. This picture was an abstract representation of the answer to the root question. Another major component of a well thought-out metric is another picture—one your customers can easily decipher. This picture is normally a chart, graph, or table. Plan to include one in your metric development plan.

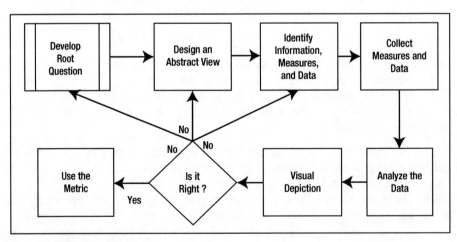

Figure 3-5. Visual Depiction

It can easily be more than one picture. If you need a dashboard made up of twelve charts, graphs, and tables—then so be it. If you've done a good job with the root question and abstract version of your metric, determining how you'll graphically represent the metric should be an easy step. The really good news is that you can't go wrong with this component. If you pick a stacked bar chart, and later realize it should have been trend lines—you can change it. No harm done.

Not only can you change the way you represent your metric if you find a different structure would tell your story better, but you may need to have multiple representations anyway. This will depend on who the customer is, how each customer will use the metric, and how you will share it. For each group, the manner in which you present the metric may vary.

This component should be fun. Let your creativity shine through. Find ways to explain visually so that you need less prose. A picture can truly tell a story of a thousand words. No matter how good it is, you'll want to add prose to ensure the viewer gets it right, but we want that prose to be as brief as possible. We want the picture to tell the story, clearly. Don't over-complicate the picture.

You may, in fact, have more data than necessary to tell your story. You may find yourself reluctant to leave out information, but sometimes less really is more. Especially if the extra information could confuse the audience. You're not required to put data into your metric just because you've collected it.

Also, experiment with different ways to depict the metric. You might even test ideas for the visuals with your metric customers.

Narrative Description

I love it when someone asks, "Do I have to spell it out for you?" My answer is frequently, "Thanks! That would be nice."

Why not? No matter how good your graphical representation is, you can't afford to risk a misunderstanding. You rooted out the question and you designed the metric so that you could provide the right answer to the right question. You cannot allow the viewer of the metric to misinterpret the story that you've worked so hard to tell.

The narrative is your chance to ensure the viewer sees what you see, the way you see it. They will hopefully hear what you are trying to tell them. Any part of the plan can be updated on a regular basis, but the narrative requires frequent documentation. Since the narrative explains what the metric is telling the viewer, the explanation has to change to match the story as it changes. The narration which accompanies the picture and documents what the metric means is critical to how the metric will be used.

Figure 3-6 shows when the narration is documented.

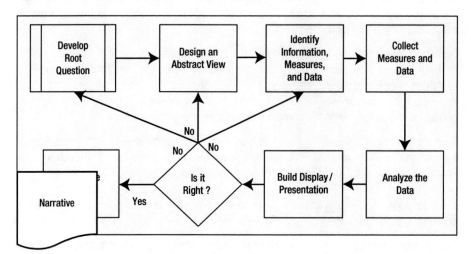

Figure 3-6. Narrative

Documentation: Making the Metric Development Plan More Than a Plan

In the end, the metric development plan should document the why (purpose statement), what (metric), when (schedule), who (customers), and how (analysis, how it will and how it won't be used).

Document it as thoroughly as possible—putting all of the details into one place. This will help you in the following three ways:

- It will help you think out the metric in a comprehensive manner.
- It will help you if you need to improve your processes.
- It will help you if you need to replicate the steps.

Figure 3-7 shows them all together in coordination with the process for developing the metric.

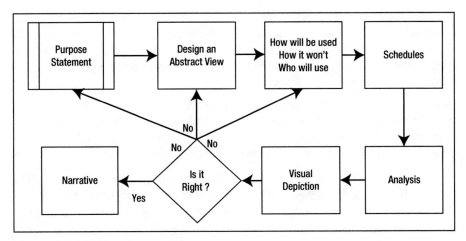

Figure 3-7. The Development Plan

Rather than prescribe a length or specific format, I want to stress the readability of the final plan. You will want it for reference and at times for evidence of agreements made. I find it extremely useful when the metrics are reported infrequently. The more infrequently the metrics are reported, the more likely I'll forget the steps I followed. The collection can be very complicated, cleaning the data can be complex, and the analysis can require even more detailed steps. The more complex and the more infrequent the process, the more likely I'll need the plan documented.

Of course, even if I perform the process weekly, the responsible thing to do is to document the plan so others can carry it out in my absence.

The plan has use throughout the life of the metric. It starts out helping me to fully think out the design and creation of the metric. It then helps in capturing the agreements made around the metrics use and schedule. It helps in defending actions (it becomes a contract between the metric analyst and the data providers and the end customer) and meeting expectations. Finally it is also critical to long-term success. It provides a historical view as well as a "how to" guide. Without repeatability you can't improve.

Without repeatability, you can't improve.

The components of the development plan need to be documented in a manner that allows easy and accurate access. Ensuring accuracy is more difficult than making it easy to access. We discussed different means of collecting data and ways to make it more accurate. The really good news is that many times, the way we make it more accurate also makes it easy to access. Less human interaction moves us toward more confidence in the accuracy of the data, and automation makes it easier to collect.

When you document the components, don't be afraid to be verbose. This isn't a time for brevity. We need to build confidence in the metric and the components. We need to document as much information around each component as necessary to build trust in the following:

- *Accuracy of the raw data.* You will be challenged on this, and rightfully so. People have their own expectations of what the answer to your root question should be. They will also have expectations regarding what the data should say about that question. Regardless of the answer, *someone* will think you have it wrong and check your data. Thus, you have to be accurate when you share the data. This requires that you perform quality checks of the data. It doesn't matter if the errors are due to your sources, your formulas, or a software glitch. If your data is proven to be wrong, your metrics won't be trusted or used.

  Most examples of inaccurate raw data can be found as a result of human error but even automated tools are prone to errors, particularly in the interpretation of the data. Errors can be found in anything from logging data incorrectly, mistakes in calculations, or assigning the wrong categories to information. If your categories are not defined properly, an automated system may report the data correctly, but it might be reporting the wrong data. If you are tracking time to resolve trouble calls, is the time equal to the time between the start and stop dates? Or is it the time from the call to the resolution (which may occur well before the day/time the trouble ticket is closed)? Are you using calendar days to track time or workdays? If you are reporting on availability, what is considered an outage? How do you determine the outage occurred, when, and for how long? The simple rule of thumb is to double (and triple) check your data. I find the best way to check my data is to have someone else look at it. I'm too close to the work to see the errors others see immediately.

When you're starting, there is nothing more important than accuracy of your raw data.

- *Accuracy of your analysis.* We'll get into methods of analysis later, but for now, it is important for you to document the processes and steps you take to analyze the data. This will enable you to repeat the process—a necessity for consistency. A simple example is the use of formulas in spreadsheet programs. I do a lot of my metric work in spreadsheet programs because they are easy, user-friendly, and powerful. I use formulas to calculate everything from the number of elapsed days to the percentage of change over time. Whatever methods you use they must be documented. Anyone looking over your work should be able to replicate your work by hand (using pen, paper, and a calculator). This documentation is tedious but necessary. Your process must be repeatable. Your process *must* produce zero defects in the data, analysis, and results.

Your process and the resulting information must be error free.

- *Repeatability of your process.* Yes, I already mentioned this in the accuracy of your analysis. But I it is worth emphasizing and clarifying that repeatability is critical not only for the analysis, but throughout the process to design the metric. The collection of the data must be repeatable—in a strict sense. The analysis of the data must be repeatable. The graphical representation must also be a repeatable step in the process. Each time, you should collect, analyze, and report the data in the same way. If you don't document the process and ensure it is repeatable, you will lose the all-important trust of your audience. This repeatability is necessary throughout the process. It's why we develop schedules. We want to do it the same way, at the same time intervals, and using the same tools. Consistency is critical.

Without repeatability you don't really have a process.

To adhere to the tenants of good documentation, you'll need to use a method for controlling versions of your data, analysis, and reports. You'll need to store your information with backups. All of the documentation listed must be safeguarded against loss or tampering. You have to ensure the accuracy of the components and you can't do this if you don't control access to the information.

First, you'll have to ensure the sources of your data are producing accurate information. When you have checked the data for quality and have attained a high level of confidence in the accuracy, you'll have to repeat the processes you used to gather that information. Once you have accurate data, you have to ensure it stays that way.

People are the greatest risk to having accurate data.

You will need a safe and secure location to store your data, your analysis, and your reports. You will need to safeguard it from others who may innocently tamper with it. You will also need to keep it safe from yourself. When was the last time you worked on something well past your bedtime? When was the last time you made errors keying data? When was the last time you lost over an hour's worth of work because you forgot to save regularly?

You will make mistakes—it's inevitable. The key is to mitigate this reality as much as possible.

How should you mitigate the inevitable mistakes you will undoubtedly make? Save early, save often, and save your work in more than one place. It won't hurt to have a hard copy of your work as a final safeguard. Along with backing up your data, it's important to have the processes documented.

Another tool for mitigating mistakes is to use variables in all of your formulas. If you're using software to perform equations, avoid any raw data in the formulas. Put any values that you will reuse in a separate location (worksheet, table, or file). Not only does it allow you to avoid mistakes, it makes modifying the formulas easier.

Reference all values and keep raw data out of the equation.

The following are a few other pointers to help you as you document your plan:

- *Don't work when tired.* Seriously. You should know yourself well enough to know when you're tired. Put the work down and come back to it when you are refreshed. There are some things you can do when tired—metrics is not one of them.
- *Stick to your process.* Don't allow short deadlines to force you to deviate from your process. You may be tempted to take shortcuts just to get the metric updated fast enough to meet an unexpected deadline. Resist this. Resist the person requesting the data before the agreed-upon schedule. Whenever you deviate from your process you run the risk of making mistakes.

Start with "no." Refuse to rush.

- *Use version control.* It doesn't have to be extensive—just effective. As long as you can track the work you've done and any changes you've made, you'll need to be able to "undo" any changes you've made and return to an earlier version you have faith in.
- *Create and use templates whenever possible.* Templates allow you to make your process more repeatable and to ensure you collect the same data, the same way. I use templates for surveys, interviews, and questionnaires. I use them for analysis and creating graphs and charts. One caution—double-check the template for accuracy.

Reuse is great! Why re-create the wheel? Just double-check that the wheel isn't riddled with broken spokes.

A Note on Process Byproducts

When you worked on the root question, you identified byproducts like goals, objectives, tasks, and measures of success, which were not essential to the metric's design. As you worked on the abstract picture of your metric, other thoughts came to mind. When you captured possible measures you'd need to fill out the picture, you identified more than what was required. The excess items you parked or stored in a to-do list. All of these byproducts have potential to help you improve your organization and could be very valuable. They should be captured and shared. Don't waste them.

Don't waste anything! Your intellectual property is valuable—treat it with respect.

Recap

I have introduced a taxonomy so that we can communicate clearly around the subject of metrics. In the second chapter, I covered the theory and concept of designing a metric and the high-level process for collecting, analyzing, and reporting the data, measures, and information that go into making up that metric. In this chapter, I covered the basics of how and where to begin. I have purposefully kept the information at a high level so that you can feel comfortable with the concept before I start getting into the weeds. In this chapter we covered:

- A metric development plan is not a luxury. It's a necessity.
- The plan not only helps in the creation of the metric, but it also provides guidance for the maintenance and final disposition.
- The metric development plan is made up of the following components:
    - A purpose statement
    - An explanation of how it will be used
    - An explanation of how it won't be used
    - A list of the customers of the metrics
    - Schedules
    - Analysis
    - Visuals or "a picture for the rest of us"
    - A narrative
- Accuracy is critical. I stressed the importance of accuracy in your data (source dependent), your collection (process dependent) and your analysis (process and tool dependent). I also offered the benefits of making your processes repeatable.

Conclusion

We have set some of the foundation for designing and using metrics responsibly. We provided some tools for the practical implementation of a metrics program. The next three chapters will cover the dangers inherent in a metrics program and I will provide warnings, mitigations, and threats to help you avoid the headaches many fall victim to. I believe this is a logical progression—because before you use a powerful and, therefore, potentially dangerous tool, it is important that you understand what it is, how it should be used, and how to avoid injury.

In almost every serious effort, you are told to document your work. It is stressed in everything from software engineering to grant writing. The problem is, it's tedious. I don't know of anyone who is passionate about documenting their work. If you fail to document everything else, I'll forgive you—as long as you document your metric.

Using Metrics as Indicators

To keep things simple, thus far I've focused only on the following basic concepts:

- Metrics are made up of basic components: data, measures, information, and other metrics.
- Metrics should be built from a root question.
- It's more important to share how you won't use a metric than how you will.

This chapter introduces another basic concept about creating and using metrics—metrics are nothing more than indicators. That may seem to be a way of saying they aren't powerful, but we know that's not the case. Metrics can be extremely powerful. Rather, the concept of metrics as indicators warns us not to elevate metrics to the status of truth.

Metrics' considerable power is proven by how much damage they can do. Metrics' worth is rooted in their inherent ability to ignite conversations. Metrics should lead to discussions between customers and service providers, between management and staff. Conversations should blossom around improvement opportunities and anomalies in the data. The basis for these conversations should be the investigation, analysis, and resolution of indicators provided through metrics.

Metrics should be a catalyst to investigation, discussion, and only then, action. The only proper response to metrics is to investigate. Not the type of general investigation discussed in Chapter 15 on research, but instead a directed and focused investigation into the truth behind the indicator.

Facts Aren't Always True

If you search the internet for things we know to be true (supported, of course, by data), you'll eventually find more than one site that offers evidence "debunking" past and present-day myths. What was thought to be a fact is proven to be an incorrect application of theory or the misinterpretation of data.

Our earlier examples of health information are a ripe area, full of things people once believed to be true but now believe the opposite. Think about foods that were considered good for you ten years ago but today are not. Or foods that were considered not to be good for you, which now are considered healthy fare. Are eggs good for you or not? The answer not only depends on who you ask, but when.

- The US Government's "food pyramid" changes periodically.
- Who doesn't remember the scenes of Rocky downing raw eggs?
- It seems like each year we get a new "diet" to follow—high protein, high cholesterol, low fat, no red meat, or fish...the arguments change regularly.

One good argument on the topic of old facts not being in line with new truths is that facts don't change, just our interpretation of them.

Let's take a quick look at a fact that perhaps isn't truth.

It concerns the Amazon book sales rankings. Michael Langthorne, one of my former coauthors, enjoys watching the sales ranking of our book on Amazon.com. He has a high level of confidence in the data and his level of excitement grows or wanes based on the numbers. The problem is that the rankings are daily and depend on not only the number of sales of our book, but also the number of sales of all the other books on the site. The sales are also only counted for individual buyers. If you were to buy a thousand copies of our book, Amazon would only count that as *one* sale toward the rankings. If you were to instead make a thousand separate orders, it would then be counted as one thousand sales, boosting the rankings. Another issue is that Amazon doesn't care who purchases the book. If I were to buy those books, it would improve our rankings, although with no bias because I'm one of the authors.

The point is simple. While the data is "accurate" (or at least you can have a high confidence level in them being accurate), the interpretation of that data can be problematic. Should Mike buy a new television in anticipation of rising sales due to the increased popularity of the book? Or should he be depressed over the lack of sales if the rankings fall drastically?

It's fairly obvious that the answer to both questions is no.

This misrepresentation of metrics as fact can be seen in instances where only a portion of the metric is relayed to the viewer.

A business example is one a friend of mine loves to tell about the service desk analyst who was by all accounts taking three to five times as long to close cases as the other analysts. The "fact" was clear—he was less efficient. He was closing less than half of the cases as his peers and taking much longer to close each case. His "numbers" were abysmal.

The manager of the service desk took this "fact" and made a decision. It may not have helped his thought process that this "slow" worker was also the oldest and had been on the service desk longer than any of the analysts. The manager at the time made the mistake of believing the data he was looking at was a "fact" rather than an indicator. And rather than investigate the matter, he took immediate action.

> He called the weak performer into his office and began chewing him out. When he finally finished his critique he gave the worker a chance to speak, if only to answer this question (veiled threat): "So, what are you going to do about this? How are you going to improve your time to resolve cases? I want to see you closing more cases, faster."
>
> Showing a great deal more patience than he felt at the moment, the worker replied, "My first question is, how is the quality of my work?"
>
> "Lousy! I just told you. You're the slowest analyst on the floor!"
>
> "That's only how fast I work, not how good the quality is. Are you getting any complaints?"
>
> "Well, no."
>
> "Any complaints from customers?"
>
> "No."
>
> "How about my coworkers? Any complaints from them?"

"No," said the manager. "But the data doesn't lie."

"You're right, it doesn't lie. It's just not telling the whole story and therefore it isn't the truth."

"What? Are you trying to tell me you aren't the slowest? You are the one who closes the cases. Are you just incompetent?" The manager was implying that he wasn't closing the cases when done.

"No, I am the slowest," admitted the worker. "And no, I'm not incompetent, just the opposite. Have you asked anyone on the floor why I'm slow?"

"No—I'm asking you."

"Actually you never asked me why. You started out by showing me data that shows that I'm 'slow, inefficient,' and now 'incompetent.'"

The manager wasn't happy with the turn this had taken. The employee continued, "Did you check the types of cases I'm closing? I'm actually faster than most of my coworkers. If you looked at how fast I close simple cases, you'd see that I'm one of the fastest."

"The data doesn't break out that way," said the manager. "How am I supposed to know the types of cases each of you close?"

The employee replied, "Ask?" He was silent a moment. "If you had asked me or anyone else on the floor why I take longer to close cases and why I close fewer cases you'd find out a few things. I close fewer cases because I take longer to close my cases. The other analysts give me any cases that they can't resolve. I get the hardest cases to close because I have the most experience. I am not slow, inefficient, or incompetent. Just the opposite. I'm the best analyst you have on the floor."

The manager looked uncomfortable.

The employee continued, "So, tell me, what do you want me to change? If you want, I won't take any cases from the other analysts and I'll let the customers' toughest problems go unresolved. Your call. You're the boss."

Needless (but fun) to say, the boss never bothered him about his time to resolve again. And luckily for all involved, the boss did not remain in the position much longer.

The only proper initial response to metrics is to investigate.

Earlier, I offered the view that metrics were not facts. You can give metrics too much value by deciding that they are facts. This is dangerous when leadership decides to "drive" decisions with metrics. This gives metrics more power than they deserve. When we elevate metrics to truth, we stop looking deeper. We also risk making decisions and taking actions based on information that may easily be less than 100 percent accurate.

Metrics are not facts. They are indicators.

When we give metrics some undeserved lofty status (as truth instead of indicators) we encourage our organization to "chase the data" rather than work toward the underlying root question the metrics were designed to answer. We send a totally clear and equally wrong message to our staff that the metrics are what matter. We end up trying to influence behavior with numbers, percentages, charts, and graphs.

The simplest example may be in customer satisfaction surveys. Even direct feedback provided during a focus group interview has to be taken with a grain of salt. And when we look at truly objective data, there is always room for misinterpretation. Objective measuring tools can have defects and produce faulty data.

Most times good managers (as well as good workers and good customers) know the truth without the data. Investigate when you see data that doesn't match your gut instinct. Investigate when the data agrees too readily with your hunch.

One of the major benefits of building a metric the way I suggest is that it tells a complete story in answer to a root question. If you've built it well, chances are, it's accurate and comprehensive. It is the closest thing you'll get to the truth. But, I know from experience, no matter how hard I try there is always room for error and misinterpretation. A little pause for the cause of investigation won't hurt—and it may help immensely.

Metrics Can Be Wrong

Since there is the possibility of variance and error in any collection method, there is always room for doubting the total validity of any measure. If you don't have a healthy skepticism of what the information says, you will be led down the wrong path as often as not. Let's say the check-engine light in your car comes on. Let's also say that the car is new. Even if we know that the light is a malfunction indicator, we should refrain from jumping to conclusions. My favorite visits to the mechanics are when they run their diagnostics on my check-engine light and they determine that the only problem *is* with the check-engine light.

Perhaps you are thinking that the fuel-level indicator would be a better example. If the fuel gauge reads near empty, especially if the warning light accompanies it, you can have a high level of confidence that you need gas. But the gas gauge is still only an indicator. Perhaps it's a more reliable one than the check-engine light, but it's still only an indicator. Besides the variance involved (I noticed that when on a hill the gauge goes from nearly empty to nearly an eighth of a tank!), there is still the possibility of a stuck or broken gauge.

I understand if you choose to believe the gas gauge, the thermometer, or the digital clock—which are single measures. But, when you're looking at metrics, which are made up of multiple data, measures, and information, I hope you do so with a healthy dose of humility toward your ability to interpret the meaning of the metric.

This healthy humility keeps us from rushing to conclusions or decisions based solely on indicators (metrics).

Metrics are a tool, an indicator—they are not the answer and may have multiple interpretations.

I've heard (too often for my taste) that metrics should "drive" decisions. I much prefer the attitude and belief that metrics should "inform" decisions.

Accurate Metrics Are Still Simply Indicators

Putting aside the possibility of erroneous data, there are important reasons to refrain from putting too much trust in metrics.

Let's look at an example from the world of Major League Baseball. I like to use baseball because of all the major sports, baseball is easily the most statistically focused. Fans, writers, announcers, and players alike use statistics to discuss America's pastime. It is arguably an intrinsic part of the game.

To be in the National Baseball Hall of Fame is, in many ways, the pinnacle of a player's career. Let's look at one of the greatest player's statistics. In 2011, I was able to witness Derek Jeter's 3,000th hit (a home run), one of the accomplishments a player can achieve to essentially assure his position in the Hall of Fame (Jeter was only the 28th player of all time to achieve this). The question was immediately raised—could Jeter become the all-time leader in hits? The present all-time leader had 4,256 hits! Personally, I don't think Jeter will make it.

The all-time hits leader was also voted as an All-Star 17 times in a 23-year career—at an unheard of five different positions. He won three World Series championships, two Golden Glove Awards, one National League Most Valuable Player (MVP) award, and also a World Series MVP award. He also won Rookie of the Year and the Lou Gehrig Memorial Award and was selected to Major League Baseball's All-Century Team. According to one online source, his MLB records are as follows:

- Most hits
- Most outs
- Most games played
- Most at bats
- Most singles
- Most runs by a switch hitter
- Most doubles by a switch hitter
- Most walks by a switch hitter
- Most total bases by a switch hitter
- Most seasons with 200 or more hits
- Most consecutive seasons with 100 or more hits
- Most consecutive seasons with 600 at bats
- Only player to play more than 500 games at each of five different positions

This baseball player holds a few other world records, as well as numerous National League records that include most runs and doubles.

In every list I could find, he was ranked in the top 50 of all-time baseball players. In 1998 *The Sporting News* ranked him as the 25th and The Society for American Baseball Research placed him at 48th.

So, based on all of this objective, critically checked data, it should be easily understood why this professional baseball player was unanimously elected to the National Baseball Hall of Fame on the first ballot that he was eligible for.

But he wasn't elected.

His name is Pete Rose. He is not in the Baseball Hall of Fame and may never get there. If you look at all of the statistical data that the voters for the Hall use, his selection is a no-brainer. But the statistics, while telling a complete story, lacks the input that was taken into account—specifically that he broke one of baseball's not-to-be-breached rules: he legally and illegally gambled on professional baseball games.

In the face of the overwhelming "facts" that Pete Rose should be in the Baseball Hall of Fame, the truth is in direct contrast to the data.

Even if we look at well-defined metrics that tell a full story, they are only indicators in the truest sense. If you fully and clearly explain the results of your investigation, you complete the metric by explaining the meaning of the indicator. You explain what the metrics indicate so that better decisions can be made, improvement opportunities identified, or progress determined. You are providing an interpretation—hopefully one backed by the results of your investigation.

No matter how you decorate it, metrics are only indicators and as such should elicit only one initial response: to investigate.

Of course, some metrics are simple enough that you will accept their story without as much investigation (like the gas gauge on your car), but even in these instances, you should keep a watchful eye in case they start to show you data that you believe is misleading or erroneous.

At the end of the day, even if you have total confidence in the accuracy of the data (pro-sports statistics, for example), you have to treat it all as indicators. Data can't predict the future. If it could, then there would be no reason to play the games!

The point is that metrics should not be seen as facts but rather as indicators of current and past conditions. Used properly, metrics should lead our conversations, help us to focus, and draw our attention in the right direction. Metrics don't provide the answers; they help us ask the right questions and take the right actions.

Indicators: Qualitative vs. Quantitative Data

The simple difference between qualitative and quantitative data is that qualitative data is made up of opinions and quantitative data is made up of objective numbers. Qualitative data is more readily accepted to be an indicator, while quantitative data is more likely to be mistakenly viewed as fact, without any further investigation necessary. Let's look at these two main categories of indicators.

Qualitative Data

Customer satisfaction ratings are opinions—a qualitative measure of how satisfied your customer is. Most qualitative collection tools consist of surveys and interviews. They can be in the form of open-ended questions, multiple-choice questions, or ratings. Even observations can be qualitative, if they don't involve capturing "numbers"—like counting the number of strikes in baseball, or the number of questions about a specific product line. When observations capture the opinions of the observer, we still have qualitative data.

Many times, qualitative data is what is called for to provide answers to our root question. Besides asking how satisfied your customers are, some other examples are:

- How satisfied are your workers?
- Which product do your customers prefer, regular or diet?
- How fast do they want it?
- How much money are your customers willing to pay for your product or service?
- When or at what hours do your customers expect your product or service to be available?
- Do your workers feel appreciated?

No matter how you collect this data, they are opinions. They are not objective data. They are not, for the most part, even numbers. You can take qualitative data and try to transpose them into more quantitative forms—turning opinions into values on a Likert scale, for example. But in the end, they are still opinions. They'll look like quantitative data, but they are not.

Some analysts, especially those that believe the customer is always right, believe that qualitative data is the best data. Through open-ended questions these analysts believe you receive valuable feedback on your processes, products, and services. Since the customer is king, what better analytical tool is there than to capture the customers' opinion on your products and services?

These analysts love focus groups and interviews. Surveys will suffice in a pinch, but they lack the ability for analysts to observe the non-verbals and other signs that can help them determine the answer to the question, "How satisfied are our customers?"

One of the most popular organizational development books in recent years is *First, Break All the Rules* by Marcus Buckingham and Curt Coffman (Simon & Schuster, 1999). This book is built on the analysis the authors performed on qualitative data. The reviews sell potential readers by promising to help us "see into the minds" of successful managers and leaders in successful companies. The overwhelming success of this book is just one modern-day example of the power of qualitative measures.

Quantitative Data

Quantitative data usually means numbers—objective measures without emotion. This includes all of the gauges in your car. They also include information from automated systems like automated-call tools, which tell you how many calls were answered, how long it took for them to be answered, and how long the call lasted.

The debate used to be that one form of data was better than another. It was argued that quantitative data was better because it avoided the natural inconsistencies of data based on emotional opinions. Then the quantitative camp argued that someone could rate your product high or low on a satisfaction scale for many reasons other than the products' quality. Some factors that could go into a qualitative evaluation of your service or product could include:

- The time of day the question was asked
- The mood the respondent was in before you asked the question
- Past experiences of the respondent with similar products or services
- The temperature of the room
- The lighting
- The attractiveness of the person asking the question
- If the interviewer has a foreign accent

The list can go on forever. Quantitative data on the other hand avoids these variances and gets directly to the things that can be counted. Some examples in the same type of scenario could include:

- The number of customers who bought your product
- The number of times a customer buys the product
- The amount of money the customer paid for your product
- What other products the customer bought
- The number of product returns

The proponents of quantitative information would argue that this is much more reliable and, therefore, meaningful data.

I'm sure you've guessed that neither camp is entirely correct. I'm going to suggest using a mix of both types of data.

Quantitative and Qualitative Data

For the most part, the flaws with qualitative data can be best alleviated by including some quantitative data—and vice versa. Qualitative data, when taken in isolation, is hard to trust because of the many factors that can lead to the information you collect. If a customer says that they love your product or service, but never buy it, the warm fuzzy you receive from the positive feedback will not help when the company goes out of business. Quantitative data on the number of sales and repeat customers can help provide faith in the qualitative feedback.

If we look at quantitative data by itself, we risk making some unwise decisions. If our entire inventory of a test product sells out in one day, we may decide that it is a hot item and we should expect to sell many more. Without qualitative data to support this assumption, we may go into mass production and invest large sums. Qualitative questions could have informed us of why the item sold out so fast. We may learn that the causes for the immediate success were unlikely to recur and therefore we may need to do more research and development before going full speed ahead. Perhaps the product sold out because a confused customer was sent to the store to buy a lot of product X and instead bought a lot of your product by mistake. Perhaps it sold quickly because it was a new product with a novel look, but when asked, the customers assured you they'd not buy it again—that they didn't like it.

Not only should you use both types of data (and the accompanying data collection methods), but you should also look to collect more than one of each. And of course, once you do, you have to investigate the results.

You may believe qualitative measures are more obvious indicators. Yet even when we ask a customer if she is satisfied with a product, and she answers emphatically, "yes," her response doesn't mean she was truly satisfied. The only "fact" we know is that the respondent said she was satisfied.

Even in the case of automated-call software, the results are only indicators.

Quantitative data, while objective, are still only indicators. If you don't know why the numbers are what they are, you will end up guessing at the reasons behind the numbers. If you guess at the causes, you are guessing at the answer.

Metrics (indicators) require interpretation to be used properly.

I advocate using triangulation (see Chapter 7) for getting a better read on the full answer to any root question. This would direct us not to take qualitative or quantitative data alone. The great debate between which is better is unnecessary. You should use some of each in your recipe.

Recap

The following are principles to remember:

- *Metrics are only indicators.*
- Metrics are not facts. Even when you have a high level of confidence in their accuracy, don't elevate them to the status of truth.
- The only proper response to a metric is to investigate.
- When you tell the story by adding prose, you are explaining what the metrics are indicating so that better decisions can be made, or improvement opportunities identified, or progress determined.
- There are two main categories of indicators: Qualitative and Quantitative. Qualitative is subjective in nature and usually an expression of opinion. Quantitative is objective in nature and compiled using automated, impartial tools.
- Metrics by themselves don't provide the answers; they help us ask the right questions and take the right actions.
- *Metrics require interpretation to be useful.*
- *Even the interpretation is open to interpretation—metrics aren't about providing truth, they're about providing insight.*

Conclusion

Metrics are only indicators. This doesn't mean they aren't valid or accurate. Even the most objective, accurate, and valid metrics should only be treated as indicators. From my days in the Air Force, I learned that "perception is reality." This is true for metrics. One of the major reasons I insist on providing an explanation to accompany your charts, graphs, and tables is to limit the variance in perceptions of your metrics. The interpretation of your metrics should not be left up to the viewer. You should do the work and due diligence, and investigate what the metrics are telling you. You should take the results of your investigation to form thoughtful conclusions based on data. These should be provided in the explanation for the metric.

You will then do your best to sell your interpretation of the metric to your audience. Even with that, you have to accept that your interpretation is open to interpretation by those viewing your metrics. You also have to accept that your well-defined and fully told story is, in the end, only an indicator. It should be a well-explained indicator and one that your diagnostics have correctly interpreted; but it is an indicator nonetheless. This requires healthy humility on your part.

Remember, metrics are only a tool. They are not meant to be more.

Using the Answer Key
A Shortcut

This chapter marks the beginning of the practical portion of the book. We've covered a lot of theory and concepts in the first part, which should provide a foundation for doing the actual work.

The Answer Key is a tool for helping ensure you have the right answer to your root question. It works with the majority of organizational improvement questions. It will also give you ideas about other areas you may want to measure. You'll get the most benefit when you use the Answer Key to work on organizational improvement efforts.

What Is the Answer Key?

The Answer Key starts with the defining point of any metric: the need for information, the root question. The Answer Key won't work for every root question, only ones concerning the health of the organization. The health of the organization covers the wide range of questions and needs we usually develop metrics for. Most root questions, especially in a business, revolve around how well the organization is functioning. Most Balanced Scorecards (see the box) and questions about customer satisfaction fit under this umbrella.

The Answer Key is a shortcut for many of the metrics you'll encounter. It includes the metrics I recommend organizations start with when they are seeking to implement a metrics program for the first time.

The Balanced Scorecard and the Dashboard

The Balanced Scorecard was introduced in 1987 by Art Schneiderman, a manager at the semiconductor company, Analog Devices. It has its most well-known proponents in Robert S. Kaplan, a professor at Harvard Business School, and Dr. David P. Norton, a founder and director of the Palladium Group. The basic concept consists of four perspectives: Financial, Customer, Internal Business Processes, and Learning/Growth. By looking at these key areas, leadership can gain a pulse of the organization through the use of measures and targets.

While I don't agree with the concept of "targets" and I have reservations on the Balanced Scorecard as a whole, it has strengths I have to respect. The Balanced Scorecard has been used successfully by many organizations and continues to be popular.

The "Dashboard" is a later promotion of metrics in a more balanced manner. Created in the spirit of its namesake, it is a dynamic metric tool. Like the Balanced Scorecard, the Dashboard employs multiple measures, but includes a more real-time component built around Key Performance Indicators. There is no shortage of metric processes and tools to choose from. The good news is that what I offer can be applied to any of these popular methods or you can embark on a personal journey where you build your own metrics from scratch.

The Answer Key helps you determine where you need to go with your metrics. It also identifies other questions that may relate to the one you're starting with. It can also help you keep from going in the wrong direction and dispersing your efforts too broadly, with no focus.

The Answer Key is made up of tiers that branch out from left to right. Each tier has more measures and data than the previous tier. The following sections will describe each of these tiers in more detail.

Answer Key: First Tier

The first tier isn't so much of a tier as it is a starting point. Is your root question an organizational information need? Does your root question deal with information about an organization; specifically, about the health of the organization? If so, your question will probably fall under one of the following two concerns:

- How well you provide services and products to your customers
- How healthy the future looks for your organization

Answer Key: Second Tier

If your root question fits within one of the first two tiers of the Answer Key, this tool will help you focus your efforts and find viable measures without spending inordinate amounts of time hunting for them. But, if your question does not fit into the Answer Key, don't change your question so you can use this shortcut!

Also don't ignore the need for developing the root question first. In other words, don't start with the key. If you do, you'll end up short-circuiting your efforts to develop useful metrics and more importantly, to answer your questions.

Tier two provides a framework for strategic-level root questions. If your root question is at the vision level, the second tier may represent actual metrics. When you find your root question is based on improving the organization, the question is often based on a need to understand "where the organization is" and "where it is going." The Answer Key shows that this need for information flows into two channels, one to show the return (what we get) vs. our investment (what we put in) and the other to assist in the management of resources. I call these two branches "Return vs. Investment" and "The State of the Union." Figure 5-1 shows this branching.

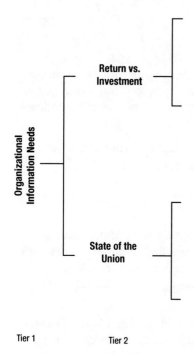

Figure 5-1. The Answer Key, tiers one and two

Return vs. Investment

Return vs. Investment is the first of the two main branches of organizational metrics. It represents the information needed to answer questions concerning how well the organization is functioning and how well it is run. Are we doing the right things? Are we doing the right things the right way? These are key focus areas for improvement and, actually, for survival. If you aren't doing the "right" things, chances are you will soon be out of business or, at the least, out of a job.

If you aren't doing things the right way, you may find that you can continue to function and the business may continue to survive, but any meaningful improvement is highly unlikely. The best you will be able to hope for is to survive, but not thrive.

Root questions around the *return* may include

- How well are we providing our key services?
- In what ways can we improve our key services?

Questions around the *investment* may include

- How much does it cost us to provide our key services?
- How well are we managing our resources?

As we delve deeper into the answer key, more specific questions will become apparent. Remember though, the breadth of your root question will determine how far to the left you'll need to go. The farther left on the Answer Key, the more broad or strategic the question.

State of the Union

Once you are effectively and efficiently running the business, you can turn your attention to how you manage your resources. The most valuable assets you have should be maintained with loving care. Yes, I'm talking about your workforce. Every boss I've ever had has touted the same mantra: "Our most valuable assets are our people." Yet it's amazing to me how poorly we take care of those admittedly invaluable assets.

I observe managers who take their BMWs to their dealers for scheduled maintenance, only use premium gasoline (regardless of the price of gas), and won't park anywhere near another car—yet do absolutely nothing to maintain their workforce. No training plans, no employee satisfaction surveys, not even a suggestion program. They rarely listen to their staff and devalue them by never asking for input. If people are truly our greatest assets, then we should treat them as such.

This view of the organization is our "State of the Union" address. It tells us how healthy our organization is internally. While Return vs. Investment tells us how healthy the organization is from a customer and business point of view, the State of the Union tells us how healthy the culture is.

Besides the workforce, we also need to focus on the potential for our future. We can determine this by looking at how we are managing our growth toward maturity. Do we have good strategic plans for our future? Are we working toward our goals?

Root questions you may encounter in this area include the following:

- How strong is the culture of recognition in our organization?
- How strong is the loyalty of our workforce?
- How well are our professional-development efforts working?
- What is the expected future of our organization?
- How do we stack up against our competition?
- How well are we achieving our strategic goals?

The further to the right you move on the Answer Key, the more specific and tactical your root questions will become.

Answer Key: Third Tier

Figure 5-2 shows the next level of the Answer Key, in which we extend the branches to include Product/Service Health (effectiveness), Process Health (efficiency), Organizational Health (employee maintenance), and Future Health (projects and strategic planning).

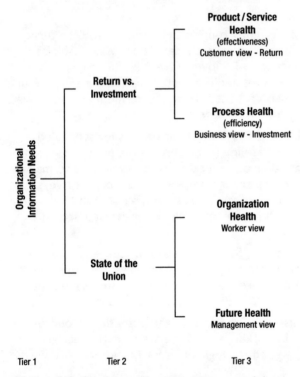

Product / Service Health
(effectiveness)
Customer view - Return

Return vs. Investment

Process Health
(efficiency)
Business view - Investment

Organizational Information Needs

Organization Health
Worker view

State of the Union

Future Health
Management view

Tier 1   Tier 2   Tier 3

Figure 5-2. The Answer Key, tiers one, two, and three

Most root questions boil down to wanting to know answers based on one of the views of the organization represented in the third tier. The titles—Product/Service Health, Process Health, Organizational Health, and Future Health—help us to understand the relationship of each branch to the other. They also help us understand where our metric fits. Along with the titles, we find an accompanying viewpoint to further assist in reading the Answer

Key. These viewpoints show that each of the titles can be looked at from the perspective of Customers, the Business, the Workers, and finally Management.

Let's figure out where your root question best fits.

Does your root question deal with how well you provide a service or product? Does it ask if you are doing the right things? Does it ask if the things you are doing satisfy the needs or desires of your customers? Is your root question one the customer would ask? If your question matches any of these, it fits into the Product/Service Health category.

Does your root question touch on how well you perform the processes necessary to deliver the services or products? How efficient you are? How long it takes or how much it costs for you to perform the tasks in the process? Is your question one a frontline manager would ask? If your question can be found in any of these, you are probably looking at a Process Health root question.

If your root question concerns human resources, the staff, or something a compassionate leader would ask, your question may belong in the Organizational Health branch. Root questions here ask about the morale of the workforce, loyalty, and retention rates for employees, among other things. How well do you treat your staff? Is your organization among the top 100 places to work in your industry?

The final area of the third tier represents root questions that are concerned with the Future Health of the organization. Is the organization suffering from organizational immaturity? How useful are the strategic plans, mission statement, and vision of the organization? How well is research and development progressing? This view is primarily one of top leadership—if your leadership and the organization are ready to look ahead.

How would you use the Answer Key to develop your metrics?

The information needed to define the Return vs. Investment is made up of the well-trod paths of "effectiveness" and "efficiency." Effectiveness is the organization's health from the customer's point of view. How well is the organization delivering on its promises? Is the organization doing the right things? This is not only important for the development of viable metrics, but for understanding and growing the culture of the organization. Some organizations may not even know who its customers are. And if the customer base has been well defined, gathering the customer's view of the components of effectiveness is not seen as important.

Sometimes organizations are forced to ask customers what they think of the company's effectiveness. Surveys are built, focus groups are formed, and the questions are asked.

- Do you use our products or services?
- Are you satisfied with the delivery of our products and services?
- How satisfied are you with our organization?

While these questions help define viable measures, they also give focus for your own growth. Does the organization have a clearly-defined and documented list of customers? Does the organization know what its products and services are? Is the organization in the business of satisfying the customer? How does the organization "serve" the customer? These are more than guidelines for gathering data points. The Answer Key helps form a picture for an organization seeking to achieve continuous improvement.

While these four sections can describe the metrics themselves (if you have a higher-level root question), chances are your root question is at this level and your metrics won't start until the fourth tier.

Answer Key: Fourth Tier

Now we'll look at the level most organizations start and finish with. When your root question starts here, you have tactical, low-level questions. This is to be expected when an organization is first starting to use metrics. The root questions you'll encounter will be very specific and may only address a small area. You may have a root question about delivery that asks, "How well are we responding to customers requests for updates?" for example.

You may have root questions around specific Process Health issues, like the amount of time it takes to produce a widget, the quality of your output, or the cost for a specific service. Where your root question falls in the Answer Key changes the character of each tier. Figure 5-3 introduces the fourth tier.

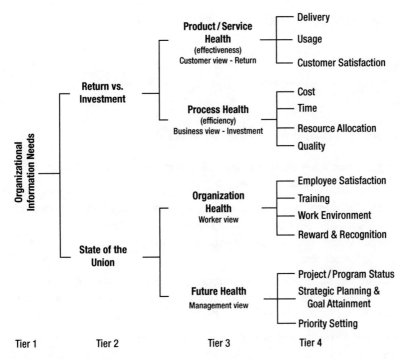

Figure 5-3. The Answer Key, tiers one through four

If your root question comes out of the fourth tier, everything to the left is context for the question. As your organization matures, you'll move your questions to the left, asking questions from a more strategic position. If your root question were in tier two, then tier three would represent the metrics you could use and tier four would represent information. The measures and data would be defined for each information set—and could become a fifth and sixth tier if necessary.

The Answer Key not only keeps you focused and helps you determine what area you're interested in; it also provides some standard metrics, information, and measures, depending on where your root question falls.

Product/Service Health (effectiveness)

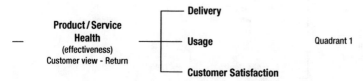

Figure 5-4. The Answer Key, Quadrant I, Product/Service Health

The following are the main components of Product/Service Health (Figure 5-4):

- *Delivery*: How well are you delivering your products and/or services?
- *Usage*: Are your products and/or services being used?
- *Customer satisfaction*: What do your customers think of your products and/or services?

Each component can be broken down into smaller bits—making it more palatable. Delivery is a good example for this as it is a higher-level concept. I tend to break delivery into the following parts:

- *Availability*: Is the service/product available when the customer wants it?
- *Speed*: How long does it take to deliver the service/product?
- *Accuracy*: Do we deliver what we say we will or are there errors involved?

The driving force behind Product/Service Health is the customer. We don't care who is "responsible" for the issue. We don't care if you have any control over the situation or condition. All we're trying to see is how the customer views our products and services. This simplistic way of looking at your organization is valuable because it makes it easy to focus on what is most important.

Process Health (efficiency)

Figure 5-5. The Answer Key, Quadrant 2, Process Health

The other component of Return vs. Investment is efficiency, or is the organization doing things the "right way?" This (Figure 5-5) captures a business view that all stakeholders should want to claim. The following, tested components of efficiency remain relevant:

- *Cost*: What is the cost-benefit of the way we perform our processes?
- *Time*: Time is akin to speed in the customer view. Many times the same data and sources can be reused for this measure. How much time does it take to perform a task or process?
- *Resource allocation*: How efficiently do we distribute the work? Do we assign work by type and amount?
- *Quality*: Quality is accuracy from the business point of view. Even if we have redundant systems providing 100 percent uptime, we will need to track that reliability (for each of those systems) so that we can best maintain them.

Many organizations focus too much on cost and forget that their concerns should first be based around whether the organization is doing the right things (effectiveness) and only then if it is doing them the right way (efficiency). Instead, many organizations latch onto any perceived faults in cost and then react without deep or critical thought. This error is compounded by the lack of information about the costs of services and production. This is especially noticeable in the soft industries. Manufacturing industries usually have a good handle on cost data, but soft industries like information technology, software development, or education find it very difficult to price out their products and services. This is logical, since these organizations normally have trouble defining what products and services they produce. Ask a dean of a given college what products and services the organization delivers. Then take a step further and see if the cost of those offerings is documented.

Time, especially when it is connected to cost as a delimiter (person/hours), is one of the most abused pieces of information. Managers jump on the metrics bandwagon when they start to believe that they can ask for data that will allow them to manage (not coach or lead) their people without having to actually talk to them or get to know them. Timesheets, time-motion studies, and time allocation worksheets come to be in vogue. In a well-constructed metrics program, you wouldn't get to this level without starting from the all-important root and all of its listed components, which should prevent one from abusing the data. Time shouldn't be used to "control" your workforce. It should be used to do the following:

- Improve the organization's ability to estimate delivery schedules
- Assist in improving process and procedures
- Round out other data, like cost and quality

If "quality" is based on the objective measure of defects, how many defects per a thousand instances equals "quality?" Is high quality the goal? Is quality a "yes or no" decision? Quality is best described in terms of defects and re-work, and like "time" it can be misused. It is not a simple way for managers to determine who should get a raise or any other human resources issue. If you abuse metrics, *quality can become a weapon instead of a tool.*

Ensure your metrics are used as a tool for improvement and not a weapon.

Quality, time, resource allocation, and cost are all components of Process Health and define the business view of the Investment the organization's processes and procedures represent. Therefore, these views should only be used to improve the business—not people. Product/Service Health was ex-clusively from the customers' viewpoint. Process Health is equally exclusive in its focus—and it represents the business view. The customer will most likely never see (and shouldn't have a need to see) these metrics. These are "internal" metrics, as are the next two areas of the fourth tier.

Metrics should be used to improve the overall business, not people.

Organizational Health

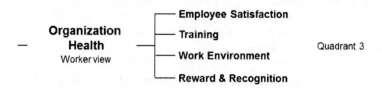

Figure 5-6. The Answer Key, Quadrant 3, Organizational Health

When we look at Organizational Health (Figure 5-6), we look at the organi-zation from the worker's viewpoint. It takes into account the following:

- Employee satisfaction
- Professional development
- Work environment
- Reward and recognition

When we ensure that our most valuable assets are treated as such, we find that the organization improves. I normally suggest organizations address the Answer Key areas from the top down, making the Organizational Health measures third or fourth. This is in part due to political concerns. When you justify the use of metrics, it's much easier to gain support if you first address the organization's health from the customers' point of view. Without customers, there won't be a business to improve. Once you've tackled the customer's view, you will need to ensure that you can afford to keep your workforce.

But in an ideal world, one in which perhaps you are the CEO, I'd argue easily that the first place to start your improvement efforts should be with your greatest assets, and then with your customers. Sound blasphemous? If you have a healthy workforce, you can work with them to better define your business model, your future, and where you want to improve.

Employee satisfaction is pretty straightforward. The more satisfied your workforce is with their situation, the organization, and the environment, the harder they will work. The more loyal they will be. The stronger your organization will become.

Along with their satisfaction, you must be concerned with developing their skills and their knowledge base. Professional development measures tell you how well you're doing in this area. Do you have training plans for each worker? What is the level of skill development for each worker? The stronger your workforce, the more you'll be able to do. It should be a criminal offense to first eliminate training whenever funding cuts come down. The only way to do more with less is to increase the capacity of our workforce to produce more and produce better. The best way to improve productivity is to improve the worker's skill set.

The work environment measures are normally captured through subjective tools—like surveys. But there are plenty of objective measures available. Square footage for workspace. Air quality. Lighting. Ergonomics. There are many ways to measure the quality of the physical work environment. There is also the cultural work environment. Is the organization a pleasant place to work? Is it a high stress environment (and if it is, does it need to be)? Again, you can find both subjective (ask the workers) and objective measures. Do workers take a lot of vacation and sick time? Is turnover high?

The final component of Organizational Health is reward and recognition. The simple questions may not require data collection. Do you have a formal reward or recognition program? Is it effective? Does it do what you want it to? How do you reward your workers? How do you recognize their accomplishments? Do you only recognize their work-related achievements? And on a more subtle note, do you inadvertently combine recognition and reward, such that recognition only occurs when there is a reward involved?

The bottom line on Organizational Health is an extremely easy one—do you treat your most valuable asset like they are your most valued asset?

Future Health

Figure 5-7. The Answer Key, Quadrant 4, Future Health

The last area of the Answer Key is Future Health (Figure 5-7). It covers the following:

- Project/Program status
- Strategic planning: How well the organization is implementing the strategic plan
- Goal attainment: How well the organization is reaching its goals
- Priority setting: How well priorities are being set, and being met

This area assumes that you are working on continuous improvement for the organization. Future Health is not listed last because it isn't as important as the others. It's last in the list because most organizations are not ready for attempting metrics in this area. Most organizations need to get the first three areas of the fourth tier under control before they start to look at large-scale improvement efforts.

Many organizations bypass this guidance and jump to measures to show how well they are working to improve processes. They jump on the continuous process improvement wagon. I don't put much faith in such behaviors since these organizations drop these same efforts as soon as funding becomes tight.

The reason you undertake an improvement effort is more important than if you succeed at it. The only way you can truly succeed is to do the right things for the right reasons.

Measures around the organization's Future Health are mostly predictive, and this makes them "sexy" to leadership. But more important than predicting the future is encouraging and rewarding true process improvement.

Program and project status measures provide insights for leadership into how these efforts are helping improve the organization. You should expect that progress in process improvement is or will be reflected in the measures captured in the other three areas. If you do a good job on continuous process improvement, the customer view should improve. The business view should also see gains, and the workforce should also benefit. If these three areas aren't improved by your efforts, you aren't improving the organization.

Strategic planning, goal attainment, and priority setting are all important things to focus on—but in themselves they are meaningless. If these are not part of a bigger effort to improve the organization, you are just spinning your wheels. These efforts are tough because they require true (and sometimes reckless) commitment to succeeding. You have to want to change. Many organizations pay lip service to this area and don't really see the effort through to the end—and when we're talking about "continuous" process improvement—there really isn't an end.

Answer Key: The Fifth Tier and Beyond

The fifth tier would introduce specific measures for each of the "information" within each of the viewpoints presented. While your root question could conceivably be here, it is unlikely. If you find your question starts here, you probably don't have a need for a metric. Instead, you probably only need a measure.

The elements you're most likely to find here are measures. For example, extending from the top branch of Usage in the fourth tier you may find the following branching out into a fifth tier:

- Unique customers by month, by type
- Number of purchases, by type
- Number of repeat customers

It is unnecessary to list possible measures for each of the fourth tier's elements. It won't make any sense to try to list each of what would be in tier six or seven—lower-level measures or data. In the examples for Usage, we might see data points as follows:

- Number of customers
- Names of each customer
- Products listed by type
- Dates and times of each purchase

How to Use the Answer Key: Identify Types of Measures

The Answer Key can be used to identify measures you can use to answer your root question. If you have done your homework and defined the root question and developed your abstract design, you are now ready for the next step—identifying possible measures to fill out the metric.

The Answer Key can help with this phase of the process. Take your root question and metric design and determine where you are on the Answer Key. If your question deals with the value of the organization, then you're on the top tier, Return vs. Investment. If your question is in the realm of managing organizational resources, you're on the lower tier, State of the Union.

We used some examples of root questions earlier. One was based on the distribution of work. This would fit under the fourth tier, Process Health–Resource Allocation. Using this tool, we not only can identify the type of measures we'll need, but we understand the area of focus of our question. Moving to the left from Resource Allocation, we can see that our question is dealing with the business view (investment). If our question is a root question, we can use the Five Whys. And now we can also ask if our concerns are bigger than just Resource Allocation (measure centered). Are our concerns actually around Process Health? Are we missing the measures around cost, time, and quality?

If your root question is answered by just one of the measures in the fourth tier, chances are you don't have the root question. You definitely don't have a metric.

Another example we used was, "What is the value of our web/teleconferencing service?" This also falls under Return vs. Investment and could fit under the (Customer view) Product/Service Health–Usage or –Customer Satisfaction. But, it also can fit under the (Business view) Process Health, especially since it is full of cost-benefit measures. Often, your metric may dictate the need for measures from more than one category. Logically they usually come from the same larger area—Return vs. Investment or State of the Union. So, many times if you have a metric for effectiveness, you may also be measuring things useful for efficiency. I find this to be particularly true with time. Consider time to resolve an issue vs. time to accomplish a task. If the task is problem resolution, the measures are the same.

Using the Answer Key allows us to do a quick and easy quality check on the measures we've identified. For example, if the metric is a Worker view (based on the root question), and you find some of the measures you identified are from the Customer view (like delivery measures), then either those measures are wrong for the metric, or, possibly your metric is not the right one for answering the question. As a general rule, I find that the measures are usually misplaced, rather than that the metric is incorrect.

One more example. We also covered, "How responsive is the help desk?" This could be time in the efficiency category (time to respond) and it can also be represented by effectiveness measures—specifically delivery. When we look at speed and availability under delivery (another measure is accuracy) we can see how measures of both would go into telling the story of how responsive the help desk is to customer needs. The use of Time to Respond/Time to Resolve would use some of the same data points, although that "view" of the data would not be useful for answering our particular question.

Bonus Material

Since this chapter introduces the practicum portion of the book, let's do a practical exercise. Upcoming is a list of possible root questions based on Bernard Marr's excellent book on performance measures, *The Intelligent Company* (Wiley, 2010). Marr offers that there are two types of root questions: Key Performance Questions (KPQ) and Key Analytic Questions (KAQ). He uses this distinction to differentiate between doing the "right things" (KAQ) and doing it the "right way" (KPQ).

As you have read, I translate these into "effectiveness" and "efficiency" respectively. While Marr gives a list of questions for each type, the reasoning for their delineation is not explained, and they don't match mine. Marr's examples actually span all four viewpoints I offer in the Answer Key, not just customer and business views. Interestingly, more than one of his questions shows up in both categories in his own book.

I hope using his questions as a basis allows you to not only practice classifying them against the Answer Key, but to also see that you don't have to believe what is offered (by any author, including myself)—you should try it out for yourself.

Review each question in Table 5-1, and using the viewpoint, determine where the question fits on the Answer Key by placing an X in the corresponding column

Table 5-1. Categorizing Root Questions

Question	Customer	Business	Worker	Leadership
Will our customers recommend us to others?				
To what level are our employees engaged?				
Are we shifting toward an innovative climate in the org?				
How much do we trust each other?				
How well are fwe successfully promoting our services?				
To what degree are we optimizing our inventory?				
How well are we reducing the waste?				
How well are we keeping our best customers?				
How well are we fostering continuous improvement?				
How well are we retaining the talent in our organization?				
How well are we managing our financial resources?				
What is the level of brand recognition?				
What are the best routes for our delivery trucks?				

Question	Customer	Business	Worker	Leadership
How well are we sharing information within the org?				
How do our customers perceive our service?				
How well are we working in teams?				
To what extent do workers feel passionate about our org?				
How well are we building new competencies?				

Hopefully you found that there were examples that fit in each of the categories. You may also find that you marked more than one column for a question (yes, this is allowed). If we remember that it depends on the viewpoint, this is easy to understand.

One question that could fit into more than one category was the final one, "How well are we building new competencies?" This could be a business viewpoint, if we want to know how well our training program is working. If we look at it from the worker's viewpoint—concerned with the training of our workers—it could be an Organizational Health question. If we look at it from the point of view of leadership wanting to know if we will be ready to deal with future requirements, it could fit Future Health. When you are dealing with your questions, you'll know (or ask) whose viewpoint is intended.

So, now, if you are like me, you're looking for the "book" answers to the exercise above. In Table 5-2, I give you my answers—with the caveat that there are no "right" answers.

The idea is to use the Answer Key to determine whether your measures are doing what they are supposed to do—that they are aligned and comprehensive. Remember that aligned means that they help answer the root question (if you find that the measures you're using don't align on the Answer Key, then they don't answer the same root question); and comprehensive means that together, you have confidence that they will answer the question (there are no missing data points).

Table 5-2. Answers to the Categorization Exercise

Question	Customer	Business	Worker	Leadership
Will our customers recommend us to others?	X			
To what level are our employees engaged?			X	
Are we shifting toward an innovative climate in the org?				X
How much do we trust each other?			X	X
How successfully are we promoting our services?	X			
To what degree are we optimizing our inventory?		X		
How well are we reducing the waste?		X		
How well are we keeping our best customers?	X			
How well are we fostering continuous improvement?				X
How well are we retaining the talent in our organization?			X	
How well are we managing our financial resources?				X
What is the level of brand recognition?	X			X
What are the best routes for our delivery trucks?		X		
How well are we sharing information within the org?				X
How do our customers perceive our service?	X			
How well are we working in teams?			X	
To what extent do workers feel passionate about our org?			X	
How well are we building new competencies?		X	X	X

Recap

The Answer Key can help you check the quality of your work and ensure that you're on the right track. And if or when you get stumped and you don't know which direction to go, it can help you get on track.

Most metrics you design, if they fall on the Answer Key, will most likely start at the third tier and belong to one of the following four viewpoints:

- The customers' viewpoint (effectiveness)
- The business's viewpoint (efficiency)
- The workers' viewpoint
- The leadership's viewpoint

As you move from left to right on the Answer Key, you move from the strategic to the tactical. Another way to look at this is that you move from the root question toward data.

Regardless of where your metric (or root question) falls, you'll have to move to the right to find the measures and data you need to answer the question. At the fourth tier we found the following:

- Return vs. Investment
    - Product/Service Health—Customer View
    - Process Health—Business View
- State of the Union
    - Organizational Health—Employee View
    - Future Health—Leadership View

The fourth tier is the most frequently used by my clients. It is far enough left that root questions starting here are worthy of metrics to answer, and far enough right that they are easy for most organizations to comprehend their use in improving the organization.

In the fifth (and any consecutive) tier, we find mostly information and measures. If we find our root question residing here, the question is probably very tactical and may not require a full-blown metric to answer. Remembering the Metric Development Plan, you should flesh out the metric by identifying not only the information and measures, but also document the individual data points needed.

Conclusion

The reason the Answer Key leads off the practical part of the book is that it is a great shortcut tool for you to implement metrics. It helps you put your root question into a context of organizational health. If you are forced to work without a root question, it can be used to ensure you are not trying to blend together incongruous measures, as well as help you to work toward a driving need.

Working from the left, moving right, you go from the high-level to the tactical. It will help you identify possible information and measures you can use to answer your root question.

Working from right to left, you can work from specific measures (or even data) back toward a driving need. Working in this direction will also help you to ensure that your metrics are logically grouped and organized. You normally don't want information from different areas (product/service, process, organizational, or future health) mixed together into one metric, as they would rarely answer any question, unless it is at the highest or leftmost levels of the Answer Key.

Remember that the Answer Key, while a useful shortcut, is still only a tool for helping you develop your metrics. It's not the whole answer and it doesn't relieve you of the need to follow the model for developing metrics.

Start with Effectiveness

The first chief information officer I worked for used to say, "do the right thing." Besides the philosophical and religious interpretations of this directive, there are also the leader's simple day-to-day behavioral expectations of her workforce. Effectiveness metrics will allow you to determine if you are "doing the right things."

I am doing more than suggest that you *start* with effectiveness. In Chapter 5, I introduced the Answer Key. I discussed the components of effectiveness metrics, the first quadrant of tier three, Product and Service Health. I'm recommending that you not only start here, but that you remain in this area of the Answer Key until your organization has matured to a point of readiness for dealing with the other quadrants.

As described in my first book on overcoming organizational immaturity, an organization may be simply incapable of dealing with a full-blown metrics program. Using metrics is an advanced behavior.

Let's look at the reasons I propose you should start (and remain) in the effectiveness quadrant for the foreseeable future. The reasons can be discussed one quadrant at a time, starting with quadrant 4, Future Health.

Let's look at the Answer Key again in Figure 6-1.

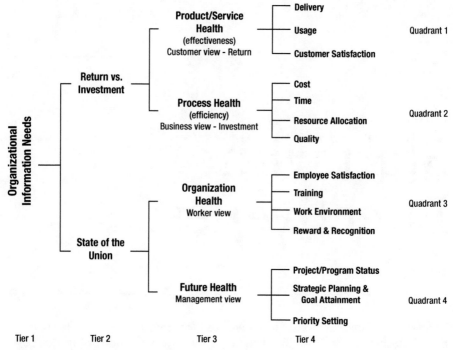

Figure 6-1. The Answer Key

Future Health

The fourth quadrant of tier three (Figure 6-2) covers Future Health or the organization's health from the view point of leadership. Before you start working on a metrics program covering the Future Health area, it would be best if your organization were ready for it.

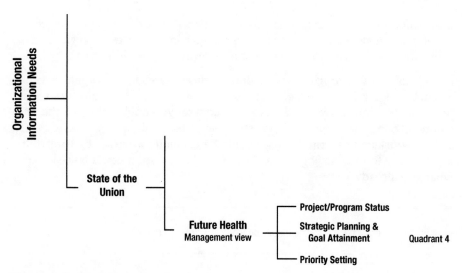

Figure 6-2. The Answer Key, Quadrant 4

The following are some questions you can ask yourself or others to determine if your organization is ready for metrics in this area:

- Do you have a mission statement? Most organizations do these days.
- If you ask five workers what the mission of the organization is, will you get the same correct answer?
- Do you have a living strategic plan? If yes, how far out is the furthest goal? Most process improvement experts will tell you that a strategic goal should be three to five years out at a minimum. They can stretch out to ten years.
- Does your organization have the majority of its goals documented?
- If you have long-range goals, are they being actively worked? (I won't ask if you know how well they are progressing, since that would require measures which lead to metrics.)
- Have the organizational concerns been prioritized? If so, are those priorities adhered to or are they routinely ignored?
- Do your goals include improving processes over time?
- Do you have a strong project management process in place?
- Is the process followed willingly by the organization?

If you can't answer these questions in the affirmative, you may not be ready. Normally there is an inner conflict around this area for an organization. The leadership, which is the main driver of metrics, wants to improve the organization in all aspects, all at one time. This drives the organization to develop strategic plans. It seems to be a requirement for every high-level leader to have a strategic plan with a mission statement and goals.

I won't take you through all the problems this creates for an organization incapable of organizational-wide change. Rather, I offer these questions to help you determine if you are ready. Of course, you could measure this area and determine that your artifacts (strategic plans, goals, and prioritized lists) are not working as intended. That could be useful information by itself, but as I am very fond of saying, most times you don't need metrics to tell you what you already know.

Most times, you don't need a metric to tell you what you already know.

I believe most organizations put together strategic plans and prioritized lists. Most even develop processes for their larger-scale efforts. Mostly because these are "the right things to do." But unfortunately, most of these organizations aren't actually ready for these efforts, so their earnest attempts result in few to no benefits; compounding this lost investment by creating metrics would be wasteful.

Future Health metrics require a readiness most organizations lack.

Organizational Health

The Organizational Health quadrant (Figure 6-3) is from the viewpoint of the worker.

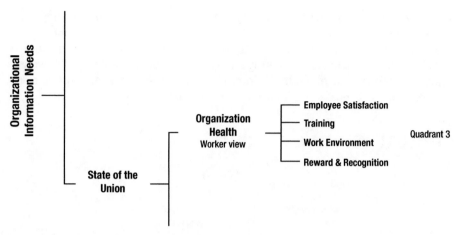

Figure 6-3. The Answer Key, Quadrant 3

Again, we can ask some basic questions to get a feel for the readiness of this endeavor.

- Do you have a rewards and recognition program?
- Do you have a suggestion program for the workforce to provide inputs?
- Would you describe your culture as one of mutual trust?
- Does each of your workers have a professional development program?

Unlike the Future Health quadrant, Organizational Health doesn't tend to be an early area of interest for leadership. In many organizations suffering from immaturity, leaders fear metrics based on this area. Leadership should know if the workforce is treated well and feel valued. They shouldn't "need" metrics to inform them about this. When the "answers" aren't known, it creates doubt and that doubt rightly worries leadership. Until there is trust within the organization, this area could be troublesome for leadership.

In most cases, *leadership* isn't ready for Organizational Health metrics.

Both Organizational Health and Future Health quadrants speak directly to the "State of the Union" of the organization. In both cases, the metrics should wait until the organization is doing the right things and pleasing the customer on a steady basis. If the organization is in turmoil or suffering from immaturity, a metrics program won't resolve the issues—to the contrary, it will probably make things worse. Starting with either of these two quadrants would be like measuring the average airspeed, altitude, and lift coefficients of a paper airplane. It is much more important to obtain better transportation before you start measuring how well a paper airplane works.

Return vs. Investment

Figure 6-4. The Answer Key, Quadrants I and 2

The top two quadrants (Figure 6-4) are where most organizations naturally gravitate when they embark on a metrics effort. Most leaders start with wanting to see customer satisfaction survey results. It's the easiest measure to start with. Without fail, every time I bring up finding out how the customer feels about services or products, the first thought is always "survey." I don't mean this is a negative—in fact, I'm happy when this happens because it's a very safe and logical place to start.

The Balanced Scorecard also has four quadrants: Customer, Finance, Employee, and Process— and most leaders jump to the Finance quadrant. The nearest equivalent in the Answer Key is the Process Health (or efficiency) quadrant.

While the right two quadrants in the State of the Union require that the organization be ready, but typically the organization is not, the Return vs. Investment quadrants can be addressed before maturity. Of course, the more mature the organization, the better—especially when developing a metric program.

Process Health

The Process Health (efficiency) measures (Figure 6-5) can cause a lot of issues, especially in an organization suffering from immaturity. If you don't have great rapport with the workforce, or if there is any lack of trust between the workers, trying to work on metrics for this quadrant can be a killer.

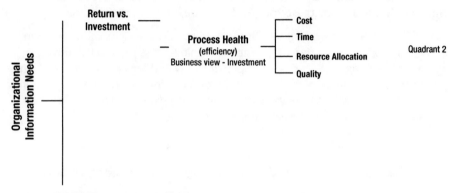

Figure 6-5. The Answer Key, Quadrant 2

The questions I would have you ask to determine readiness for efficiency measures include the following:

- Does your workforce trust management?
- Does your first line of supervision trust upper and/or middle management?
- Does management trust the workforce?

To be able to use efficiency measures safely requires trust. Honest and accurate data is impossible to achieve in a culture lacking trust. Most pundits think that a culture of trust is predicated on how well the top leaders of an organization walk the talk. Does the workforce trust the top leaders to follow through? To do what they say they would? To keep to their agreements and commitments?

I find the answer to the trust question to be much more direct and simple. Does the workforce believe that their direct supervisors have their best interests at heart? They care much less about the top leader's level of authenticity. They care about their direct manager above all else. As you move further away from the direct manager, the amount of trust required lessens.

So, rather than preach to the CEO of the company that she must gain the workforce's trust, start at the lowest levels and ensure that there is a culture of trust from the bottom up.

When you decide to measure how efficient the organization is, your employees clearly hear that you want to measure how efficient *they* are. They will not "hear" that you want to improve processes and procedures. At least, they won't unless they trust you. And by "you," I mean their boss.

My CIO usually followed up his admonition to "do the right thing" with an equally important directive to do the right things "the right way." If management is strong, it will seek to improve the way things are done—not improve those who are doing the work. If you rush into working with efficiency measures, you risk not only gathering inaccurate data due to mistrust, but worse, you run the risk of seeding more mistrust.

Process Health metrics require a level of mutual trust rarely found within most organizations.

Remember, Organizational Health metrics speak to the workers' situation, which most leaders are not ready to hear. And even if the leadership believes it is capable of hearing the feedback, if there is a lack of trust, most workers are not ready to share.

That same lack of trust makes collecting accurate data on how well the business is run (Process Health) hard to accomplish.

Product/Service Health

So, that leads us to the Product/Service Health quadrant (Figure 6-6). This is not only the safest place to start, it's also the most logical.

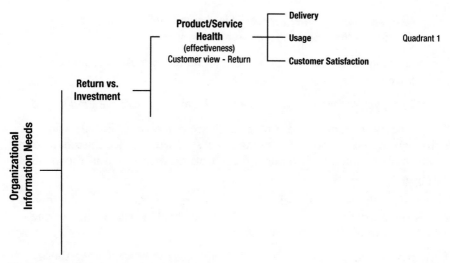

Figure 6-6. The Answer Key, Quadrant I

Let's look at the following questions, which you should ask to determine if you're ready for effectiveness measures:

- Do you know who your customers are? (This should be a no-brainer, but it's actually worth asking. I am rarely surprised by what is not known.)
- Do you know what your customers consider important?
- Do you know your customers' expectations?

Does this sound a lot easier than the other four quadrants? That is because it is. You need less maturity in the top half of the tier, and there is less risk involved in Product/Service Health than with efficiency measures. At a minimum, you should know who your customers are and be able to determine their wants, expectations, and needs.

You might ask, how could you *not* know who your customers are?

I'll admit, I found it hard to fathom at first. But, it can actually happen. A story a colleague enjoys relaying centered on a clerk in an admissions office in a college. The clerk had been dealing with freshmen for at least two years too many.

On one of these occasions, a freshman was giving the clerk the common refrain that he was her customer and deserved better than he was getting. He ranted about how she should be doing everything in her power to satisfy his needs since he was the reason the school existed.

"Where is your customer service?" He shouted one last time, enjoying the attention the other students were giving him.

She calmly waited for him to pause. She wanted to make sure he heard her clearly.

"Deary, you're mistaken. You're not the customer, you're the product."

You might be thinking, "nice retort" or "cute comeback." But the bad part is that my colleague was a faculty member. And worse, those listening found it extremely humorous. Of course, I can't blame them—it was a funny line. But, how true was it?

Do we sometimes confuse who our customers are? Another well-known joke is the grocery clerk who argues that "we could get a lot more done if we didn't have to deal with customers."

If it is obvious who your customers are and what they want, then there wouldn't be so many customer service courses and seminars. It may be one of the most basic axioms: the truth is not always obvious.

The truth is not always obvious.

You would think the opposite to be more likely. Falsehoods and lies should be hard to find. The truth shouldn't be hard to find. The truth shouldn't be hidden or obscured by extraneous data. The truth *should* be obvious.

What should be obvious—like the truth or who your customers are—is not always obvious.

So how do you determine who your customers are? Since it's the prerequisite for developing effectiveness metrics, I think it is worth covering a simple process for determining who your customers are.

One simple view is that your customer is who pays your salary. This allows you to determine your customer on a personal level (as well as an organizational level). Let's start with the obvious (but not necessarily the "truth"). You are paid by your organization. But how is that funding derived? If you are a for-profit, it most likely comes from the sale of a product or service. The buyer of that service or product may likely be a vendor or distributor. The next logical question is, who pays the recipient of your product or service? You should follow this logic until you've identified the end user or purchaser.

Let's look at a car's airbags. The worker who quality-checks the airbag believes his customer is the automobile manufacturer who has the contract with his division. That is accurate, but not the truth. It's neither the car manufacturer nor the dealership that buys the cars. This is clearer when we look at the buyer who is the rental car agency. The rental car agency then rents the vehicle to a final end user (customer). Is that the true customer? Yes, but there is another customer. The passenger who sits in the "shot gun" seat who actually benefits from that particular airbag is a truer representation of that customer. That of course can be extrapolated out to include those who love that passenger. The passenger's children, parents, and spouse.

If the person quality-checking the airbags sees the underlying truth about the real customer for their work, how would it change that worker's behavior patterns? How would it change that worker's self-esteem?

In a not-for-profit organization, this process still works. Consider Habitat for Humanity. When you volunteer your time to Habitat for Humanity, is the site supervisor the customer? Or is it the Habitat for Humanity organization? Or is it the person who will eventually take possession of the home? Or is it the children who will have a "real" home to live in for the first time in their lives? You could go even further and ask if the real customer is society. Without becoming too philosophical, I suggest that we go as far as the direct end user. In this case, it's the family who ultimately lives in the house.

When we look into this reality far enough, we resolve to accept that our customers are much more than the first purchaser of our products or services. When we look this deeply we find the truth of who our customers are.

Of course, when we look at the effectiveness measures of delivery, usage, and customer satisfaction, it is usually good enough to determine the immediate customer. You'll need to know who they are so you can ascertain what the customer considers important. You will also need to determine what their expectations are and how to meet those requirements.

The Customers' Viewpoint

Starting with the customers' viewpoint makes total sense. It's the right place to start collecting, analyzing, and reporting data, measures, and information. Let me tell you a story about a restaurant owned by Tom. He was a hard-working man who loved good food.

Tom's restaurant was doing all right, but he wanted to do better. He wanted his restaurant to be the best in the town, perhaps even a prototype for a chain of restaurants. His menu was made up of old family recipes—home cooking that appealed to everyone. He thought an even better restaurant would provide a good future for his family.

He wanted to know how well the business was actually doing and how to improve. He decided to collect metrics; not only to determine how well he was doing, but to also better predict if his vision had a chance of coming true.

Tom knew very little about organizational development or process improvement. He knew even less about metrics. He was a great manager/owner and his passion for the business, the product, and customer service made him a natural. His compassion for his staff was born from a history working low-end jobs, saving and scrimping, and then taking the biggest risk of his life—putting all of his savings into his own restaurant. He knew what it was like to be underpaid and underappreciated. What he didn't know was how to take his dream to the next level.

When he thought about gathering information about his restaurant, he immediately thought of customer satisfaction surveys. He created a comment card, which he had each waitperson give to the customers along with the menu. He wanted to give customers a chance to critique their restaurant experience from the beginning to the end.

Tom knew there were many good and bad points to the survey. It was good in that it would provide quick feedback from his most important critics—his customers. The feedback would help the staff and remind them to keep the customers' happiness at the forefront.

On the other hand, he knew customers might not always provide the information needed to help him improve because many people don't like to complain—unless they are extremely dissatisfied.

Besides the qualitative information a survey provides, Tom needed objective input regarding the quality of his services and products. This information was readily available.

Tom had empirical data on his customer base—since most customers used credit cards, he could determine the number of repeat customers and how often these customers frequented his restaurant. He also could determine the menu items they ordered. He knew when his busy times were and when the restaurant was slow. He actually already had a wealth of usage information. This information in conjunction with the customer satisfaction survey results should give a good picture of how well his business was doing.

Tom was happy with all this information, but felt he was missing an objective measure of how well his restaurant was satisfying the customer without asking the customer for input. He thought the comment cards were enough of an intrusion.

Tom reviewed the quality of the food by bringing in local food critics. He reviewed the service of his staff by personally observing them and getting their opinions on the restaurant. He reviewed the speed of the food preparation and delivery, as well as the check out speed for the customers. He compared this information to that of other top restaurants in the area.

With these inputs Tom felt confident that he had good indicators of the quality of his restaurant from the customers' point of view.

And for the most part he was right. There are other measures he could use, like availability (restaurant hours), reliability (consistency in taste, quality, and time to table), and accuracy (getting the food orders right). These would help round out his metric and give him a more comprehensive picture. But his customer satisfaction and usage data were a good start.

Removing Fear

By looking at the customers' viewpoint, Tom removed the basis of fear, which plagues efficiency metrics, while focusing on Return vs. Investment—the area most managers desire deeper understanding of. Fear is born of the unknown. The unknown factor in most early metrics programs (especially in an organization suffering from immaturity) is how the information will (and won't) be used. That is why I push for all metrics efforts to clearly communicate how the metrics will and won't be used.

Even if you promise that the measures you collect and report won't be used improperly, unless you have a strong culture of trust in your organization, the workforce won't believe, and fear will rule. At least if you use efficiency measures. If instead you start with effectiveness measures, it is easy to convince others that the information won't be used against them. This is because all of the measures will reflect the customers' point of view.

A real life example follows.

No matter how often I argue that metrics won't be used improperly, the only way I've won over my clients is to show them the metrics. Let's take accuracy in the form of rework. When designing the metric, if you stick to the rule that it has to be from the customers' viewpoint, you won't even collect data on internal rework. You will only deal with rework from the customer's point of view.

When I was designing effectiveness metrics for our printing services, the question arose around what constituted rework.

"If we have to send the printer back to the vendor three times before they fix it, is that rework?"

I answered with a question. "Does the customer know you sent it back three times?"

"No."

"Then no, it's not rework."

"How about if we get the wrong parts from the vendor?"

Again, I replied with a question, "Does the customer know?"

"Nope."

"Then it's still not rework."

"How about if we fix a printer jam, and when the customer tries to print, we find out there was also another problem?"

"Does the customer know?"

"Yes, but it wasn't our fault..."

"Then, yes, that's rework."

"But it wasn't our fault..."

"I understand that. But the metric isn't used to place blame. The metric is simply a way for us to understand what the customer sees. If the customer would consider it rework, we want to know. We can't solve a problem if we don't know it exists."

Effectiveness is not used to judge or place blame. Effectiveness metrics provide us the customers' view of our services and products.

Focusing on First Things First

You have to start at the beginning, while keeping the end in mind. The end is a well-functioning, comprehensive metrics program. To get there though, we have to have a mature organization. We have to have a culture of trust. We must have open communications in all directions. We have to be pretty well ahead of the curve. As David Allen said in his book *Getting Things Done* (Penguin, 2002), about his consulting services, "those who use [his methods for improvement] need it the least."

So for the rest of us, we have to start at the beginning. And the first thing you'll need to do is see your organization as your customer sees it. Effectiveness measures do that.

Recap

Start at the beginning. It keeps you out of a lot of trouble when you start at the beginning. Jumping into mature behaviors that your organization is not ready for can lead to a ton of trouble. The proper and safest place to start is with Product/Service Health, or effectiveness, metrics. This will allow you to build a rapport with the organization and improve your customer relationships.

By starting with effectiveness measures, you will also allow your organization to ease into using metrics with less fear, less uncertainty, and less doubt. The organization will still have some worries over what you're introducing, but by starting with the customers' viewpoint, you mitigate most of the risk. You can also use these metrics to produce high returns—understanding and pleasing customers are really the foundation of long-term business success.

It is convenient that the best place to start is also the easiest and safest, while the other possible choices require more effort, damage control, and has the highest risks for failure.

The following are important points to remember:

- Future Health metrics require a readiness most organizations lack.
- Organizational Health metrics speak to the workers' situation, which most are not ready to hear; and if there is a lack of trust, most workers are not ready to share.
- The lack of trust that makes measuring Organizational Health difficult makes collecting accurate data on how well the business is run, Process Health, unlikely.
- Product/Service Health metrics require knowledge of the customer—who the customer is, what they see as important, and what they expect.

Conclusion

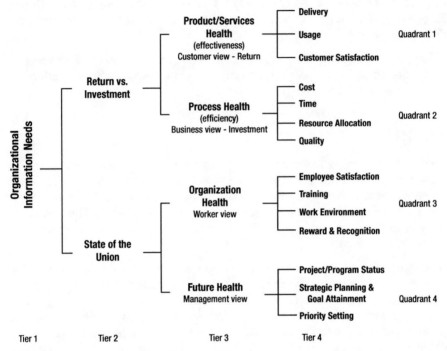

Figure 6-7. The Answer Key, with tiers and quadrants

While the Answer Key (Figure 6-7) offered multiple options for metrics development, the right place to start is with Product/Service Health (effectiveness), the customer's viewpoint. Not only is this the safest course of action, it is also the best since it builds a foundation for the other quadrants in the third tier. If you create a working, and thereby useful, metrics program around the effectiveness of your product and service health, you will build the trust necessary to branch into efficiency metrics.

Once you've tackled the Return vs. Investment quadrants, you'll have a basis of maturity preparing your organization for the State of the Union quadrants. The conclusion is as follows:

1. Start with the customer view (effectiveness measures). Take your time and fully realize the benefits of this level of metrics. Let it become an accepted part of the organization's culture.

2. Use the business view (efficiency measures) sparingly and when needed to investigate further into ways to improve effectiveness. (I'll provide more insights into this later.)

3. After you have built a healthy level of trust within the organization and a successful effectiveness-based metrics program, branch into other quadrants.

4. While management will want to go to the business view next, except for those measures necessary to improve effectiveness, I recommend skipping efficiencies and moving to the workers' viewpoint (Organizational Health). This will help build trust and result in greater and faster overall gains to the organization's effectiveness.

    If the workforce is truly the greatest asset—after developing metrics to improve the customers' experience, the next priority should be to improve the workforce's. Address Future Health metrics primarily as a tool to determine the likelihood of achieving the organization's goals. Then use them to determine if the goals were achieved. If you focus on the strategic plans portion of Future Health, you can create another safe haven for metrics.

In Chapter 11, Employing Advanced Metrics, I will go into more detail on the benefits and means for developing metrics in each of the third tier's quadrants. For now, it is enough to promote Product/Service Health as the correct starting point and to stress the need to wait on the other areas until the time is right.

Triangulation

Essential to Creating Effective Metrics

And so it was, Momma mouse gave birth to three beautiful, but blind, mice. Once they were of age, the farmer's wife took pity on them and decided to help them survive in the world. A world made much more dangerous due to their lack of sight.

The farmer's wife decided it would be helpful if the mice learned which animals were friendly, and which ones might prefer to eat them than to partake in a visit. Since she was originally a city girl, she packed the three mice into her minivan and headed off to visit the museum of natural history. She thought using the exhibits would be safer than introducing them to the real things.

Although there weren't too many African wild animals on the farm where they lived, the farmer's wife thought it would be better to be "safe" than sorry.

> They started with the tiger. She reasoned it was just a bigger version of the barnyard cat. The first mouse was on the back left paw. "It's got claws and big feet," he shouted. The second mouse was on the tail. "It's got a long strong tail." The third mouse, the oldest by three seconds, was at the face. "It has big eyes, big teeth, and whiskers."
>
> The farmer's wife smiled. "So, what is it?"
>
> "A very big cat" they all said in unison.
>
> "Very good. How about this one?" They all went over to the next animal.

"It's not an animal at all. It's a tree trunk," said the first mouse.

"No, it's a snake hanging from a tree," said the second.

And the third, again at the face of the animal, said, "It's a giant bird from the feel of the powerful wings."

"Put all of those together children," the farmer's wife advised.

They thought for a bit and finally shouted together in perfect harmony, "An elephant!"

"Very good."

They continued this way through the animal exhibit, identifying wolves, dogs, lions, and bears. They learned about all types of animals, domestic and wild. Finally, they came to one they could not solve. It seemed to have the head of a lion, the body of a goat, and a snake's tail.

"We've looked over the animal from head to toe and back again," they all agreed, "and we can't agree on what it is!"

"That's a chimera" said the farmer's wife. "I am very impressed by you three. With an understanding of animal physiology, you have success-fully identified every creature, using very different inputs."

The three mice beamed.

"But, we didn't get them all right," said the third mouse, thinking of the chimera.

"No, but even with varying, complementary, solid data from multiple sources, you can't always get to the 'truth.'" She was very pleased with how well they had done. Sometimes it's just not possible to derive the correct answer, even with a lot of data. Of course, it helps if you can ob-serve the item yourself.

Researchers are the ultimate data users.

Triangulation—a Historical Perspective

The mice were forced to use triangulation to identify the animals. They compared different pieces of information gathered using different methods to determine the answers to their question (what is the animal that we are touching?). If the mice looked at only one piece of information, they'd have the wrong answers.

I bow to Norman K. Denzin, a professor of communications and sociology at the University of Illinois at Urbana-Champagne, for his using "triangulation" to mean using more than two methods to collect data in the context of gathering and using research data.   My definition is much like it—using multiple measures, as well as collection methods, for processing the information used in a metric.

A major reason for using triangulation, according to Denzin, is to reduce (if not eliminate) bias in the research. By using triangulation we ensure that we have a comprehensive answer to the question.

In his book, *Sociological Methods: A Source Book*, Denzin describes the following four types of triangulation:[1]

- *Data source*: Using multiple data sources.
- *Investigator*: Using more than one person to collect, analyze, or interpret a set of data.
- *Theory*: Using multiple perspectives to interpret a set of data.
- *Method*: Using multiple methods to capture the data.

But even Denzin would have to agree that it was not his "invention" since he cites a paper by Eugene J. Webb in which Webb offers a triangulated approach to sociological research. Denzin offers that as you increase the number of differing measures used to provide insight on a single issue, the definitions move from an abstract thought, to validated concept, and finally to proven reality. Although Denzin may not have been the first to coin the term "triangulation," I like his explanation. It matches very closely to how I use the term in the context of a metrics program.

Denzin's four types of triangulation aren't an exact match to the different types that I use for metrics—and that is partly due to the nature of the use of our results. While Denzin is giving guidance for sociological research that has the purpose of finding deeper truths within his field and having

---

[1] Norman K. Denzin, *Sociological Methods: A Sourcebook* (Chicago: Aldine Publishing Co., 1970).

those truths debated and challenged within the scientific community in journals and experiments—our needs (yours and mine) are much simpler and more practical.

The need for different investigators is relatively unnecessary in my field, although it is critical in the field of research to avoid bias in the analysis. I agree with having different data sources, different perspectives, and different methods. I refer to perspectives as viewpoints. Let's now look at my version of triangulation.

Triangulation as a Practical Application

In 2003 I developed a concept of using multiple measures to construct a comprehensive metric. I was developing a metrics program for my IT Department and I needed to create a complete story that answered two questions posed by the top executive officer. His first question was: "How are you doing?"

He was inquiring about the health of our IT organization. A simple but driving question. It created not only a set of metrics, but it sent me on a journey that culminated in documenting many of the methods and theories that I've captured in this book.

The executive's second question was a great companion to the first: "How do you know?"

I think I liked these questions more for their simplicity and directness than anything else. They drove our organization toward a viable, practical metrics program.

Triangulation of Measures

I focused on the Effectiveness quadrant of the Answer Key (Figure 7-1), choosing to qualify the question as being from our customers' point of view—because the executive asking it was our top-level customer. While the executive may have cared about how efficiently we were conducting our affairs, his first primary concern was how well we were serving our customers.

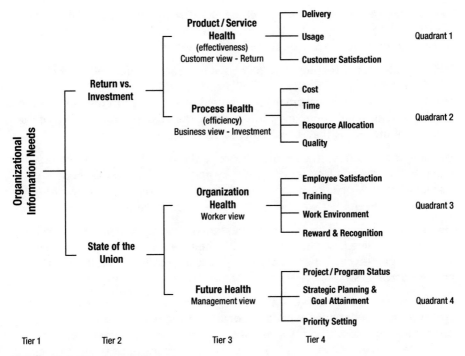

Figure 7-1. The Answer Key

When I developed the metrics to answer these questions, I knew it was critical to produce an answer that would be accepted as accurate. Besides the need to have controls around the collection and analysis, I needed a basic construct for the metric.

I knew the quadrant. I knew the possible measures that would fit (or at least a starting point). I also knew how to test the measures for alignment with the Product/Service Health quadrant.

But to ensure we gained a comprehensive picture, I fell upon triangulation—the use of three or more measures to answer the question. In the case of effectiveness, we identified the primary ones—Delivery, Usage, and Customer Satisfaction—from the Answer Key, as shown in Figure 7-2.

Figure 7-2. The Product/Service Health quadrant

Rather than select one or two, I determined that we should use all three, which would provide a fuller picture. Each measure had different characteristics in their sources and methods of collection.

Delivery addressed the need for objective measures of how well we provided our services and products. This measure would capture data on our effectiveness without customer involvement. The best source would be the trouble-tracking and reporting tools used by the IT department. One of the benefits of metrics is that it highlights tools you are already using.

By using the data from these tools, it drove the units to capture the data more accurately and frequently than they had been. Before the metrics program, the tools were not being used to their best levels and the resulting data was not useful—it was GIGO (garbage in, garbage out).

Usage was a means of capturing the customers' viewpoint unobtrusively, in this case watching how they "voted with their feet." This could be represented by unique customers (how many customers do you really serve) or repeat customers.

Customer satisfaction surveys allow you to ask how well you served the customer and understand what's important to them, but you can also ask open-ended questions to get direct input on how you can improve. While the IT department already had satisfaction surveys for each trouble case, these only gathered information from customers who expressed a problem with our service or product and were already using our product or service.

We also wanted to hear from those who hadn't had any issues with our service and perhaps even more importantly, those who had not yet tried our services. We needed to know why potential customers weren't turning to us to help address their needs. An organization can only grow so much from marketing to current customers. At some point, it needs to bring in new customers.

So, besides the trouble ticket follow up surveys, the IT department conducted annual surveys to the entire customer base. Depending on your business, you may need to partake in a sampling of potential customers.

Each area investigated had a customer viewpoint and addressed a different type of feedback—objective and independent customer feedback, indirect customer feedback, and direct customer feedback.

It would be nice if you could introduce the concept of triangulation and it would be accepted. It would be nice if you could introduce any of the concepts I've offered so far—from root questions, to the metrics framework and taxonomy, to the use of documentation, how to use and not use metrics, the Answer Key, starting with Effectiveness—without having to fight for their acceptance.

When I attempted to create a metrics program for my own organization, I ran into a lot of resistance. I believed it stemmed from the "no prophet is accepted in her own village" syndrome. But after helping others develop and implement metrics programs, I now believe it's deeper than that. While the syndrome does make it difficult, even if you are an outside consultant, the refrain will be raised—"Just ask the customer! Our customer satisfaction surveys are enough!" Not only will it be shouted, a chorus will rise up in strong harmony.

Even today, I have to fight for a multi-measure metric. Not just using more than two measures, but in using ones from different views within the same quadrant.

Triangulation of Collection Methods and Sources

Triangulation also requires different collection methods, as follows:

- Delivery is objectively collected and without customer involvement. In other words, the customer won't know you're collecting the data. You won't be using any opinions (all quantitative data). Most times I also try to use automated collection methods for these measures (like trouble call tracking systems, monitoring systems, or time accounting systems). It is important to note that these do not measure customers, but how well the organization delivers the products and services. I will explain shortly.
- Usage is a measurement based on customer behaviors. What do they buy? Who do they call? How often do they use our services? How did they find out about our services and products? How many one-time customers do we have vs. how many repeat customers?
- Customer Satisfaction is the most customer-centric measurement group. Here, we directly ask the customer for their opinion. A better title for this item would be "customer direct feedback." You ask the customer what they thought of the service and product, but you also ask for ideas for improvement. These questions can be asked in a survey, through focus groups, or through individual interviews. There are pros and cons to each, from varying costs to differing

volumes of data collected. You should pick the methods that work best for you. Many times the customer base will dictate the best feedback tools.

Remember our three blind mice? When they "observed" the elephant, they had a hard time figuring out what it was until they were allowed to communicate what they observed (triangulation). Since they were able to identify the animals correctly, it would seem that there was no need to vary this strategy or methodology—only the sampling and source. A more accurate form of triangulation uses multiple methods and strategies. If the elephant were alive rather than a museum exhibit, one mouse could use touch, another smell, and the third could ask the elephant a well-thought-out set of questions.

Triangulation dictates that you use different sources, methodologies, and types of measures. Table 7-1 reflects the possibilities.

Table 7-1. Triangulation to Create Effective Metrics

Measurement Area	Source	Methodology	Type
Delivery	Distributor's feedback, objective data collection tools (machine counting, defect counts, returns, time accounting tools)	Process/product results (defect rates), Automation (preferred)	Objective
Usage	Unobtrusive observation, receipts, inventories, usage counters	Observation, Automation (preferred), Counting	Objective
Customer Satisfaction	Customer feedback, customer actions (amount of tip or smiles), customer referrals	Survey, Questionnaire, Observation	Subjective

You can use other groupings for triangulation. I offer these because I know they work, and they are simple to implement. The idea is to address at least three different viewpoints, sources, and methods of collection.

The concept of triangulation can be used at each level of the metric. I don't suggest you go too deeply or you may find that you are collecting thousands of different measures. I want you to use triangulation at the top level—in the case of effectiveness metrics, at the Delivery, Usage, and Customer Satisfaction level. But, you can use the same concept at the next level.

For Customer Satisfaction, you could use the following three different methods of collection: surveys, focus groups, and interviews. This can be very expensive, especially interviews. But you could also use two different surveys—the annual survey given to a large portion of your customer base, and the trouble call survey. You can also use work-order surveys—questionnaires provided to customers when you deliver your service/product. This is another survey of your active customer base, but it doesn't require a problem. You can also administer satisfaction surveys three to six months after delivery to see if the customer:

1. Continues to be satisfied with the service or product now that the initial excitement may have worn off

2. Has new insights to the strengths or weaknesses of your product or service

3. Has recommended your service or products to others

Usage also allows for multiple measures. You can measure the number of unique customers, repeat customers, and the frequency of customer "purchases" of your services and products. I recently bought a new laptop from Best Buy and the experience was so enjoyable that I took my adult daughter there the next week. She bought a laptop for herself (nothing at all like the one I bought) and I couldn't help but buy a wireless keyboard and mouse (which I'm using to type this). Not only was I a repeat customer, but I referred someone else the next week (actually I drove her to the store, helped her pick out a computer, and offered to carry it to the car for her). All of this could be used to measure usage.

I saved Delivery for last because it is the one most easily triangulated. In the program I developed for my organization, I broke delivery into the following three major factors:

- Availability
- Speed
- Accuracy

Availability is straightforward and not always applicable. Is the service or product available when the customer wants or needs it? In the case of telephone services, when you pick up the handset, do you get a dial tone? I just suffered through five days without my home service (I still have a landline for our home) due to a malfunction to the phone line outside the house. The service (product) was unavailable for five days. My wife and I both found this unacceptable. Availability can also be triangulated (remember, I warned about going too deep)—in this case, total outages, partial outages, and degradation of service are three viable measures.

Speed is one of the most powerful of the delivery measures, especially in our present society, even the global society—we all want things faster. Patience is mostly a lost virtue. So in my project, we measured speed to resolve, speed to restore, and speed to complete work orders. We also measured speed to deliver projects, software contracts, and new products. Another favorite at many companies is speed to respond—how fast do you return messages, answer the phone, or respond in person? Speed can easily be related to availability. For example, we not only wanted to know the number of outages there were and how long they lasted, but how fast did we respond, resolve the problem, and restore the service?

Patience is mostly a lost virtue, so expect many of your Product/Service Health metrics to be related to speed.

In the case of my phone outage, I was unhappy with the time to respond (five days to have the technician show up at my door), but I was pleased with the speed to resolve. The technician fixed the problem in less than 30 minutes.

The last area I used for Delivery was accuracy. This was normally captured in the form of rework. How many cases were reopened after the customer thought it was resolved? Others could include defects per products delivered. There are also errors in service. Did we deliver the right things? Did we deliver to the right people? At the right time? At the right location? There are many areas in which an organization can make mistakes. Accuracy measures the quality of your products or services from the customer's viewpoint.

Triangulation of Perspectives

Triangulation is a simple concept. Use multiple sources of data when you can. Use more than one type of measure. More than one collection method. More than one perspective. In the case of the quadrants you are addressing, the differing perspectives is *not* referring to the following four viewpoints

1. Customers'

2. Business's (managers')

3. Workers'

4. Leadership's

Instead, I'm offering the following perspectives:

1. Objective, non-customer involvement
2. Customer behaviors (observation) and
3. Direct customer feedback

In the case of Effectiveness metrics (the place I recommend you begin), you are only dealing with the customer's viewpoint.

"The simultaneous consideration of intrinsic and extrinsic test factors forces every researcher to be self-consciously aware of how his every action can influence subsequent observations. From this perspective research becomes a social act."[2]

What if metrics became a "social act?" What if metrics, through triangulation coupled with open sharing of findings, were to become a collaborative event? A social act within the organization's society? It would help eliminate misuse and abuse of data, allow for multiple viewpoints to ensure accuracy of the data and, more importantly, lead to more meaningful interpretations of the metrics (answers). This social act may also lead the organization to ask better questions.

Demographics Don't Count

You may mistakenly choose to triangulate your metrics based on demographics. This is not a true triangulation of the data, but decomposition. For example, at institutes of higher learning, we frequently look at the data based on a demographic of our customer base faculty, staff, and students. Not every customer fits cleanly into one of these three categories, so we also look at non-institute affiliates, officers, and family. While this provides multiple and different data, they are not different views, sources, and methods. They are just a breakout of the data already gathered. This decomposition could be very useful (especially when wanting to know a specific constituent's feedback) but doesn't constitute triangulation.

These breakouts are very good for analyzing a subset of your customer population and allows you to address specific needs of each demographic. But it doesn't satisfy the requirement for triangulation.

---

[2] Norman K. Denzin, *Sociological Methods: A Sourcebook* (Chicago: Aldine Publishing Co., 1970), pp. 471-472.

According to Denzin, using multiple forms of triangulation within a single investigation leads to higher confidence in the (observed) findings. He also offers that the more diversity in the measures, the methods of collection, the people interpreting the data, and the sources directly correlates to the level of confidence. The higher the level of triangulation, the higher the level of confidence. The lower the level of triangulation, the lower the confidence.

I agree with this concept and would happily argue that you can have higher confidence in any metric made up of multiple measures than one made up of less. Answers derived from other metrics encourage an even higher level of confidence.

I don't propose that we seek out this level of confidence by demanding meta-metrics (metrics made up of other metrics) at every turn. Remember, some questions may not dictate even a single metric. Some may simply need a yes or no answer. Others may need a measure (or two) to provide the necessary insight to make a better decision. But, the more complex and critical the question, the more likely a higher level of confidence is called for. If your root question will be used to help decide on the future direction of the entire organization along with a considerable investment, you might demand a higher level of confidence in individual data used to build the metric and in the metric's overall conclusions.

Conflicting Results

Because we use varying methods and data sources, we run the real risk of obtaining conflicting results. But, rather than see this as a negative, you should see it as a positive.

Let's look at our restaurant example. If our restaurant's effectiveness metric is made up of Delivery, Usage, and Customer Satisfaction, we may expect that the results of each of these measurement areas should always coincide. If we have good service (Delivery) we should have high Customer Satisfaction ratings. And if we have high Customer Satisfaction, we could assume that we should have high levels of repeat customers, and high usage. We also expect the opposite. If we have poor Customer Satisfaction, we expect that customers won't come back. If we don't deliver well (too slow, wrong items delivered, or the menu items are unavailable) we would expect poor ratings and less usage.

These are logical assumptions, but many times incorrect ones. Each of the permutations tells us something different. In Table 7-2, let's look at each measure with a simple high vs. low result. Of course, the real results of your measures may be much more complicated—especially when you remember that each can also utilize triangulation. Delivery could have high availability and speed to deliver, but poor accuracy. You could have high usage for one type of clientele and low for another. Customer satisfaction could have high marks for some areas (courtesy of staff) and low for others (efficiency of staff). Rather than complicate it further, let's look at the measures at the higher level, keeping in mind the complexity possible when taking into account lower levels of triangulation.

Besides the interpretation of each of the individual measurement areas, the triangulation itself offers information you would lack if you only collected one or two areas.

Using our restaurant business as an example, let's interpret some possible measures. In Table 7.2, you can see how different permutations of the results of the measures can tell a different story. While each measure provides some basic insights, it is more meaningful to look at them in relation to each other.

Table 7-2. Interpreting Measures: An Example

Delivery	Usage	Customer Satisfaction	Possible Interpretation
High	High	High	Generally, life should be good. There are other factors to investigate—other metrics to create. It may be time to look at other quadrants in the tier like: Employee Satisfaction and Turnover. Of course, the owner may want to measure how well the business is doing counting the bottom line—is it making money? Future Health would be another area to investigate.
High	Low	High	In this scenario, the issue of low usage is likely due to something other than delivery or customer satisfaction. It could be you have too high of a price point. Your business could be in a poor location. You could suffer from inadequate marketing and advertising.
High	High	Low	You may be the "only game in town." The customer may perceive that you are the only choice for the service/product you offer. Your assessment of your delivery may be correct or out of touch with the customer. If your assessment is correct, then you may be offering a product/service that your customers "need" but not necessarily want. Like flu shots.

Delivery	Usage	Customer Satisfaction	Possible Interpretation
High	Low	Low	This case could describe a situation where your menu doesn't fit your clientele. Perhaps your menu is misplaced in the primary neighborhood your restaurant is in. Your pricing could be too high for your customer base.
Low	High	High	You may be the only source for a niche market. If there is no competition for your product/service, you may likely receive good marks from customer satisfaction. Once again, you may have a monopoly-like situation. When AT&T was Ma Bell, and you only had one choice, customer satisfaction may have been higher, even if customer service wasn't the best. Most times, customer satisfaction isn't an objective observation—it is based on your expectations. If the customer doesn't expect a lot, even mediocre service may rate high.
Low	High	Low	It is even more likely that you have the "only game in town." This could be based on price point (the cheapest food in town), or based on your product or service. If after the largest snow to hit your area stops—you may be very willing to pay the only snow removal service regardless of the quality, speed, or level of customer service.
Low	Low	High	This could be representative of an excellent staff. If you have the nicest wait staff but lousy food, you could see this mix of rating. It could be the customer likes you personally and doesn't want to hurt your feelings, but is unwilling to continue to spend money in your establishment. But it could also be that your delivery expectations are too stringent and you're in a lousy location.

You may argue that triangulation seems to make the results more confusing, not clearer. But in actuality, triangulation assures that you have more data and more views of that data. The more information you have the better your answers will be. But in all cases the next step should be the same. Investigate, investigate, investigate. The beauty of triangulation is that you already have so many inputs that your investigation can be much more focused and reap greater benefits with less additional work.

Imagine if all you measured was Customer Satisfaction. If you ratings in this area were high, what could you determine? You could think life was good. But if you're not making enough money to keep your business open, you'll wonder what happened.

Triangulation not only allows you to use disparate data to answer a single question, it actually encourages you to do so.

Recap

Triangulation is a principle foundation for a strong metric program. Triangulation has many benefits. The more triangulation used, the stronger the benefits. But the saying "all things in moderation" is also true with triangulation. You can overdo anything. You'll need to find the happy medium for you. Let's look at some of the following benefits:

- Higher levels of confidence in the accuracy of the measures used to form the metric
- Higher levels of confidence in the methods used to collect, analyze, and report the measures
- A broader perspective of the answer—increasing the likelihood of an accurate interpretation of the metric
- Satisfaction in knowing that you are "hearing the voice of all your customers"
- A more robust metric (if you lose a measure, data source, or analysis tool you will have other measures to fall back on)
- Confidence that you are "seeing" the big picture as well as you can

It is important to use triangulation in more than one aspect of the measurement collection and analysis, including the following:

- Multiple sources of data
- Multiple collection methods
- Multiple analysis methods (across measures and the willingness to apply different analytics to the same measures)
- Multiple areas (like Delivery, Usage, and Customer Satisfaction) or categories

With all of this diversity it is important to stay focused. Collecting data from different quadrants in the Answer Key would not fit the principle of triangulation. If you dilute your answers by mixing the core viewpoint, you will run the risk of becoming lost in the data. If you lose focus and collect data from disparate parts of the Answer Key, it is probable that you are trying to answer multiple questions with only one answer. While meta-metrics use other metrics as part of their input, they must still stay within the context defined by the root question.

A solid metric can lead you in time to metrics in other areas of the Answer Key, but only after you've done your due diligence in answering the questions at hand.

Conclusion

The concept of triangulation is not unique to the development of metrics and has been proven to be an effective guiding principle for using data.

Triangulation is a major principle in creating a viable metric program. It offers many benefits in return for the effort it takes to collect and analyze more data, from more sources, in multiple ways. Using triangulation on the Product/Service Health quadrant of the Answer Key garners you a robust set of measures to build your metric.

By concentrating on using a blend of sources, measures, and methods you end up with a comprehensive metric. You will have to still assess the metric for completeness to the question, but triangulation helps you get there with much less fuss and frustration.

Figure 7-3. The Product/Service Health quadrant

A quick review of the Product/Service Health quadrant (Figure 7-3) demonstrates this, as follows:

- Product/Service Health
    - Delivery
        - Availability
        - Speed
        - Accuracy
    - Usage
        - Unique users
        - Repeat customers
        - Referrals

- Customer Satisfaction
  - Annual surveys
  - Trouble resolution feedback
  - Interviews

You can have more than three components for any of these. For example, you could include "reliability" in Delivery or "frequency of use" under Usage. Many times, the measures themselves dictate different methods of collection and analysis. Surveys are inherently different than interviews. While trouble resolution feedback is normally in the form of a survey, the types of questions asked are drastically different from the general survey administered annually.

Each piece of information (Delivery, Usage, and Customer Satisfaction) has a different collection/analysis methodology, but within each set you can further vary the tools, processes, and methods of collection/analysis.

When you combine the focus of the Answer Key with the comprehensiveness of triangulation, you will find yourself ready to promote a practical metric program to the organization.

CHAPTER

8

Expectations
How to View Metrics in a Meaningful Way

If the Answer Key is the secret to unlocking the development of a useful metric program, the use of expectations is the keychain. Expectations allow you to change many of the common negatives toward measurement into productive improvement.

Don't Choose Poorly

I love the line in *Indiana Jones and the Last Crusade* (1989) when the Grail Knight matter-of-factly announces, "he chose poorly." There were dozens of cups to choose from and the villain chose the wrong one. It was understandable, though. He chose the most ornate, jewel-bespeckled chalice on the table.

Managers often pick the flashiest looking tools, and are disappointed by their inadequacy. I want to help you avoid "choosing poorly." The fear, uncertainty, and doubt around all metric programs stem from the misuse and abuse of the measures, in turn causing harm to those who are asked to provide the data. At times, this is a result of misguided or malicious management practices. Because I am an optimist and believe fully in the greater good, I believe that the misuse of metrics is rarely due to intentional actions. Most of the time, the abuse of metrics occurs because leaders are misled by any one of the deficient management techniques that use metrics improperly. These include the following:

1. The use of stretch goals

2. Measures as goals

3. Targets and thresholds

4. Incentive programs based on measures

These techniques may seem quite innocent and proper. There are authors, experts, and consultants who promote each, if not all, of them. Even successful CEOs will applaud the use of these "tools" for improvement. Do not be fooled: these are misuses of metrics, and any success attained by these paths is temporary.

Let's look at each briefly, and then introduce a simpler solution.

The Use of Stretch Goals

Using goals to strive for success is a good thing. The misuse of this concept by creating "stretch goals" and using measures as goals is where leaders fall astray. Goals in themselves can be a great tool. Vision, mission, and goals are a potent combination for steering an organization forward. But the misuse of goals can cause an organization's efforts to crash and burn.

Invariably, stretch goals are not independently identified for self-improvement. In business I find that managers think it's a good tool for motivating the workforce. Achievable goals aren't enough. "Stretch" goals are the latest silver bullet. The leader sets stretch goals for a department or staff member— and voila! The goal is attained. The leader looks brilliant, the department/ worker is applauded, and everyone is happy. Except that in most cases, the stretch goal was dictated (rather than collaboratively agreed upon) and the workers have no ownership. No ownership means less pride in the accomplishment.

The stretch goal is typically a big task to be achieved. This is fine if it ends there. But the school of thought is to upgrade the first stretch goal with a tougher, bigger stretch goal the next year. And so on, and so on. The workforce eventually catches on to this.

I can clearly hear the orator in the coliseum announcing, "Let the games begin!"

The manager keeps pushing to see how much he can get out of the workforce. The workforce wisely realizes how late they have to achieve the goal within the required time period (finishing early would mean a new stretch goal before the year is out—better to deliver on time than early). Stretch goals do not belong to the organization—and they definitely do not belong to the workforce. No, these goals are solely owned by management.

Another unintended consequence of stretch goals is that other work will suffer. Work that may have been performed to an exemplary level is reduced to "good enough" since it is not a part of the stretch goals. It is hard to stay focused on the big picture when mini-goals are set up as the standard of excellence.

Measures as Goals

Another common problem lies in the misuse of the measures of success (MoS) as the goal itself, instead of focusing on the identified requirement. Sometimes this becomes a slight nuance in meaning. If your task is to sell five thousand units of the new product are you measuring to the goal or to the MoS?

If you said the goal, you'd be mistaken. A simple test is, if you sold one more (or one less) than the "goal," would you be happier or not? How about ten more (or ten less)? One hundred? If it matters, then you're using the measure of success as the goal.

Where this becomes important is when the workforce needs to understand the purpose, the big picture, the mission and the vision of the organization. When you treat the worker as a partner in improvement, you don't attempt to manipulate (motivate) them by assigning "stretch goals" or by having them chase the measures instead of achieving the goal.

The true goal may be to improve the bottom line. Increasing sales is one possible task toward that end, and the idea of selling any particular number of any particular item would be a subtask. The number of items sold would constitute a measure of success.

When you chase the MoS you lose focus. You may reach the measure while failing to achieve the guiding goal. For example, you may sell five thousand units of the new item, but sales could drop significantly in the other product lines. This would not end up helping you achieve the goal.

Another way to look at it is to remember that any measure of success (or full blown metric) is only an indicator. Therefore, you should not celebrate the meeting of a MoS since it is not the goal; it is only an indicator of possibly reaching the goal.

Even when measures of success are properly used, managers occasionally make them tools for abuse by setting targets and thresholds.

Targets and Thresholds

Targets, like stretch goals, have the nasty habit of being re-written each time they are achieved. If you have a target, you can bet that it will be reached at the eleventh (if not final) hour. Again, there's no benefit to the workforce in achieving the target earlier than asked for since the most common response (after the small celebration and reward) is a new target to reach.

Targets (when misused) aren't moved as a result of logical, data-driven decisions. They are moved based on their achievement, or lack thereof. This means that the new target is set based only on how well you met the previous one—again using a poor indicator as the "truth." The workforce again will come to understand the rules of the game quickly. If they reach the target early, the reward is usually the same as if they reach it at the last possible moment. Some managers reward last-second heroics more than they reward early achievement. Early success is seen as the manager's underestimation of the capabilities of the workers. The target wasn't "tough" enough, so why highly reward for reaching it?

And the games continue.

It behooves the workers to barely reach the target. The manager sees himself as an astute judge of the workers' capabilities and a shrewd motivator. The workforce is seen as hardworking and able to be encouraged. Everyone is happy.

Thresholds are the same as targets, but from a negative point of view. Instead of setting a bar higher each time and trying to reach it, the threshold sets the minimum acceptable performance and challenges the workforce to stay above it throughout.

Again, the workforce is smarter than the manipulators believe. They will stay above this minimum, but barely. If they exceed it too significantly, the minimum will be raised until they fail, at which time they will incur the unjust wrath of management for being incompetent.

The stories of workers telling new hires to "slow down" because the over energetic rookie will make them look bad is not a myth. Workforces learn the rules of the game and quickly adapt to the motivational tools used by poor managers.

You're probably wondering what the problem is with clearly articulating the acceptable levels of performance. It would seem to be good communication to make this clear to the workforce. And you'd be correct. But, when targets and thresholds are misused, they never stabilize—they constantly move in reaction to their achievement. As the saying goes, it's hard to hit a moving target.

Incentive Programs Based on Measures

The last misstep I'll cover is building incentives around measures. Again, as with stretch goals and using measures of success as the goal—the emphasis (and reward) is placed on the wrong thing. There was an Olympic weight lifter who was given a large monetary reward for every weight-lifting record he broke. Not surprisingly, he broke his own world records incrementally—with the smallest increase in weight allowed to count as a new record. He was able to break world records many times. This was probably not exactly what the establishment was trying to motivate with their incentive program. But since the measure was the focus, rather than the goal, the results were naturally off center.

More enterprises than you can imagine have gone out of business due to misplaced focus. This absence of focus includes forgetting who the customer is, forgetting why the organization exists, and forgetting the goals of the organization. Focusing on individual acclaim rather than organizational success, on incentives rather than overall excellence, on measures instead of the goals, and on thresholds, targets, and incentives around measures—are misaligned with what is important.

Expectations

The use of expectations is not a conceptual or theoretical breakthrough. It is not a silver bullet. It, too, can be abused and misused.

Expectations help you stay focused on what is important. They provide the ultimate context for your metrics—based fully on the customers' point of view.

Expectations provide the ultimate context for your metrics—based fully on the customers' point of view.

Expectations are a clear description of what the customer expects from your service or product. Of course, you can use expectations for any of the views in the Answer Key, but we're focused on effectiveness, so we'll stick to the first quadrant.

The following are the questions that you will ask:

1. What level of service does the customer expect?
2. What is the quality of product that the customer expects?
3. Will exceeding these expectations benefit the organization?
4. Will failing to meet these expectations hurt the organization?
5. Why does the customer have these expectations?

With expectations, we start with the assumption that the customer has a range of expectations that you will provide. Let's look at the service center/help desk again as an example.

When a customer calls the service center seeking advice, he has some general expectations. For example, when I buy a product online and consequently need to get help from a service center, my expectations are rather low. My first expectation is that I won't be able to easily find a phone number to call on the company's web site. I am rarely disappointed—it seems not matter what link, icon, or button I select, I am given more opportunities to buy something. After a diligent search and more keystrokes (and clicks) than I want to count, I find the phone number. After dialing it, I expect that I won't get to speak to a living person until I spend at least five minutes navigating the auto-response call system. Of all the choices provided, (1 for new service, 2 for extending your service, 3 for adding a service, etc.) none of them will be, "speak to a service representative." So, without listening to all the choices, I press 0. Then, I get the "sorry that is an invalid choice, please try again." So I press 0 again and before the same recording can apologize for my mistake again, I press zero once more and, yes, I finally get a living, breathing representative to answer my call!

Now, my expectations change: how long it will take for a technician to actually engage me in conversation? Once I've explained my problem to the technician, how long will it take him to assist me? How well will the technician's solution work? These are all expectations that will help the organization define the measures used for performance.

If you're measuring time to respond and time to resolve—two natural measures for a help desk, then you will need to understand expectations from the customer's point of view, not management's.

If you simply look at the measures without expectations, you will quickly realize something is missing. Figure 8-1 shows this.

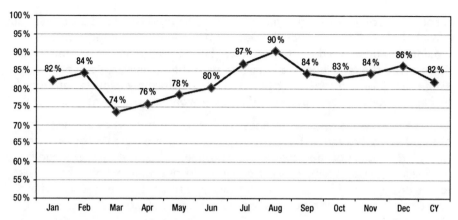

Figure 8-1. Cases resolved in less than 8 work hours

Figure 8-1 is a chart showing the percentage of help-desk cases resolved within eight hours. Does the chart tell a good story or a bad one? Are the results in March acceptable? Are the results in August acceptable? Is the overall percentage for the calendar year (CY) within acceptable parameters?

Without expectations, we don't know if the story is a good one or a bad one.

When you gather the expectations, you'll need to determine what "meets expectations" means. This should almost always be a range, and not a single value. In the scenario of "time to resolve" we may have different expectations based on different criteria—like the level of the problem. If the customer's issue is a simple one, the expectations are for a quick resolution. If the issue is a complicated one, then the expectations won't be as stringent.

Let's continue with a simple problem: you need a password reset. How long should this take? My expectations are that I should have it reset within an hour from whenever I actually get to speak to a living person. I expect that I will have to prove who I am—the proper "owner" of the account that I have lost the password to. Once I've answered the required questions, I expect to receive an e-mail (another security measure) with a new password. While most times I get this e-mail within minutes, I'm willing to accept up to an hour. So, my expectations range from five minutes to one hour.

Those are *my* expectations. Meeting these expectations would make me a satisfied customer. I don't require more, and I would be dissatisfied with less (if it took more than an hour, I would likely call the help desk back). If the resolution took less than five minutes, I'd be happy. Happy and surprised. But I would not expect it to happen the next time. And more importantly, I wouldn't be dissatisfied if it took longer (but still within my hour time frame). If I received the e-mail before I hung up with the technician, I'd probably even remark on the speed. Again, it wouldn't change my expectations, but I'd be happy about the unexpected. I'd actually wonder how it was possible.

This is the other essential difference with expectations—they are not changed easily or readily. When an expectation is met, the customer is satisfied. When it is not met, they are dissatisfied. When they are exceeded, it is truly a surprise. A happy surprise, but a surprise nonetheless. The customer doesn't raise her expectations every year, or if her expectations are constantly met. Meeting expectations doesn't necessitate their change—it affirms them.

Let's see what happens when we add expectations to the chart. Figure 8-2 shows the same data as in Figure 8-1, but with expectations added.

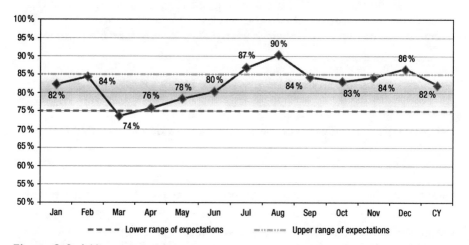

Figure 8-2. Adding expectations

The dotted and dashed lines indicate the direction the expectations flow. Expectations are met when they remain within the boundaries. Anomalies above or below the range of expectations are worthy of investigation.

How do you determine the customers' expectations if your customers are a large, diverse group? For example, in the case of international companies like Amazon.com, McDonalds, or Ford Motor Company? Even if it were possible to ask each customer about personal expectations, everyone would not come to a consensus. Therefore, it is important for you to come to a decision about the general expectations of the customer base.

From the organization's point of view, it is important to meet customers' expectations. If the organization cannot do so, it has to change so that it can. This is the foundation for a Service/Product Health metrics program. When the organization fails to meet expectations, further investigation should take place to see if the cause can be avoided in the future. Most organizations strive to do this already. Unfortunately, these same organizations forget to celebrate the times they meet expectations—and instead expend their energies punishing themselves for the few times they fail to meet expectations. These organizations also celebrate and reward times when they exceed expectations. But, if the expectations are correctly identified, *any* deviation—whether below (failure to meet) or above (exceeding)—should be investigated.

If there's a failure to meet expectations, determine if the occurrence can be prevented in the future. Perhaps a change in process or procedure can eliminate the occurrence.

If results exceed expectations, determine if the occurrence can be replicated—within manageable costs. Since exceeding expectations is not normal, chances are that something else was sacrificed to achieve this level of service or product quality. Either a different service was neglected, extra time was required, or extra expenses were invested. If this is not true, it would not be an anomaly, it would be the norm. And it would be within the customers' expectations.

There is a small nuance differentiating targets and the upper limit of expectations. If you consistently exceed expectations, then either your determination of what the customer expects is not ambitious enough or your service/product quality levels are such that the customer will truly expect more from you.

The scenario I gave about my expectations in re-setting my password was true. But if I were to discuss my expectations of a third-party delivery for a product I bought online vs. my expectations for Amazon.com's Prime sales (two-day, free delivery), they would be extremely different. As would be my expectations if I paid for overnight delivery vs. standard shipping. Overall though, whenever I see that a product I purchased is supplied by Amazon (vs. a third-party choice), I have higher expectations of the speed of delivery and the quality of the packaging.

The same will happen with your customers if you consistently exceed expectations. The question is: can you afford to do so consistently? The best-case scenario is that you are exceeding expectations because of a change to your processes or procedures. If your continuous process improvement efforts (Total Quality Management, Kaizen, or Six Sigma, for example) are successful, you may be delivering better and faster than before, without degrading other services or increasing costs.

If this were a "target," management would look at even one occurrence in which you exceeded the target and demand that you do so increasingly often each year. Or it may raise the target the next year.

When you exceed expectations, it is as much an anomaly as when you fail to meet them. Granted, the customer is not dissatisfied, but you will still need to investigate the causes, because your organization may not be able to afford these anomalies. Therefore, don't automatically applaud them as a good thing. Leadership must be as curious about the causes behind exceeding expectations as about failing to meet them. Granted, exceeding suggests that you are not running the business into the ground (Efficiency Measures) or that you are not causing poor customer experiences in other service or product areas. But this is why you cannot afford to push for or reward exceeding expectations.

Meeting expectations is truly the preference.

A more thorough representation of the measure would make the expectations band stand out. And don't use the classic green is good and red is bad style. Figure 8-3 presents a clearer picture of the expectations for cases to be resolved within eight work hours.

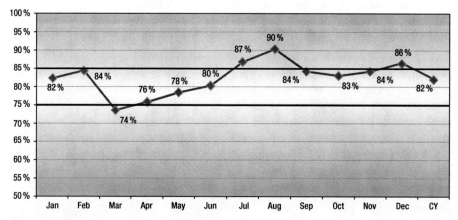

Figure 8-3. Neutrally colored expectations

Discovering Expectations

Many times when I'm helping a department define their metrics, the managers don't know the customers' expectations. I usually push and prod with questions like, "What would make your customers dissatisfied?" Or, "What would make them take notice?" I'll use their customer satisfaction surveys (remember, almost everyone already has these in place) to see what customers have said about speed, availability, or accuracy.

Normally, using a little investigative tenacity, I can create an initial range for the customers' expectations. Once I've analyzed enough data, and considered anything usable from satisfaction surveys, the norm is easily identified.

This norm provides insight to the stability of the processes and to the level of service normally provided. I use this as a guide to work with the department to create expectations. This is necessary because usually the customer base is just too large to query a complete representative body. After I've determined the norm, I ask the department if it seems right.

Figure 8-4 shows an example of data—call it trouble calls resolved within eight hours or less—collected over three calendar years.

Note: If you don't have historic data, you may not be able to conduct this exercise until you have collected enough data to compare to.

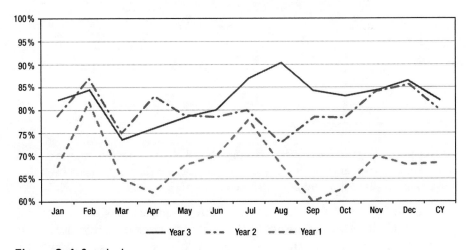

Figure 8-4. Sample data

When there is data for multiple years and several data points, it becomes easier to determine expectations. In the case of Figure 8-4, I would ask the customer if Year 1 was a "normal" year. Usually, the answer is that it was a below-par year for them. The poor results, compared to other years, were usually caused by a change in process, leadership, or system. Regardless of the reasons, I only want to know if, what took place during that year could be considered normal.

I then check Year 2 and Year 3. Chances are that these years were more normal and the department felt good about its overall performance during these periods.

Using only Years 2 and 3, I work with the department to see what the data is showing as "normal." This is seen in Figure 8-5. I disregard Year 1, the "abnormal" year. Even if it had been an exemplary year—with results consistently close to 90 percent, I would remove it because that, too, would not be "normal."

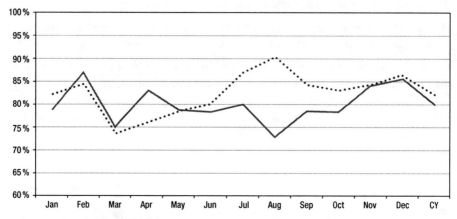

Figure 8-5. Two-year sample

At this point, I again ask the department to use their collective memory and tell me if the lows and highs were abnormal. Rather than try to get them to set a range, I just ask them about the extremes.

- "In August of Year 2, you were below 75 percent. Was that normal?" If the answer is no, I will ask about March of that year.
- "It seems that March is traditionally a 'bad' month—is that right? Were the past two Marches abnormal for any reason?"

I will ask the same questions about August of Year 3, in which the unit reached its highest numbers, and then work my way down. You can also use statistical analysis for this purpose, but I find using the charts of the data much less intimidating to the department. Also, statistics give the impression that creating the range is not up to the department.

It is important to give the unit ownership of both the metric and the team's performance. By having the members of the department collaboratively determine the customers' expectations, you gain benefits from the start, as follows:

1. Ownership of both the processes and team performance levels

2. A common understanding of what the customers expect

3. An open discussion of the previous highs and lows—without negative or positive connotations. The department learns to view metrics as input, rather than drivers of consequence.

Figure 8-6 shows an example of what I estimate to be the performance norm for the unit.

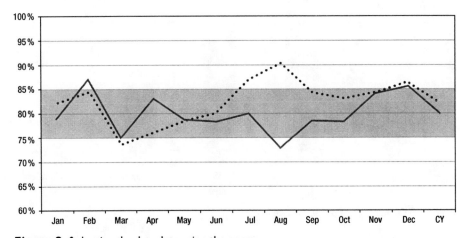

Figure 8-6. Letting the data determine the norm

At this point, I would ask the department if the chart (Figure 8-6) seems correct.

"Would you agree that your customers' expectations lie between a 75 percent and an 85 percent rate of performance?" I usually get an affirmative nodding of heads. That isn't enough, though. I want to get as close to correct as possible, but I'm willing to accept what amounts to a good guess to start. I say this because regardless of where we set the expectations, we must stay flexible regarding the definition. We may obtain better feedback from the customer. We may change our processes in a way that the expectations would have to change (rarely do customers grow to expect less—most times they will only expect more).

I ask, "So, would the customer be surprised if you delivered over 85 percent? " If I get a yes, I ask the logical follow up question, "How did the customer react in February of Year 2 and August of Year 3?" And, "How did you achieve these results?" I'd ask the same questions about March of Year 3 and August of Year 2. Depending on the answers I might readjust the expectations.

I mentioned that you could use statistical analysis. Let's look at an example. Figure 8-7 shows the same data analyzed using Microsoft Excel's Data Analysis Add-in tools.

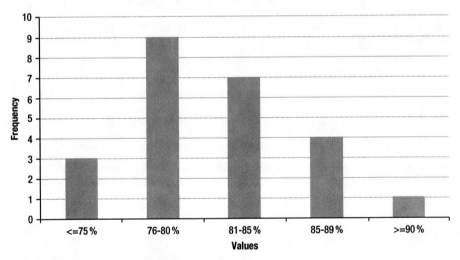

Figure 8-7. Histogram of the two-year sample

Based on the histogram, my guess of 75 to 85 percent would seem acceptable. More exact may be greater than 75 percent and less than or equal to 85 percent. If we look at a simpler view of the data spread, we find that the range offered is quite reasonable and probable. But again, the main test will be to check our ideas against customer feedback.

A simple frequency chart of the same data, shown in Figure 8-8, tests the visual interpretation and affirms the guess.

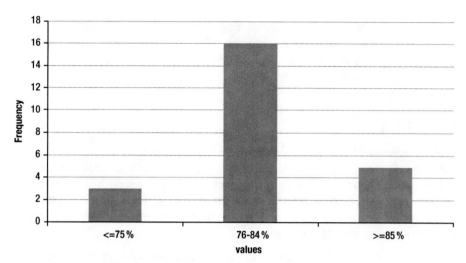

Figure 8-8. Frequency chart of two-year sample

Recap

The existing schools of thought on performance measures—specifically the concepts of targets, thresholds, and using measurements as goals—should be replaced by a collaborative approach that gives ownership of service and product quality to the workforce. This is accomplished by determining customer expectations.

- Expectations are almost always a range.
- Meeting expectations is what you want to do on a regular basis.
- Failing to meet expectations is an anomaly that should be investigated to determine causes.
- Exceeding expectations is an anomaly that should be investigated to determine causes.
- Positive and negative anomalies should both be of concern to the organization. Whether you are exceeding expectations or failing to meet expectations, you need to investigate further.
- When setting expectations, look to the data to help identify the norm. The question then becomes, "Is the norm equal to the customers' expectations?" If yes, then the data should reflect that. The purpose is to be able to identify the anomalies that fall out of the norm or outside of the range of expected behavior.

- Treasure anomalies—because anomalies are where your metrics earn their return on investment. The main reason to adjust the range of expectations is to ensure that you are properly identifying the anomalies.

Conclusion

The old school-of-thought doesn't work. Using metrics as a form of motivation falls closer to manipulation than collaboration. You'll need to develop a solid rapport with your workforce and fully team with them to use metrics properly. Setting stretch goals, targets, thresholds, using measures as goals, and rewarding reaching a measure as an incentive are examples of using the wrong tool for the job.

Meeting customer expectations is the real goal. Anomalies to the expectations can provide useful information.

Expectations provide a clear context and are the key to open the doors to improvement.

Creating and Interpreting the Metrics Report Card

I struggled for a long time trying to decide how to introduce the Report Card to you. I debated if I should present it as another tool (like the Answer Key), or offer it as a methodology. What I settled on was to offer it as a real-life example of how metrics, when used within the constructs I've offered, can evolve and take shape.

I will relate to you the three-year journey to develop a viable metric program for an organization in which I had to clearly articulate the overall health of the organization and the health of each of its core services. I made mistakes along the way, learning, changing, testing, and trying. I will share with you the journey of discovery and the final destination I arrived at. Hopefully you can learn from my mistakes and benefit from the final product as either a template or example for your use.

The top-level executive asked a straightforward question of our CIO, "How healthy is your organization? And how do you know?" This fit in well with the curiosity of my CIO, who wanted meaningful information about the organization's health, but didn't know how to communicate the need.

With this root question in hand, I endeavored to find a way to build a metric program that would provide meaningful answers. The "we" I refer to is a metric project team made up of Ernst & Young consultants and myself.

To instill a metric program in an organization that was not truly ready for it was a difficult proposition. One that was actually impossible to succeed at. I say that with all humility because even with the level of success we enjoy today with the Report Card, it's still not used to its full potential. But we are getting better, and the Report Card has lasted longer than any other reporting tool our organization has used to date.

To succeed at this challenge while keeping to the principles and values I've laid out so far in this book was even more difficult. To make this possible, especially when working with a mandate (perhaps one of the worst ways to implement any specific improvement effort because it removes the chance for "buy-in" of the workforce), required a metric program that would have benefit to the data owners, the executive requesting the answers, as well as all the people in between.

Along with a metric system that would provide meaningful information to all levels, I wanted it to be easy to understand and require as little translation between levels as possible.

As I've written earlier, you can't do this on your own. It would have been impossible for me to succeed at this by myself—not only because the effort was too large for one person, but because I wouldn't be able to obtain buy-in on my own. The service providers wouldn't buy in and believe how the information would (and wouldn't) be used if I didn't involve them throughout the process. Management wouldn't buy in to the idea that whatever solution I developed was going to work, since I was already a member of the village. No prophet (or metrics designer) is accepted in his own village. So I ended up with a team of outside consultants, myself, and heavy involvement of each service provider.

Concept

First, you may be thinking, "Why a Report Card and not a Scorecard? After all, many organizations track metrics using them." I started with the thought of using a scorecard. The scorecard methodology included using measures from different areas (which fit the concept of triangulation), but the areas were not even within the same family of measures (see Answer Key). The other problem was that Scorecards mixed in the more "risky" efficiency measures along with effectiveness ones. Without a doubt, I wanted to stay in the Service/Product Health area, since I'd be working hard to break through enough barriers without fighting the war that would ensue with efficiency measures.

What I liked about the scorecard (and dashboards) was the combination of measures to tell a fuller picture. That fits the definition of a metric rather than just a bunch of measures.

But think about the name itself: the scorecard represents a means of knowing "who's winning." In the fall of 2011, I watched the University of Notre Dame lose its opening football game 23–20 to the University of South Florida. What was amazing was that Notre Dame "won" in every imaginable category, and not by just a little. Offensively, defensively, all categories except one: turnovers. In the end, the only statistic that matters is the final score, and that is determined by points. Those points are normally predictable through other measures.

So, the scorecard will tell you quickly who is winning, and who has won. It won't tell you, though, who is performing better in specific areas. A fan may only be concerned with the scorecard, but I was working with the equivalents of the coaching staff. The offensive, defensive, and special team coaches, along with the running backs, receivers, and linebackers coaches would all want to know how their units were performing.

I wanted the best of both. I wanted a final score and indicators of the quality of performance that led to that score.

What we came upon is the concept of a Report Card. This metric would be like a college report card, where the student receives feedback throughout the year on how well his education is progressing. There are quizzes, tests, and papers to be graded. At periodic intervals (mid-semester and at the end of the semester) grades are levied. Based on the feedback the student knows if he is doing well, if he needs to improve, or if he is exceeding expectations.

In each case, the organization, like the student, has decisions to make, based on the entire report card. It's not enough to celebrate the exceptional grades (A+) and denigrate any poor grades. It requires more information before a decision can be made. Was the A+ obtained at the expense of a different subject? What is the benefit for the A+ over an A or even a B? Is the poor grade in a subject that the student needs/actually wants? Can the class be dropped? Is it required for the major?

For our purposes, we treated the metric we developed in the same way as a report card. While we may be happy to get higher-than-expected grades, we only want the following results:

1. Those that don't require more than an acceptable effort (for example, if the student is neglecting other subjects or the student is burning the midnight oil to the point that his health is suffering).

2. The student obtained the grades without "cheating." In the organizational context, cheating equates to doing things outside the acceptable standards, policies, or processes.

3. The student earned the grades. We don't want grades that were not earned—positive or negative. The metric should reflect the performance of the service from the customers' viewpoints.

When we look at grades that fall below expectations (the failure of a quiz or test, for example), we also have to ask the following:

1. Was the failure due to an avoidable circumstance? This might include poor study habits, not doing the required work, or a lack of prerequisite coursework?

2. Was it due to a lack of effort or focus?

3. Is the subject actually required for the major? If not, is it a course that can be dropped? If the service is not part of the organization's core services, can it be dropped? Are results "below expectations" acceptable?

Let's look at how the Report Card is built, from an individual service to the overall organization's health.

Ground Work

All organizations have customers. In our case, to answer the questions posed by our executive leadership, we chose to answer it in the context of how well we delivered our services to our customers. We could have taken the question to mean how efficiently we were producing our products and delivering our services...but using the Answer Key we chose to start at the more critical focal point of how well we were satisfying our customers (Service/Product Health). This focus allowed us to design a program from the bottom up.

By focusing on the customer's viewpoint (effectiveness), we found it possible to introduce the metrics at the staff level, mitigating the fear, uncertainty, and doubt normally encountered with metrics. We were able to assure the workforce, including supervisors, middle-managers, and directors, that the information we were gathering, analyzing, and eventually reporting would not reflect how well any one person in the organization was performing, nor any unit. It would instead communicate how the customer saw our services and products.

The Information would be valuable to everyone at every level. Without "blame" being involved, we could address the customers' concerns without distraction. Not only wasn't blame ("who" wasn't important, only the "why"), but the information we had wasn't considered fact—it was the customers' perception that mattered more than any argument about fact.

This helped address the normal arguments against collecting certain data: *"But we have no control over that,"* and *"It's not our fault."*

We agreed to use the following major categories of information suggested by the Answer Key:

1. Delivery

2. Usage

3. Customer Satisfaction

We further agreed that Delivery, for most services, would be further broken down into Availability, Speed, and Accuracy. This was especially useful since the most contentious measurements resided in the Delivery category. Most of our service providers were already collecting and reviewing measures of Customer Satisfaction through the trouble call tracking system surveys. Usage was a "safe" measure since rarely does anyone consider usage numbers a reflection of their performance.

Since we expected the most pushback from the Delivery measures, we hoped to ease the resistance by using the three areas just mentioned (triangulation).

So, the root question, and our higher-level information needs were identified easily. Of course we still had to then identify individual measures and their component data. Before we did this, we needed to know which services would be included in the report card. We needed to know the organization's key/core services. A service catalog would have helped immensely, but at the time, this was lacking. In many organizations suffering from organizational immaturity, much of the prerequisites for a solid metric program may be missing. This is one of the reasons that using a metric program is considered a mature behavior.

While trying to implement a mature behavior (like a metric program) in an immature organization can be rife with problems, if done carefully it can actually act as a catalyst for moving toward maturity. In our case, the metric program clearly helped the organization think about and move toward developing a service catalog. While it had been identified as a need long before the metric program was launched, the metric effort helped focus on the deficiency.

Another behavior encouraged by the Report Card would end up being the more consistent and accurate use of the trouble call tracking system. Since a large amount of data (for almost all of the services included in the Report Card) relied on this system, the organization had to become more rigorous in its use of the system.

Until the organization documented a service catalog, we did our best to identify the services that would be considered core by the majority of the organization.

Being an information technology organization we had a lot of services and products to choose from. Some of the key services we chose included the following:

- Service Desk
- E-mail
- Calendaring
- Network
- Telephone

These services were easily accepted as part of the core services we provided. For each of these services, we built a template for collecting measures in the areas identified. This template would include the service, the type of information (category) to be used in the analysis of the health of the service, and specific measures that would be used to answer the root question. The results are shown in Table 9-1.

Table 9-1. Services and their associated measures.

Service	Category	Measure
Service Desk	Availability	Abandoned call rate
	Speed	Time to Respond
		Time to Resolve
	Accuracy	Rework

Service	Category	Measure
	Usage	Unique customers
		Preferred provider rating
	Customer Satisfaction	Survey results
E-mail	Availability	% of Uptime
	Speed	Time to Resolve issues
		Time to Receive
		Time to Send
	Accuracy	Rework (of problem resolutions)
		SPAM filter accuracy
	Usage	*Not applicable*
	Customer Satisfaction	Survey results
Calendaring	Availability	% of Uptime
	Speed	Time to Resolve issues
	Accuracy	Rework (of problem resolutions)
		Calendar system errors (dropped appointments, functionality issues, etc.)
	Usage	% of Features utilized
		Frequency of use
	Customer Satisfaction	Survey results
Network	Availability	% of Uptime
		Degradation of service
	Speed	Connection speed
		Upload speed
		Download speed
		Time to Resolve issues
	Accuracy	Rework (of problem resolutions)
	Usage	Frequency of use
	Customer Satisfaction	Survey results

Service	Category	Measure
Telephone	Availability	% of Uptime (system)
		% of Uptime (individual devices)
	Speed	Time to Resolve issues
	Accuracy	Rework (of problem resolutions)
		Lost calls
	Usage	% of Features utilized
	Customer Satisfaction	Survey results

You may have different services to look at. You may be, for example, in an entirely different industry than the one I'm using in the example. Even if you have the same services, you may have different categories of information and therefore different measures.

I'm going to focus on only one area, Service Desk, to continue this example, but I want to first explain the "not applicable" measure for usage of e-mail. Our organization provided the e-mail for our customers—basically as a monopoly. Our customers had no other choice for their work e-mail. They could use other e-mail services (Gmail, for example), but it would have to go through our system first and then could be auto-forwarded. So we started with "not applicable" and didn't measure usage for e-mail. We also did not measure usage for Calendaring, Networking, and Telephone, for the same reasons. While *we* didn't use a measure for usage in these cases, there are measures that could have been used.

For e-mail we could have used Percentage of Use and the Number of Customers who Auto-Forwarded their e-mail to a different e-mail provider.

For Calendaring we could look at Frequency of Use, and Percentage of Features Used. Calendaring was a new enough service that it would have been worthwhile to know the level of usage (acceptance by our customers) of the features.

Measuring the Frequency of Use of the internet and telephones still seems meaningless since they are high-use services that we held as a monopoly.

The following are two points that I want to make clear:

1. Some of the measures can be "not applicable." Although triangulation dictates that you attempt to have at least three measures from different viewpoints, it is not mandatory.

2. Just because you can think of measures, doesn't mean that you have to use them.

Just because you can think of measures, doesn't mean that you have to use them.

So, back to the Service Desk. Let's look at the specific measures which were identified for this service.

Table 9-2. Service Desk Measures.

Service	Category	Measure
Service Desk	Availability	Abandoned call rate
	Speed	Time to Resolve
	Accuracy	Rework
	Usage	Unique customers
	Customer Satisfaction	Survey results

As explained in Chapter 5, the Delivery measures of Availability, Speed, and Accuracy would be measured objectively through information gathered from the service provider. The great news for us was that the manager of the department was (and still is) an extremely compassionate leader. Where much of the dangers and warnings I've written about come from fear, uncertainty, and doubt—the realization of those trepidations occurs most times because the manager misuses the metrics. In the case of our Service Desk, I didn't worry that the manager would misuse or abuse the information we provided. If I told her the data showed that a worker was negligent, lazy, or incompetent, rather than take premature action, she'd investigate to first find out the "truth" behind the data. Then if the interpretation I offered was accurate, she'd work with the staff member to address the issues—compassionately.

The manager's attitude made the Service Desk an excellent service to start with. We had a high confidence level in her ability to help us sell the program to her staff and become a solid example for other service providers.

Another positive from starting with this service provider was the large amount of data easily attained. The Service Desk was the highest user of the trouble call tracking system. The majority of the data would be through this system. The Availability data (abandoned calls) was available through a totally automated call system, making it an objective set of measures. Customer satisfaction was handled by a third-party survey organization. So, this service provider had all the data we could want and most of it was through objective collection methods. All of it was obtainable without intruding on the departments' day-to-day operations. An ideal service to start with.

Speed would be tracked with a little less objectivity than Availability. Since it was based on the speed of resolution, it would be derived from the time to open and time to close trouble-call cases. This required that the analyst answering the call logged in the call accurately at each phase—opening and closing. Since the manager believed in metrics, she encouraged (and ensured) the workers logged cases accurately.

Accuracy was also measured using the trouble-call tracking system. Rework was defined as cases that were prematurely (incorrectly) closed. We could try to identify errors (defects) throughout the solution process, but since much of finding solutions to customer problems included trial and error, this was not an easy place to start. Even with the manager's compassion, I didn't want to ask the analyst to track how many different guesses they tried before they got it right. This would require a high level of trust (for the worker to not believe it would reflect about herself), a trust I hadn't developed yet. Another problem with this possibility was that the information might not reflect the customer's view point. Most customers expect a fair amount of trial and error, and hunting around for the right solution.

In each case—Abandoned Call Rate, Time to Resolve, and Rework, the data would reflect the customer's view point.

Moving from Delivery to Usage was, in this case a more difficult set of measures. Since the Service Desk was an internal service provider (the customers were not paying for the service), usage did not reflect income to the organization. The manager had a very healthy big picture view of the mission of her department. If usage was "high," that might reflect the instability of the IT systems, services, and products. It may also reflect the ineffectiveness of IT-related training. In most businesses and services, high usage would be a good thing. In the case of the Service Desk, high usage might be as bad as low usage. Also, if the usage was "low" it wasn't clear if this reflected that the training was excellent, and the systems stable or that the customer didn't find the Service Desk a meaningful, useful provider.

As with most measures, the information derived from it would have to be interpreted. Further investigation should be carried out rather than jumping to any conclusions. Any extremes could be a negative in this case—but the information was still useful. Since we had data, measures, and information from a decent span of time (over three years), we could determine if there were changes in the customers' patterns of usage. By looking at unique customers, we could determine if there were anomalies—up or down. These spikes may not indicate a good or bad thing. Instead they would indicate only that something had changed.

To be meaningful, I had to have longitudinal data for comparison; otherwise anomalies could not be identified. In some cases it isn't as important—but in the case of usage, it was. The key is to be able to determine anomalies—measures that fell out of the range of normal expectations. After we identified the proper measures and data points, we had to identify expectations.

The task is to identify anomalies—measures that fall out of the range of normal expectations.

This highlights an important facet of the metric program. Your information is only indicators and shouldn't be acted upon without further investigation. Rather than expect these metrics to be the impetus for action, it more often is the indicator that something is amiss, something has changed, or something needs to be investigated.

Customer Satisfaction was another example of data that was easy to attain. The department utilized a third-party survey company that sent survey invitations (via e-mail) to the customer of every closed trouble call. The vendor collected the responses, tabulated the results, and sent a weekly report to the department. I was given a monthly copy of the results for inclusion in the Report Card. All of the measures we had identified were collectable unobtrusively, with no disruption of the department's workflow. This is not always possible, but it is always a goal.

Since most of the data was attainable through automated systems, the data we had was readily available and had a high level of detachment from human error. The few places where humans did interact with the data, the team's desire to produce accurate information made us very happy to have this service as our flagship.

Recall the Metric Development Plan. We realized it was important to identify the source, the data (each component), how and when to collect, and how to analyze it. In the case of the Service Desk much of this was already done. Table 9-3 takes the categories and measures identified for the Service Desk and further breaks them down into the data needed, where that data will be found, and some basic analysis of the data. This analysis can be programmed into a software tool for display.

Table 9-3. Development Plan collection and analysis.

Category	Measure	Data	Source	Analysis
Availability	Abandoned call rate	Total calls	Automated call system	% of total calls abandoned (abandoned ÷ total calls)
		Calls abandoned	Automated call system	
Speed	Time to Resolve	Date/Time case was opened	Trouble call tracking system	Closed–Start–Stop time
		Date/Time case was closed		
		Stop time		
Accuracy	Rework	Total cases	Trouble call tracking system	% of cases re-opened (reopened cases ÷ total cases)
		Number of cases reopened		
Usage	Unique customers	Customer name	Trouble call tracking system	Number of unique customers
Customer Satisfaction	Courtesy of the analyst, skills/ knowledge of the analyst, timeliness of the resolution, and overall satisfaction	5-point Likert scale—on level of satisfaction for each topic/ question	Third-party survey company surveyed every trouble call customer	Ratio of promoters (5s) to detractors (1s, 2s, 3s)

This was our starting point. We identified these measures easily. Some of them were already being collected and analyzed. As with most things, there were other options to choose from. After looking at the analysis, we re-evaluated our draft of the measures.

Let's return to the Metric Development Plan, which consists of the following:

- Purpose statement
- How the metrics will be used
- How the metrics won't be used
- Customers of the metrics
- Analysis
- Schedules
- A Picture for the Rest of Us
- Prose

Purpose statement. Our purpose statement was defined for us—how can we communicate to our leadership how healthy our services and products are?

How will it be used. You might think this answer would be simple and obvious; it would be used to answer the questions. In this particular case, it would be used to communicate the health of the Service Desk, from the customer's point of view.

How it won't be used. Most people want this to be obvious also, expecting not to have to answer the question. Of course I had to answer it.

- It would not be used to differentiate between analysts
- It would not be used for performance reviews
- It would not be used to push the team of analysts to reach different levels of performance—in other words, the measures wouldn't become targets to be achieved.

Customers of the metrics. The customers of this metric (Health of the Service Desk) was first and foremost the service desk itself. The manager and the analysts were the owners of the data, and they were the "rightful" owners of the information derived. Another customer was the director of our support services (who the manager answered to), the CIO, and finally the executive. All of these were customers. Each customer needed different levels of information.

The data owners (analysts and manager) could benefit from even the lowest levels of the data. The director would need to see the anomalies. She would want to know what the causes of those anomalies were. The CIO would want to know about anomalies that required his level of involvement. If the Service Desk determined that it needed an upgrade to their phone system, a new automated call system, or an expert system, the funding would have to be approved by the CIO. The data would help support these requests.

The CIO would also want to know about any trends (positive or negative), or anomalies that might reflect customer dissatisfaction. Basically, the CIO would want to know about anomalies that his boss (the executive) might ask about. Most of the time the executive would ask because a key customer or group of customers complained about a problem area. The CIO shouldn't hear about the anomaly from his boss.

The same can be said of the executive. If the service's health was below expectations, and it ended up reflecting back on the parent organization, the executive would rightly want to know why and what was being done to make things better (either repeat the positive experiences or eliminate the negative).

Analysis. Besides the planned analysis, the results of the information would have to be analyzed for trending and/or meaning. Now that we had the ground work laid out, it was time to dive a little deeper. We had to collect the data and analyze it to ensure our initial guesses of what we'd use were on target.

Availability

We started with the abandoned call rate for the service. When we looked at the data shown in Figure 9-1, I asked the manager (and the staff) to perform a simple litmus test. I asked the manager if she thought the department was unresponsive to the customer. Was the abandoned rate too high? If it was higher than expected, was it accurate? If it was, why was it so high?

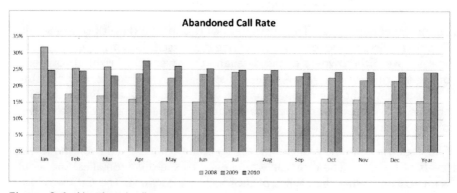

Figure 9-1. Abandoned call rate

The manager had heard many times before that abandoned rates were standard measures of performance for call centers. When she looked at the data she said it "didn't feel right." Not because it cast the department in an unfavorable light, but because she had confidence that her unit was more responsive to the needs of the customer than the rate showed (the data showed that the department was "dropping" more than two out of every ten calls).

This prompted the proper response to the measures: we investigated. We looked at two facets—the processes and procedures used to answer calls and the raw data the system produced. The process showed that calls that were not answered within two rings were sent to an automated queue. This queue started with a recording, informing the caller that all analysts were busy and one would be with the caller shortly. It was telling that the recording provided information about any known issues with the IT Services like, "the current network outage was being worked and should be back up shortly," is one example. Most days, the recording's first 30 seconds conveyed information that may have satisfied the callers' needs.

Upon further inspection, we found that the raw data included the length of the call (initiation time vs. abandoned time). This allowed us to pull another measure, as shown in Table 9-4.

Table 9-4. Development Plan collection and analysis – Abandoned calls less than 30 seconds.

Category	Measure	Data	Source	Analysis
Availability	Abandoned calls less than 30 seconds	For each abandoned call, length of call	Automated call system	% of abandoned calls less than 30 seconds in length

The measure was charted in Figure 9-2. We looked at it compared to the total abandoned rate to see if it told a clearer story.

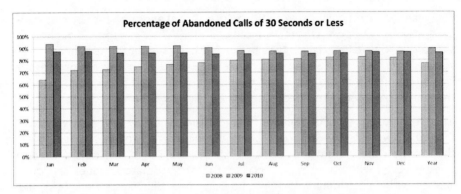

Figure 9-2. Percentage of abandoned calls less than 30 seconds in duration

As with all measures, a major question is how to communicate the measure (what graphical representation to use). In the case of Availability, we started with an Abandoned Call Rate in the form of Percentage of Calls Abandoned. When we added the more specific Calls Abandoned in Less Than 30 Seconds, we again used a percentage. We chose to show it in relation to the total *or* only show the Percentage of Abandoned Calls with the qualification that "abandoned" was defined as calls abandoned after 30 seconds.

After a year of looking at the measures in conjunction with improvements to the processes (including a shorter recording), the department chose to drop the Total Abandoned Rate and use only Abandoned Calls Less Than 30 Seconds. This was a better answer to the question of availability since it would allow for the following:

1. Wrong numbers

2. Questions answered/problems resolved by the automatic recording

3. Customers who changed their mind (They may have chosen to use the new e-mail or chat functions for assistance. Perhaps their problem solved itself while the customer was calling.)

While the assumption that a caller who didn't wait more than 30 seconds was not disappointed by the wait was only an assumption, it was believed that this would provide a more accurate account. This would have to be compared with the Speed (see the additions to the Speed measures) and the customer satisfaction measure of "timeliness." Of course, the only ones filling out the survey were ones who stayed on the phone long enough to have their call answered.

With a solid start on Availability, let's look at Speed. Speed started as Time to Resolve, which was known to be a concern with customers. Not that the organization was deficient in this aspect, but that the customer cared about how long it took to resolve an issue.

Speed

We started with the open and close times for cases tracked in the trouble call tracking system. This data required human input. It required that the analyst be religious in his behaviors and adherence to the processes, procedures, and policies established around trouble-call tracking. If the manager were almost any other manager, I would have had to spend a considerable amount of time ensuring that the workforce understood that the information would not be misused and that it would be in the best interest of the department, each and every worker, and the manager for the data input into the system to be as accurate as possible. Regardless of the story that it told. If the analyst "fudged" the data so that it wouldn't "look so bad" or so that it "looked extra good," the information would be rendered useless. Wrong decisions could be made.

In this case, I trusted the manager and only spent a minimal amount of time communicating at a staff meeting the importance of accuracy in the data and how the resulting measures and information could be used to improve processes—and would not reflect on individual performance. The key to this explanation was consistent with any of the measures and any of the units I worked with.

The data, then measures, then information, and finally metrics should not reflect the performance of an individual.

The metrics, moreover, did not reflect on how efficiently the department was run.

What the data, measures, information, and metrics did clearly reflect was the customers' perception of the service. Regardless of what the "truth" was, the department would benefit from knowing the customers' perception. This is especially true in speed.

Depending on the tools you use for capturing speed, you can report the exact time it took to resolve a problem. For example, you could use the automated call system to identify the time the call was initiated (instead of when the analyst opened the case file in the trouble call system). You could use another call system to log the day and time the analyst completed the final call to the customer, closing the case (assuming it took more than one call). You would have to have a means of connecting the case information to the call system. This level of accuracy is unnecessary in most cases—it is enough to log the time the case was opened and closed. But even if you had the accuracy described, the customer may "perceive" the resolution to take longer than it actually did.

I can assure you, showing the customer "proof" that the case actually took less time than he perceived it to take will do nothing to improve the customer's level of satisfaction nor change his opinion of how fast the department works. To the customer, perception is reality. And while it is useful to know the objective reality—you also have to address the customers' perception.

Even if you meet your Service Level Agreements (SLAs), assuming you have them, a case may be perceived as taking longer than expected.

Note: If you can get SLAs for your services, these are great starting points for documenting the customers' expectations for a service or product. If you have them, stay alert. You may find that although the customer agreed to the SLA, it may not reflect their expectations, not as time passes. It may not even reflect their expectations the day they are written.

For our metric, I collected the time the case was opened and time closed. Our trouble call system had the capability of toggling a "stop clock" switch. This function captured the amount of time the switch was toggled in the "stop" position until it was toggled back to "active."

This was very useful as it allowed the worker to capture the span of time the customer did not expect work to be performed. This was *not* used to subtract evening hours or weekends when the desk was closed. The customer, while not necessarily expecting work to get done during this time, did consider "down time" as part of the total time to correct their problem. The stop clock was used for specific, well-defined instances, such as

1. The customer was not available (on vacation, out of town) so the case, while resolved, could not be closed.

2. The customer requested that the resolution not be implemented until a specific time. Like installing new software because she didn't want the upgrade to mess up her current work.

In the case of a scheduled fix, I used another data point, scheduled resolution time, which was used as the start time in the formula. I rarely found the stop clock being used in this instance although it could also work. If you use the stop clock or scheduled resolution times, you still must capture the start time and close time. You have to keep the source data because you don't know when you'll have a customer argue that the real time should have been from the time of the call, or you may find that you want to show how far in advance you're getting the requests for future resolutions. Are you getting the request a day before? A week? Or a month before it's needed? What are your processes for dealing with these requests? How do you ensure the work gets done on schedule? The source data, including actual start and close times will help in checking your process.

So we started by looking at the Time to Resolve compared to the customers' expectations as shown in Figure 9-3.

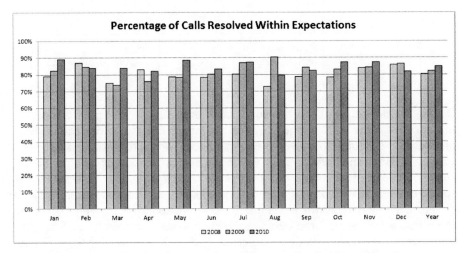

Figure 9-3. Time to Resolve: the percentage of cases resolved within expectations

For Speed we also had to make a decision on how to represent the data. We could show the data as the number of calls resolved within expectations. This could also be a percentage. You may notice a trend here. Percentages are an easy way to depict data, especially when combining it with the number of instances used to determine the percentage. Normally all that is required is the totals (the specifics can then be derived if necessary).

Like Availability, the service provider decided that there was part of the story missing. Besides the time it takes to complete the work, the customer also cared about how long it took before they were able to talk to a living, breathing analyst instead of listening to the recording. So, we needed to collect data on time to respond. Table 9-5 shows the breakdown for Time to

Respond. It's a good example of a measure that requires multiple data points to build.

Table 9-5. Development Plan collection and analysis – Time to Respond.

Category	Measure	Data	Source	Analysis
Speed	Time to Respond	Date/Time call was initiated	Automated call system	(Answered/Abandoned— initiated)
		Date/Time call was answered		
		Date/Time voicemail was received		
		Date/Time call was returned		(Call returned—voicemail receipt)—non work hours between

During the definition of this measure, it became clear that there were other measures of Time to Respond. Besides the length of time before the analyst picked up the phone, there were also call backs for customers who left voicemail. Since the Service Desk was not open on weekends or after hours, customers leaving voicemail was a common occurrence. So, the Time to Respond needed to include the time it took to call the customer back (and make contact). The expectations were based on work hours (not purely the time the message was left). If the customer left a message on a Friday at 5:15 p.m., the expectation wasn't that he'd be called back 8:00 a.m. on Monday. The expectation, as always, would be a range—that the Service Desk would attempt to call him back within three work hours for example. The tricky part was to determine if the call back had to be successful or if leaving a message on the customer's voicemail constituted contact, and therefore a response.

Time to Respond was an addition much later in the development of the metric. It wasn't used the first year. Flexibility is one of the keys to a meaningful metric program.

Flexibility is one of the keys to a meaningful metric program.

Accuracy

The defects produced in and by the system are traditionally examined. Those caught before distribution are part of "efficiency." Those that reach the customer (and which they are aware of) are part of the measures we were developing. We needed ways to represent faulty production or service delivery. In the case of the Service Desk, I looked for a simple measure of accuracy.

Rework was an easy choice. Using the trouble-call tracking system, we could track the number of cases that were reopened after the customer thought it was resolved. As long as the customer saw the reopening of the case as rework, it would be counted. We found that occasionally cases were prematurely closed—by the service desk or by second-level support. Later the customer would call the Service Desk with the same problem that was believed to have been resolved. The analysts were doing an admirable job of reopening the case (rather than open a new case making their total cases-handled numbers look better and keeping accuracy from taking a hit). This honest accounting allowed the Service Desk to see themselves as their customers saw them. Table 9-6 shows the breakdown for Rework. You should notice that the analysis is very simple in all of these cases. In the appendix on tools I will discuss briefly the place statistics plays.

Table 9-6. Development Plan collection and analysis – Rework.

Category	Measure	Data	Source	Analysis
Accuracy	Rework	Total cases	Trouble call tracking system	% of cases reopened (reopened cases ÷ total cases)
		Number of cases reopened		

Figure 9-4 shows Rework. You may have noticed by now that the charts all look somewhat alike. If you look closer, you'll see they look exactly alike. The only difference so far has been the data (values) and the titles. This consistency should benefit you inasmuch as those reviewing the measures get used to the presentation method and how to read them.

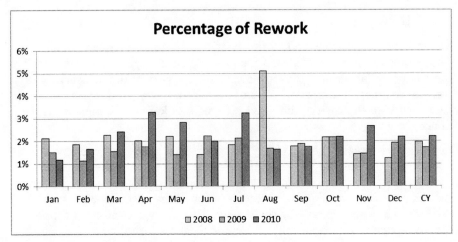

Figure 9-4. Percentage of cases reopened

Now is as good a time as any to point out how triangulation helps deter "chasing data." Organizations often find themselves chasing data to try and put a positive spin on everything, to have only good news. The analysts could have taken every legitimate rework call back and logged them in as a new case. Doing this could nearly (if not totally) eliminate rework. But it would artificially increase other data. The number of calls handled would increase. The number of cases worked would also increase. And customer satisfaction with the knowledge of the analyst would likely drop. If the customer knows that it's rework, but sees another auto-generated survey come across his e-mail for a new case—as if the worker didn't realize it was the same problem— would eventually result in lower ratings for Skills/Knowledge of the analyst.

Of course, Speed to Resolve could also look better, since no cases would show taking the time it took to rework an issue. Without triangulation this could easily happen. Of course, I had an ace in the game. Even without triangulation, the manager of the department and her workforce were all believers in serving their customers. Not only providing the service, but doing so as well as possible. They were believers in continuous process improvement and in service excellence. Even without triangulation, I have total faith that this department would not chase the data.

But by using triangulation, and not looking at measures in isolation, it helps even the less committed departments stay true to the customer's viewpoint.

If we saw spikes in other categories because of false reporting in one category, we'd find anomalies that would require explanation. Besides these anomalies, Rework would be so low (or non-existent) that it too would be an anomaly. This is another reason (besides wanting to replicate successes) we investigate results that exceed expectations, as well as those that fail to meet them.

Usage

For Usage, we captured the number of unique customers each month and also ran it as a running total. Using the potential customer base, we were able to derive a percentage of unique customers using the Service Desk. I've heard arguments that some data is just impossible to get. In this case I enjoy turning to Douglas W. Hubbard's book, *How to Measure Anything* (Wiley, 2007). Not because it has examples of all possible measures, but because the methods offered give readers confidence that they can literally measure anything.

Unique customers should be able to be measured against the customer base, regardless of your service. If you are a national service desk—say, like Microsoft or Amazon.com or Sam's Club—the customer base can be still determined. As you know by now, exact (factual) numbers may not be obtainable, but getting a very good and meaningful estimate is very feasible. The customer base can be estimated by determining how many sales of the software in question were made. If Microsoft sold 150,000 copies of a title, how many calls, from unique customers, were received about that software? Amazon.com has information on the total number of customers it has. Same can be said for Sam's Club since it's a paid membership outlet. Walmart, McDonalds, and the neighborhood supermarket have a more difficult time.

In the case of Walmart and McDonalds, their national call center can use the marketing data on "number of customers." Each has information that can be used. Not necessarily unique customers, but even so, they have a good idea of how many repeat customers they have and total customers, so the numbers can be derived.

The neighborhood supermarket can determine either the number of customers or consider the populace of the neighborhood (based on a determined radius using the store as the center) as the potential customer base.

In the case of the Service Desk, we had identifying information for each customer (when provided). Of course, this data was only as accurate as the analyst's capture of it (misspellings of names could be an issue) and the honesty (or willingness) of the customer to provide it. One hundred percent accuracy wasn't necessary though. Good data was good enough.

Sometimes "good" data is good enough.

Looking at the data over a three-year period showed that the customer base usage was pretty steady, and we felt more confident that anomalies would stand out. In Figure 9-5 you can see what we saw. The last year showed a steady increase. But not an unexpected one, since the last year showed a lot of new technologies, software, and hardware put into use.

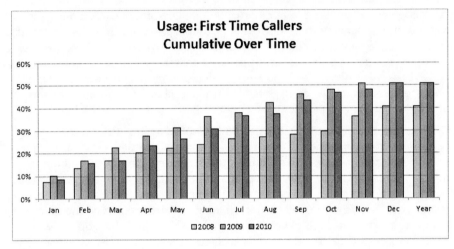

Figure 9-5. Percentage of unique customers

As with the two previous measurement areas, Usage was represented in percentages. Besides the ease of reporting, it is also easy to understand. Another benefit is consistency for the viewer. When you report multiple measures from various sources (triangulation), you can make it seem less complex by keeping the reporting of the measures as consistent as possible.

An immediate improvement to the Usage measure came through the inclusion of a survey result. We had revamped our annual customer satisfaction survey and added a question on how customers obtained assistance with information technology issues. We asked who the preferred source for help was: "When you have an IT problem, where do you turn to first?" The answer could be selected from the following choices:

- Friend
- Coworker
- Internet (search engines, general information web sites, etc.)
- Vendor/manufacturer web sites
- Hardware/software manufacturer service desk
- The IT service desk
- Other

- None of the above—I don't seek assistance

While the data resulting from this survey didn't directly reflect actual usage, we used it in this category since it provided answers in the spirit of why we sought usage data. Were our customers happy with our service? Did they trust our Service Desk to provide what they needed? Was our Service Desk a preferred provider of trouble resolution?

Table 9-7. Development Plan collection and analysis – Preferred Provider Ratings.

Category	Measure	Data	Source	Analysis
Usage	Preferred provider ratings	Number of respondents	Annual survey	% of respondents who chose the Service Desk as first choice to call
		Number choosing Service Desk as 1st choice		

As you'll see in Figure 9-6, one interesting result of the survey collection was the higher percentage in the first year.

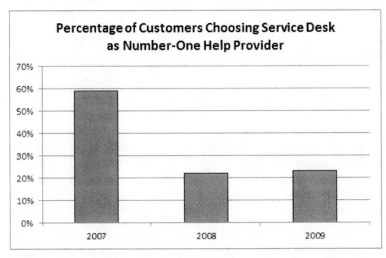

Figure 9-6. Unique users as a percentage of customers who chose the Service Desk as their first choice for assistance

The only difference in the survey from 2007 and the following two years was the number of options the respondent was offered. In 2007, there were only three choices and in the two subsequent years there were eight.

Another Usage measure we could use to round out the picture was unique customers for the abandoned calls. Regardless if they were counted against availability (greater or less than 30 seconds), it would be useful information to know how many unique customers were calling our Service Desk. In the case of those who didn't stay on the line to speak to an analyst and hung up before 30 seconds had expired, we were assuming that their need was satisfied. If they stayed on longer than 30 seconds and then hung up, we assumed their problems went unresolved.

So, for the calls under 30 seconds, we could count those as serviced customers. Looking at the number of calls abandoned could be a significant number of customers we were missing in our data pool. The data would also be useful to the manager of the Service Desk in other ways. If the same number was calling and hanging up before an analyst responded, the manager could contact that number and see if there was a specific need that was going unfulfilled. This would require that the automated call system captured the calling number without the phone being answered by an analyst. At the time of creating these metrics, this was not possible with the current phone system. So, the need was captured as a future requirement if and when the call system was changed.

Customer Satisfaction

The last set of measures we used to round out our metric involved the classic customer satisfaction survey. Our organization had been using a third-party agency for the administration, collection, and tabulation of Trouble Call Resolution Satisfaction Surveys for a while, so the data was readily available. The questions were standardized for all users of the service, allowing us to compare to the average for their clients—within our industry, and overall. This pleased our management and higher leadership immensely. They thoroughly enjoy the ability to compare their services against a benchmark. They like it even more when their services compare favorably (as ours did).

To keep to the same style of measure—percentages of a total, would be possible. We could have reported the percentages of fives, fours, threes, twos and ones. This would prove to be too complex, especially over four questions. Instead we opted to show the percentage of customers who were "satisfied." We defined satisfied as a 4 or 5 on the 5-point scale.

Other options included using Reichheld's "Promoter to Detractor" ratios. This was actually attempted for over a year before I finally gave into the inevitable. (I couldn't get the third party to use a 10-point scale and the concept of promoter to detractor was too complex for some of the managers.) The consistency provided by using percentages quickly became expected by the workforce. I still believe in the value of the promoter to detractor analysis, but for the purpose of the report card, I added percentage satisfied to the measurements for our particular audience.

FREDERICK REICHHELD'S PROMOTER-TO-DETRACTOR SCALE

According to Reichheld's *The Ultimate Question* (Harvard Business Press, 2006), the most important question you should ask is: "Would you recommend this service (or product) to a friend or coworker?" Using a 10-point scale for the answers, with 1 being "definitely not" and 10 being "definitely yes," if a respondent gives you a 9 or 10, she is considered a "promoter"—someone who would encourage others to use your service (or buy your product). If the respondent gives you a score of 6 or less, she is a "detractor." Detractors will actively discourage others from using your service (or buying your product). Numbers 7 and 8 are considered "neutral" answers—meaning that you can't predict if they will promote or detract from your reputation. You need to have a ratio of two promoters for every detractor to translate to growth (neutrals are not counted). The higher the ratio, the better your word-of mouth-advertising, and the more likely your business (the number of customers) will grow.

Figure 9-7 shows the ratio of promoters to detractors. This ratio can be a negative if you have more detractors than promoters. In the Service Desk case, we had a high ratio. For example, in December 2009, for every detractor (1-3 rating) the Service Desk had over 50 promoters (those rating them as a 5).

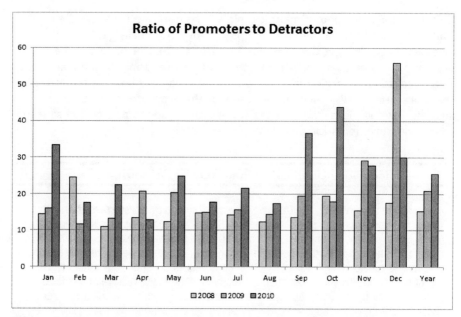

Figure 9-7. Ratio of promoters to detractors for overall customer satisfaction

The ratios were impressive. I took some liberties translating Reichheld's methodology. The 5s equated to 9s or 10s and 1 through 3 equated to 1 through 6. The 4s equated to 7s and 8s. I stopped using the terms "promoter" and "detractor" since we weren't using the proper question. It was more meaningful to simply say that the measure reflected the ratio of "Highly Satisfied" (5s) to those who could not say they were satisfied (3s or less). This in itself was more meaningful than an average, but still not as clear as I would have liked.

"What about 4s?" was a common question that I received when I revealed the data this way. Explaining that 4s were "truly neutral" didn't sway most people. The service provider thought we were losing the "satisfieds" and that a 3 was neutral. My correlating the values to Reichheld's formula was hard for them to accept. I believe this was in large part due to fear of the measures and that they wouldn't look as good as they could.

Using the ratio of highly satisfied to not satisfied may seem logical to you (it does to me). But I found that this wasn't the norm for customer satisfaction surveys. The Service Desk had been reporting this data for over a year and they always reported it as an average score like 4.7 (out of 5). It seemed as if the best way to show the results would be to use a Likert Scale.

I looked at all Service Desk reports for the past three years. The first year showed an average score of 4.7 for the year. The following year was 4.76 and a 4.8 for the most recent year. Besides a slight upward trend, I couldn't figure out what the data meant. Was the average good or bad? Well, the third party provided benchmarks for our industry and for all users of their service. So now we could see that we were above average in the case of our scores. But, I still felt a little lost. I didn't see how 4.8, 4.9, or 4.58 meant anything. Granted, if the average were 5.0, I could know that all scores were fives. This would mean that 100 percent of the customers were highly satisfied with our services. But as soon as the average score fell below that mythical result, I had trouble knowing what it meant. Even when I added in the total number of responses, I did not know what the average rating meant. Figure 9-8 shows why it was hard to comprehend the meaning.

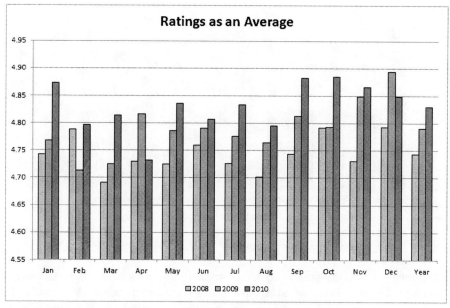

Figure 9-8. Customer satisfaction rating score as an average

So, the average score lacked meaning and comparing the highly satisfied to the not satisfied was a little confusing. A third choice was to use the percentage satisfied. I could understand quickly that a certain percentage of our customers (those who used our service) were either satisfied (4 or 5) or not satisfied (1, 2, or 3). Even with this I received arguments about the nuance of the meaning of "not satisfied." I had more than a few managers who wanted 3s not to be counted since they thought on a 5-point scale that 3s were neutral.

I had to explain that "neutral" meant the respondent, while not "dissatisfied" couldn't say "satisfied" either. The chart wasn't comparing satisfied to "dissatisfied"—but satisfied to "not satisfied." Notice that the same managers who wanted to include neutral scores in the first ratio (5s to 1–3s) wanted to drop neutral scores if they thought it would make their department look worse. Figure 9-9 shows why "percentage satisfied" was a simpler way to interpret the data.

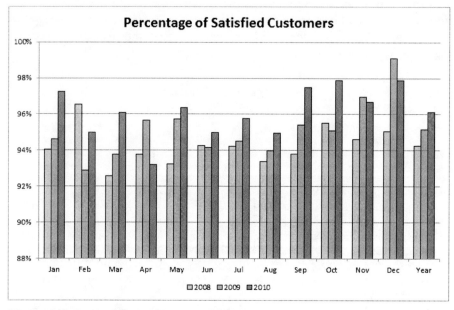

Figure 9-9. Percentage of satisfied customers

We were on a pretty steady streak of adding measures to the original plan, so we had no reservations when it came to customer satisfaction. We realized that we were only looking at feedback from those who had problems. This could give us a skewed view of our customers' overall satisfaction with our services. We would never hear from customers who wouldn't call our Service Desk because they didn't like our services. Or we could miss those who liked our services, but either didn't choose to fill out a survey or just hadn't used it in the current year. Basically, we wanted to hear from customers who hadn't called into the Service Desk. We wanted to hear from the rest of our customer base, which was not reflected in our Usage measures.

The answer was an annual customer satisfaction survey. We sent a survey that not only asked the basic questions about satisfaction with our services, but also which services were seen as most important to the customer. This helped with the other services we included in the report card. We also asked the "who is the preferred source for trouble resolution" question, which we used for Usage. This annual survey provided many useful measures besides customer satisfaction. Table 9-8 shows the first breakout of data for this category.

Table 9-8. Development Plan collection and analysis – Customer Satisfaction Survey Ratings.

Category	Measure	Data	Source	Analysis
Customer Satisfaction	Courtesy of the analyst, skills/ knowledge of the analyst, timeliness of the resolution, and overall satisfaction	5-point Likert scale—on level of satisfaction for each topic/ question	Third-party survey company surveyed every trouble-call customer	Percentage satisfied (4s and 5s of the total responses)

For the annual survey we were able to show the same percentage satisfied, but pulled from a different context. This may not seem too important, but it was very useful to allow for different viewpoints. One telling result was that the scores from the annual survey were considerably "lower" than those for trouble resolution. This flew in the face of what the departments expected (this rang true for all of the services). The staff incorrectly predicted that the scores for trouble resolution would be worse than those for annual surveys. They figured that customers filling out the trouble-resolution surveys were predisposed to be unhappy since they had a "problem," whereas the annual survey had a good chance of catching the customer in a neutral or good mood.

But the data proved them to be totally wrong. The resolution survey scores were significantly higher than the annual survey. This led to further investigation to determine why there was such a drastic difference (and one that went against the predictions). The investigation wasn't intended to improve the annual survey numbers—it was intended to provide understanding and, from that understanding, possible ideas.

One conclusion was that the resolution was done so well, (fast, accurate, and with a high rate of success) that the customer was so pleased that he gave great ratings. Conversely the annual survey reflected simply ambivalence at the time. It wasn't that the annual survey numbers were bad—they were still very good. But they were low in comparison to the astronomically good scores received for trouble resolutions.

Another conclusion was that some of the respondents to the annual survey (especially a considerable amount of negative scores) were given by respondents who hadn't used the IT services—especially in the case of the service desk. Since the IT organization had a poor reputation from a few years prior when service delivery was way below par, the respondents were rating the IT department based on this poor reputation. This is akin to the perception of Japanese manufacturing in the mid-20th century. If you said "made In Japan" it meant that the item was junk. If it broke easily, didn't work, or failed to work more often than it did work—you would say, "it must have been made in Japan."

Today, that reputation has been essentially reversed. Now "Made in Japan" describes the height of quality. Japanese-made cars are more respected for quality than American-made automobiles. We won't get into the story of how an American helped make this happen (look up the story of W. Edwards Deming) because he couldn't get our own manufacturing industry to listen. The point is that the Japanese had to overcome their negative reputation. It wasn't as simple as just delivering higher-quality products. Their potential customer base had to be convinced to give them a try. Those who only knew Japanese products as the answer to a joke had to be won over. The same was true for a good portion of our customer base.

Unfortunately those detractors Reichheld discusses can seriously damage your organization's reputation. If a good portion of your customer base is bad-mouthing your services and products, you will need to counteract that. Hoping and waiting for them to come around through attrition is a dangerous path to travel. You may find yourself out of business well before the customers realize that their perception is outdated and that the reality is that you were providing a healthy service.

The measures and follow-on investigation pointed to the need of a marketing program, and not a change in the service, processes, or products.

The Higher Education TechQual+ Project: An example

Timothy Chester's Higher Education TechQual+ project is a great example of how an annual survey can help provide not only satisfaction data, but also insights into what the customer sees as important . Tim is the CIO of the University of Georgia, and for the last six years, his pet project has been the development of the TechQual+ Project. The purpose of the project is to assess what faculty, students, and staff want from information technology organizations in higher education. It is primarily a tool for a higher education organization to find out its customers' perceptions of its services.

The TechQual+ project's goal is to find a common "language" for IT practitioners and IT users. This is part of what makes Chester's efforts special. But, the first brick in the project's foundation is "that the end user perspective" is the key to the "definition of performance indicators for IT organizations." In other words, the customers' viewpoints are critical to the success of the IT organization and the meaningfulness of any metric program.

Chester writes, "With end-user-focused data in hand, one can easily understand failures in service delivery as one-time mistakes, as opposed to urban myths of recurring problems in IT."[1]

In the *Protocol Guide for TechQual+*, Tim Chester explains that the tool's key purpose is to allow "IT leaders to respond to the requests of both administrators and accreditation bodies, who increasingly request evidence of successful outcomes." The project intends to give IT organizations a tool for compiling evidence to answer these requests.

Chester goes on to explain, "[For] IT organizations, demonstrating the effective delivery of technology services is vital to the establishment of appreciation, respect, and trustworthiness…"

This project lists the most crucial inputs for its purpose as valid and reliable effectiveness measures of IT services. Chester also believes that while standardized performance measures are highly needed, the higher education IT industry is still far off from meeting this need.

TechQual+ attempts to provide measures that can be understood and used by the organization's customers, provide a database for comparing results between institutions, and an easy to use survey tool for producing the data. One of the defining points of the project is that TechQual+ defines outcomes

---

[1] www.techqual.org

"from an end-user point of view." Chester understands the need for more than a customer satisfaction survey and uses his tool to capture the customers' viewpoints on any and all facets of what the Answer Key identifies as Product/Service Health.

This project fits in well with what I've presented in this book. It is a great way to "ask the customers" for their input. It can provide a means for gathering not only the customer's evaluation of how well a service is provided but what the customers' expectations are. Where I have relied on the service provider to interpret the customers' expectations, the methods offered in TechQual+ can be used to build a range from customer responses. This is definitely a methodology worth looking into.

TechQual+'s approach is based on evaluating the following three measures:

1. The minimum acceptable level of service (Minimum Expectations)

2. The desired level of service (Desired Expectations)

3. How well the customer feels the service meets these expectations (Perceived Performance)

The results of these measures are used to develop a "Zone of Tolerance," an "Adequacy Gap Score," and a "Superiority Gap Score," described as follows:

1. *The Zone of Tolerance*: The range between minimum and desired expectations (what the Report Card calls simply "Meets Expectations").

2. *The Adequacy Gap Score*: The difference between the "perceived" performance and the minimum expectation.

3. *The Superiority Gap Score*: The difference between the desired and perceived performance.

You should see how these "scores" correlate to the Report Card's scores. If you look at the charts offered for each measure in the Report Card, you could determine the Zone of Tolerance (the range of Meets Expectations) and those values that represent a positive or negative Adequacy or Superiority gap score.

The beauty of the TechQual+ Project is that the results reflect not only the customers' expectations (gathered through a survey instrument) but also the perceived service health (also through a survey). It is an excellent feedback tool. I highly recommend that you look into using the tool (it's free) or implementing the concepts offered by it, in your survey instruments. When used in conjunction with your objective measures (Delivery and Usage) it gives a fuller picture of the health of your service. You can use the Tech-Qual+ or other survey tool for the Customer Satisfaction part of the Report Card. While it is labeled "Customer Satisfaction," you'll see that the questions you can ask in the survey are not restricted to this area. You can (and should) ask for feedback on the importance of the services you're measuring. It can be especially useful for getting input on the range of expectations.

Two major areas of difference between the Report Card and TechQual+ should be obvious. The Report Card attempts to use objective measures collected in other ways besides the survey method. Triangulation demands that you use different collection methods and different sources. The Report Card, while also using expectations, treats "Superior" (exceeding expectations) performance as an anomaly.

The conclusion? The TechQual+ Project (and other survey-based innovative tools) should be looked into—especially as a solution for the Customer Satisfaction part of the Report Card and for gathering information on the expectations for all of the measures.

Applying Expectations

You may have noticed that the charts offered throughout this chapter are "meaningful." Part of this is the inclusion of the expectations for each measure. Imagine if the measure lacked this qualifying characteristic. Go back and look at the Customer Satisfaction chart (Figure 9-9) again. Notice it doesn't have expectations. I left them out for two reasons. The first is that we didn't have them when we started, but we could still produce the basic charts you've seen so far. Secondly, as mentioned earlier, many times the data can help you determine what is "normal." When we look at "normal" coupled with the service provider's assessment of the level of "normality" of the performance during the reported time period, we can make a good estimate of the expectations.

Now let's add the percentage values, for at least the most recent year. This makes the chart (Figure 9-10) easier to read.

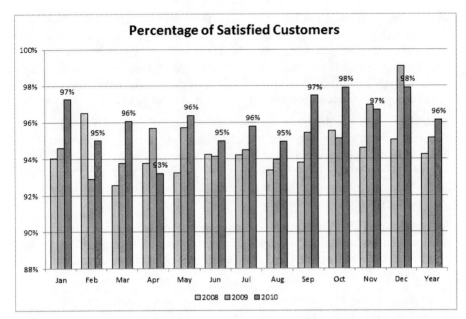

Figure 9-10. Customer Satisfaction: the percentage satisfied with the values for the last year

A little easier to read. At a glance we can see how we faired vs. the previous year. We can also see if we have upward or downward trends (three data points in succession that move up or down). While you can still see trending (up or down) you won't know if the data is "good," "bad," or "indifferent." So before we get to expectations, this chart already tells us to look at Aug–Oct 2010 . What was happening? What was causing the steady incline? Was it something we needed to look at more closely?

One of the most important steps we had to take was to develop expectations. As explained in the chapter on expectations, you can't always ask all of your customers for their feedback on this topic. Depending on the size of your customer base, the expectations can range widely. SLAs help, but they don't always reflect the customers' expectations. Sometimes they only represent the contractually agreed-upon requirements.

If the Service Desk didn't know what the expectations for this should be, we could use the data to tell us. You can start with the SLA if you have one, collect customer feedback, and then bounce that against the department's opinion. I have invariably found that the department's expectations are always higher than the SLA or what I would propose. Most people are harder on themselves than their customers are on them.

We sat down with the Service Desk department. We met with the manager, the analysts, and the department's director. Our task was to develop a set of expectations for each measure from the customer's point of view. If the customers' expectations needed to be calibrated, a separate marketing effort might be required, but until they were successfully adjusted, we had to go with the current customer viewpoint. Figure 9-11 shows Customer Satisfaction with expectations added. As you can see, we set the expectation level between 90 and 95 percent satisfied.

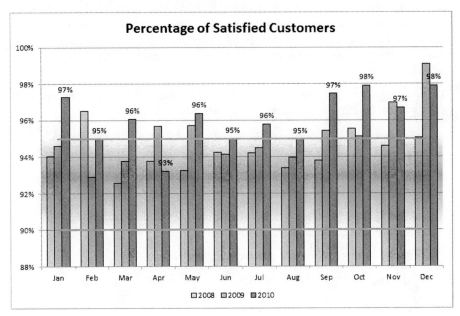

Figure 9-11. Customer Satisfaction with expectations

As you can see in Figure 9-11, it is easy to see which points require further investigation. Besides the upward trend from Aug–Oct 2010, we can also look into the anomalies above 95 percent satisfaction. This was, for the most part, uneventful. Discussion was healthy and it was educational for everyone to see what each other thought of as the customers' expectations.

You can imagine how the discussion around how fast the customer expected the phone to be answered (by an analyst) ran. Some thought 60 seconds was adequate. Others thought that customers were willing to wait minutes. Others thought if it took more than 10 seconds in today's "now" culture, it would be considered far too long.

In the end, we came up with ranges of expectation for each measure. The key was to find a common language so that the expectations would be consistently presented. For each measure, we not only identified what was "good" or "bad" but what percentages would be expected.

Let's look at abandoned call rates, for example. The first question was, what is good and bad? Lower abandoned rates were good. Higher rates were bad. After we had established the direction of "good" and "bad," we had to determine what the expectations were. What percentage of calls could be abandoned and not upset the customer? What percentage was "expected" from a healthy (good) service? What percentage would represent dissatisfaction? When would the customer say "That's too high an abandon rate. Fix it!"? What rate would be so low that the customer would be impressed? Even surprised?

When we had trouble identifying the expectations, we'd play the estimation game. I'd start with the obvious: What exceeds expectations?

Someone would respond, "I can't tell you what exceeds expectations…"

"OK. Let's work on it together," I'd reply. The reluctance to offer an estimate has many possible causes. Luckily you don't have to eliminate the causes, just deal with the effects.

I asked questions to help get to an estimate: "Would no abandoned calls be above the customers' expectations?"

"You mean that they would always get through?"

"Sure. No waiting on hold."

"They'd love that!"

"Sure," I'd say, "but would they expect it?"

An analyst would say, "No. They know we aren't manned with enough people to do that."

"So they wouldn't expect that level of service?"

"Nope."

"How about getting through within 30 seconds?"

"Yeah, they should expect that."

I'd ask: "But do they?"

"Well, yeah," someone would say, "for the most part. They know sometimes it's busy."

"So sometimes they expect that it will take longer than 30 seconds?"

"Sure, like on Mondays, or when a system is down, or we're installing new software."

"OK," I'd say, "So how often is that?"

"Maybe 10 percent of the time."

I'd sum up: "OK, so far, we can say then that 90 percent of the time they expect to speak to an analyst in less than 30 seconds?"

"I'd say they'd be happy with that."

Since we always want ranges (not targets or thresholds) I pressed for more. "So, would they be happy with 85 percent of the time? Or 80 percent? If they call ten times in a month, they should expect to talk to an analyst within 30 seconds eight of those ten times, and the other two times would take longer?"

"Sure...that'd be OK."

"How about three out of four times? Would they still be happy or would they not be satisfied?""

"Well, they may not like that. I mean, it's close."

Again I sum up: "OK. Let's say then that the customer would expect to get through to an analyst within thirty seconds, 75 to 90 percent of the time. Does that sound about right?"

"Sure."

Eventually I got to numbers that fit expectations. Once we plotted those expectations we performed the litmus test explained in the chapter on Expectations. We did this with each of the measures. We looked at the data over the years and checked the expectations against the department's perception of how well the service was provided during that time period. They knew when they had had a bad month. The relationship between the measures and the expectations should reflect their independent assessment of the quality of the service for that time period.

If we go back to the Metric Development Plan, you see the need to identify the schedule for collection and reporting. These items are not addressed separately. While we were defining the measures to use, we worked on the expectations. While we worked on the expectations we also identified the frequency of reporting and the time span for evaluation. We opted for monthly across-the-board reports, with roll-ups to the calendar year. It could have as easily been weekly, quarterly or only calendar, academic, or fiscal year.

Recap

In our real-life example, you can see that even when a mandate is given to implement a metrics program, you can get to a root question to allow the effort to be driven by a foundational need. In the case given, I was lucky that the leadership's information need was easily interpreted as a Product/Service Health question. This led cleanly to the development of effectiveness metrics for each key service.

Being able to stay in the first quadrant of the Answer Key mitigated much of the risks with implementing a large-scale metrics program in an organization that had not successfully done this in the past. It also made it possible to focus the effort. This focus allowed me to develop the Report Card methodology.

The use of triangulation and expectations were critical to the success of the program—partly because it gave a better picture of the answers to the root question and partly because they helped to remove much of the fear, uncertainty, and doubt that normally accompanies metrics.

Conclusion

Now that I've laid the groundwork for the Report Card, it's time to finish the effort. I needed a way to make the "big" picture the groundwork supported meaningful for the director's level, the CIO, and beyond. If the organization was to publish the metrics for its upper leadership, it would also have to be ready for other audiences, including shareholders or stakeholders. Customers might also want to see results of how well the organization serves them.

This requires that the metric be easily modified to show different views for different audiences. Of course, it also had to be meaningful to the service provider.

Final Product: The Metrics Report Card

Chapter 9 introduced the metrics I developed to answer the leadership's question for our organization. If only the service provider and the executive leader were to be viewers of the results, I could have moved directly to publishing the metric. But since the metrics would go through rigorous review throughout the management chain, and also be seen by customers, I had to find a way to make the results usable (if not readable) at each level.

I worked with a team of consultants and the service providers to develop what became the Report Card. This means of interpreting the metrics allows for it to be viewed at different levels, and at different degrees of aggregation, while still preserving the concept of expectations.

Now that basic measures were developed, we (the team of consultants—the service providers and me) needed a way to make them into a Report Card. What we had was a set of charts. But we needed to find a way to report on the overall service health, while still preserving the individual measure categories of Delivery, Usage, and Customer Satisfaction. Being at an academic institution, it seemed logical to use the Report Card concept as a template.

In the case of a Report Card, students can take totally disparate courses—everything from forensic anthropology to fine art printmaking. The grades obtained can be based on totally different evaluation criteria, but the grades are still understandable. An A means the student is exceeding expectations, doing very well; a B means doing well; a C means the student is surviving; below a C means the student is failing to meet expectations. Quizzes, tests, research papers, and classroom participation can be used to make up the grade. Other less normal evaluation methods can be used—like reviews of art produced, presentations to committees, and panel reviews of materials produced in the course of the class.

In all cases, the student gets a letter grade that can be transferred to a number for grade point averages. We wanted something similar that a high-level stakeholder could glance at and grasp immediately.

We settled on E, M, and O. We had to figure out how to evaluate and determine each measure and piece of information as either **E**xceeding Expectations, **M**eeting Expectations, or an **O**pportunity for Improvement. Availability was in the form of percentage (of abandoned calls or abandoned calls less than 30 seconds). So we could smoothly transition this to a common measurement view.

Delivery

Remember, for this discussion I've broken delivery into "availability," "speed," and "accuracy."

Availability

For each measure, expectations have to be identified. Table 10-1 shows the expectations for Availability.

Table 10-1. Expectations: Availability.

Category	Measure	Exceeds	Meets	Opportunity
Availability	% of Abandoned calls	<10%	10%–20%	>20%
	% of Abandoned calls < 30 seconds	>90%	75%–90%	< 75%

This made the results simple for analysis. Placing the measures into the grid would give us a "grade" of O, M, or E. This could then be used to develop a grade point average. We could roll up the Grades at the Availability level. We could also roll up the grade at the Delivery level (Availability, Speed, and Accuracy together). And hopefully we would be able to roll up the grade to an overall Service grade.

The first decision we had to make was how to roll up the two different grades. We opted to give each grade (E, M, or O) a value. It was important to us to have our results be beyond reproach. Since we knew errors might seep in from many different quadrants, we had to ensure our intentions were never in question. Trying to make what could be a complex problem into something manageable, if not simple, we worked off a 10-point value scale. An E was worth 10 points; an M was worth 5 points; and an O was worth zero. We then averaged the numerical values. So if we had two values to use, as in the case of Availability we would get the following:

- E = 10, M = 5, O = 0
- An E and an M averaged 7.5 points
- An E and an O averaged 5 points
- An M and an O averaged 2.5 points

Now we took the calculated grade and turned it back into an evaluation against expectations. A grade of 8 or greater would be an E. A grade between 5 and 8 would be an M. A grade below 5 would be an O. So, another way to look at it is as follows:

- An E and an M averaged 7.5 points, which was an M
- An E and an O averaged 5 points, which was an M
- An M and an O averaged 2.5 points, which was an O

We liked the way this worked. You had to exceed in a measure to balance out an Opportunity for Improvement. We felt this was in the spirit of "erring on the side of excellence" as my friend Don would say.

Err on the side of excellence.

A possible drawback was it made the Opportunity for Improvement a "bad" thing and the Exceeding Expectations a "good" thing. As I covered earlier, they are both anomalies. What we want are Meets Expectations. Another drawback was that the combined grades could hide anomalies. If you had an equal number of Es and Os it would roll up to Ms and look like you were doing just what was wanted—meeting expectations.

The positives were that we could show an overall grade, giving a "feel" for the health of the item. Another positive was that we could deal with the "hidden" grades by simply flagging any Ms or Es that had Os buried in the data. That would allow the metric customer to know where to dive deeper to find the Os and see what was happening in those cases.

The bad vs. good thing we could not overcome as easily. In the end we decided to deal with it on a case by case basis, ensuring that we stressed that both were anomalies. We accepted this because, no matter how much we stress the negatives to Exceeding Expectations, in the end, the fact that expectations were exceeded wasn't in itself a bad thing. It was only "bad" based on how you achieved the grade—like if you neglected other important work/services or applied too many resources to attain it. But if you achieved this grade by a process improvement or simply focusing properly on a different area, it was not only a good thing, but we could change the customers' expectations because we would be able to deliver at this higher level consistency. It could become a marketing point for our services over our competitors. Opportunity for Improvement, the other anomaly, couldn't be said to be the same. If you failed to meet expectations, most times the fact that you weren't meeting the customers' expectations made it a bad thing. Even if you found that it was due to natural disasters or things out of your control, the customer still saw it as a negative. So while I wanted both anomalies to elicit the same response—further investigation, the purpose of that investigation was clearly different.

One investigation was essentially conducted to see if the occurrence could be avoided in the future, while the other was to see if it could be replicated.

This led to the decision that we would roll up the values using the translation, and if there were Os below the level we showed, we marked the grade with an icon. (Note: As we continually worked to improve our tools and processes, we adapted the icon when there was *any* anomaly hiding in the grades with an E or an O!)

Figure 10-1 is the Translation Grid we used to convert a grade to a letter grade and back again. We originally colored the values as Green for Exceeds, Blue for Meets, and Red for an Opportunity. This made it very hard to convince anyone that Opportunity for Improvement (red) were just as much an anomaly requiring investigation as an Exceeds Expectations (green).

10	Exceeds Expectations (E)	10
9		
8		
7	Meets Expectations (M)	5
6		
5		
4	Opportunity for Improvement (O)	0
3		
2		
1		

Figure 10-1. Translation Grid

So looking at the Availability charts we added the expectations, so that visually we could tell where we were in terms of health of availability. This visual depiction happens at the measurement level, before we aggregate the grades with other measures of availability (to create a final grade for the category) and before we look to roll up grades into delivery. Figures 10-2 and 10-3 show the abandoned rate and calls abandoned in less than 30 seconds, with expectations.

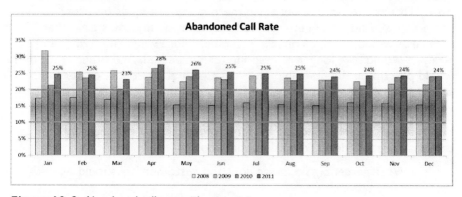

Figure 10-2. Abandoned call rate with expectations

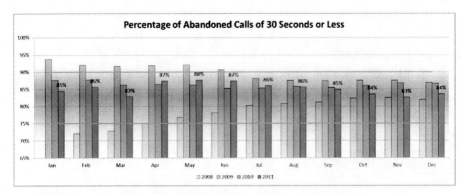

Figure 10-3. Percentage of calls abandoned in 30 seconds or less

Speed

Speed wasn't as simple as Availability. We could measure how many cases were responded to (or resolved) faster than expected, within expectations, and slower than expected. The problem was determining what that meant. What was good? We could have said any case that fell out of the Meets Expectations range (above or below) was an anomaly and should be investigated. That sounds logical, but since there were thousands of cases, it was not practical. And when I interviewed the department, it was clear that anomalies would happen from time to time. There were times when the Analysts would take longer to respond than expected. And other times they would pick up on the first ring. This was a natural byproduct of the nature of the work and the environmental factors that influenced performance as well as workload.

So for these cases, we decided to determine what was expected by the customer at a second level. We asked the following:

- What percentage of cases does the customer feel should exceed expectations?
- What percentage of cases does the customer feel should meet expectations?
- What percentage of cases does the customer feel is acceptable to fail to meet expectations?

So we looked to define the expectations in the form of length of time to respond and the time to resolve.

Time to Respond

- *Exceed*: Responds in less than 5 seconds
- *Meets*: Responds in 6 to 30 seconds
- *Opportunity for Improvement*: Responds in greater than 30 seconds

Time to Resolve

- *Exceed*: Resolved in one hour or less
- *Meets*: Resolved in 24 hours or less
- *Opportunity for Improvement*: Resolved in five days or less

For each we needed to determine the customers' expectations. What percentage of the cases would the customer expect to fall into each of the categories listed, as shown in Table 10-2.

Table 10-2. Expectations: Speed.

Category	Measure	Exceeds	Meets	Opportunity
Speed: Time to Respond	Responds in less than 5 seconds	>50%	25%–50%	<25%
	Responds in 5 to 30 seconds	>75%	50%–75%	<50%
	Responds in greater than 30 seconds	<10%	10%–25%	>25%
Speed: Time to Resolve	Resolved in one hour or less	>75%	60%–75%	<60%
	Resolved in 24 hours or less	>95%	75%–95%	<75%
	Resolved in five days or less	>97%	90%–97%	<90%

Figure 10-4 shows percentage of cases resolved in less than one hour. While this is a good measure, all three are necessary to get the full picture. Looking at only this measure would give a skewed view of how healthy the service was (in terms of speed).

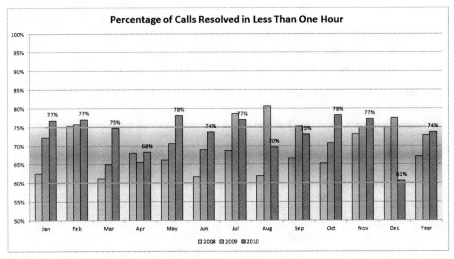

Figure 10-4. Percentage of calls resolved in less than one hour

This second level of expectations allowed us to use percentages, and allowed us to look at anomalies only when they added up to a significant (as defined by the expectations) amount of cases. It's worthwhile to note that the third measure for Speed: Time to Respond, moves in the opposite direction of the other measures. This will also be the case with rework, where less is better.

Accuracy

Rework turned out to be the best measure of accuracy for the service desk. Figure 10-5 shows Rework in the form of percentage of cases.

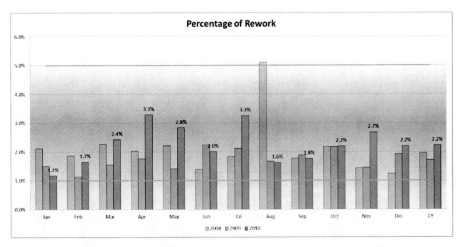

Figure 10-5. Percentage of Rework

It may be worth noting that the picture or impression the viewer of your metric gets can be affected by the way you present it. Let's look quickly at a couple of different representations of the exact same data for Rework. Figures 10-6 and 10-7 have the same data as 10-5, but I've changed the coloring on the first and the scale on the second.

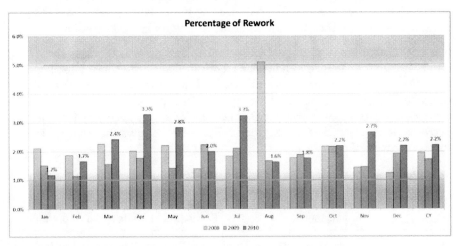

Figure 10-6. Percentage of Rework background colors reversed

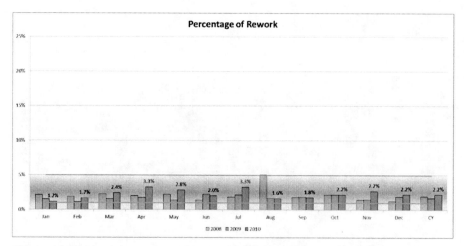

Figure 10-7. Percentage of Rework with scale increased from 0 to 6% to 0 to 25%

You can imagine the many permutations possible that can affect the viewer's perception of the data. One may make you feel the data is "bad," another that the data is "all right," and another may make you see it as "good."

The interpretations of the metric based on how it is presented must be limited. This is done through consistent and thorough communications on what you are looking for—anomalies. You cannot get caught up with how things look; not with how the charts look or how they make you or your unit look.

It is critical that you understand expectations and how to evaluate the charts presented. You're looking for trends and anomalies, not a feeling of "goodness" based on the colors or values. This is the reason I have attempted to give these charts only neutral colors and even leave off any obvious demarcations of the values that constitute an Opportunity for Improvement vs. Exceeding Expectations. Table 10-3 shows the expectations for percentage of rework.

Table 10-3. Expectations: Accuracy.

Category	Measure	Exceeds	Meets	Opportunity
Accuracy	% of Rework	<1%	1%–5%	>5%

We again were able to use percentages—which provided a consistent view of the different measures. While we used various measures (triangulation), we simplified it all by using a consistent form, a consistent view (the customers') and a consistent set of "grades" for each. We were able to keep to this established set of norms with Usage.

Usage

Usage was defined by the number of unique customers (Table 10-4). The number (data) by itself was meaningless. But simply putting it into context in the form of a measure, percentage of customer base, made it more useful. When we started measuring it, we looked at a year at a time. We showed the number of unique customers per month (a running total) so we could see slow months from more active ones. When we showed the measures over time, we started with a blank slate each year. This always put us below expectations at first, and showed a steady increase over the year until at the end of the year, we were well within expectations (see Figure 10-8).

Since this always gave the impression (and grade) of an Opportunity to Improve until the second quarter, we relooked at the presentation of the information. Not because it "looked bad" but because it was telling the wrong story. Our usage wasn't lower at the beginning of the year—we were incorrectly starting with a clean slate each year.

Table 10-4. Expectations: Usage.

Category	Measure	Exceeds	Meets	Opportunity
Usage	Percentage of first time callers for the year	>50%	20%–50%	<20%

Figure 10-8 shows how the usage, when viewed over a year's time, gives the impression that there is an anomaly for the first three months.

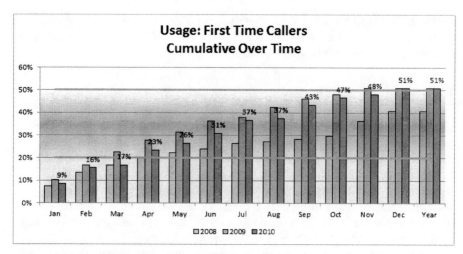

Figure 10-8. Usage: first time callers cumulative over time

So, a better representation was to have the measures shown over a running period of time. We could show it over a full year's time (since we had enough historical data, or a smaller span of time. Options included showing a running three month or six month total as well as the twelve month total. Whichever we chose, we'd have to determine the expectations—what percentage of unique customers do we expect to use our services in a year, half a year, or a quarter?

Another factor to consider was the expected frequency of use for the service. For services that were likely to be used only once a year (like a car tune up), the service provider would measure first time callers over an annual period.

If the service were a semi-annual one, say more like an oil change, it would make sense to measure it at that interval. The point being, it would depend on how often you would expect customers to come back to use your service or buy your product. Even a restaurant would work in this manner. A higher-scale restaurant may expect to see repeat customers on a monthly or quarterly basis, while a fast-food restaurant may expect a higher frequency.

The measure of unique customers can easily be combined with repeat customers. Most businesses rely on repeat customers for the majority of their income. Repeat-customer rates speak directly to the relationship the business has with their customers. To grow, much less survive, the business must satisfy their customer base so that they earn their trust. If the customers like your services or products, they will eventually come to your business again.

In the case where you are selling only one product or service, and the need for repeat purchases are rare, the satisfied customer is still your best salesperson. Rather than measure repeat customers, you may want to measure referrals. Remember the story of my laptop purchase (Chapter 7)? A week later, because of the selection, price, but mostly the customer service, I brought my daughter to the same store to buy her laptop. Normally I wouldn't buy another computer for three or four years.

Of course, this store sold more than computers and they should measure whether I return to buy other technology from them. A purer example would be my first book. I'm proud of *Why Organizations Struggle So Hard to Improve So Little*. It is a good read. But how many sales should I expect to the same customer? In this case you might think total sales are the only measure I need. But, I could learn from looking at usage measures also. Imagine if I could get the number of books ordered by one person or one organization; or the number of referrals—sales in which the buyer was influenced to buy my book from the encouragement of another reader. Another measure could be the number of reviews and the ratings that accompany those reviews. Of course, if I sell another book (like this one), I would want to measure repeat customers if I could. How many people buy both books? If the reader liked one, hopefully they liked it enough to read the other, expecting a certain level of quality and information.

The reason Fred Reichheld's predictors of promoters and detractors has merit is because word of mouth advertising—the kind you can't buy—is critical to a business's growth. New customers are nice to have, but repeat customers become your foundation for continued success and future growth.

In the case of our Service Desk, we expected customers to run into information technology issues on a quarterly basis. If they were calling only once or twice a year, it might indicate that they are using a different source for solving their IT problems. This might include just trying to solve their issues on their own. If they were calling weekly it might mean that the organization's product line and service catalog had too many defects or faults—requiring frequent assistance.

The expectations can be the same, but since we were looking originally at the expectations for a full year, we logically shouldn't expect as high an amount of first time callers (unique users) for a three month period. Since the department felt that the usage was healthy for the period reported, we chose to review the data first. If you aren't sure, a simple tool is letting the measures tell you what the expectations should be.

Figure 10-9 gives us the picture without expectations so that we can use the data to determine what is "normal."

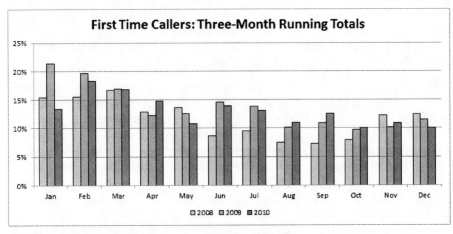

Figure 10-9. First time callers: three-month running totals (without expectations)

Based on the picture presented by the measures on a running three-month total, the norm looked to be between 5 percent and 15 percent. When I spoke with the team, they felt that five percent was too low. Even though this would create a picture that showed them having Opportunity for Improvement more often, this felt "right to them." They also felt that the Exceeding Expectations should be set at 20 percent, making the expectations range from 10 percent to 20 percent. Because of the measures, I pushed them to find out why they chose 20 percent. The answer was that "15 percent was just a little too low." So, I pressed some more. "So, why 20 percent?" And as you may have guessed, the answer was, "it's the next value."

So I set the range at 10 percent to 17.5 percent. Don't let conventions keep you from setting the correct expectations.

Don't let conventions keep you from doing the right thing.

Figure 10-10 shows the three-month running total expectations for first time callers.

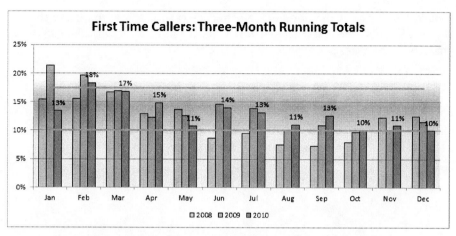

Figure 10-10. First time callers: three-month running totals (with expectations)

Table 10-5 captures the expectations in table format.

Table 10-5. Expectations: Usage.

Category	Measure	Exceeds	Meets	Opportunity
Usage	First time callers: three-month rolling	>17.5%	10%–17.5%	<10%

Once we finished determining the proper measures for unique customers, and their expectations, we looked at our other measure for usage. Another choice was the percentage of respondents who chose the Service Desk as their primary service provider in our annual survey. Table 10-6 shows the expectations we identified for the survey results.

Table 10-6. Expectations: Usage as preferred provider.

Category	Measure	Exceeds	Meets	Opportunity
Usage	Preferred provider rating: % of people who picked Service Desk as first choice	>60%	25%–60%	<20%

Figure 10-11 shows the percentage of survey respondents who listed the Service Desk as their first choice when seeking assistance with their Information Technology problems.

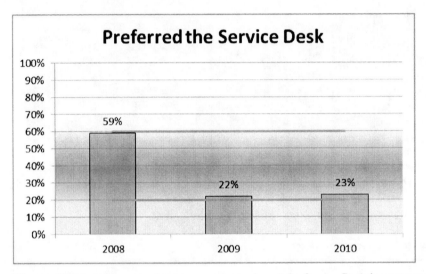

Figure 10-11. Percentage of customers who preferred the Service Desk for assistance

Although the results for 2008 were not an anomaly, the results were so different from the following year that we had to investigate to find out why. The only determination of cause we could find was that in 2008 respondents were asked to pick their top three preferences. The Service Desk was listed as one of the top three choices for 59 percent of the respondents. The next two years the question only allowed one answer—the top choice/preference. You've seen how the charting can change the perception of the measures. This is another strong example of how measures can be totally different based on how the data is collected.

As mentioned, we could also add a measure on repeat customers. If we wanted to stick with percentages, we could produce a measure of the percent of repeat customers compared to the total customers for the given period. Again this could be on a three-, six-, or twelve-month cycle. The really good news is that this measure could be derived from the same data set that gave us the count of unique customers. Where unique customers were compared to total possible customers (customer base), repeat customers would be compared to the total customers for a given period.

The final category of measure we used was what most people think of as the first to collect—customer satisfaction surveys.

Customer Satisfaction

Again we were lucky since the data was already being collected, compiled, and analyzed for us. As mentioned, we had to decide which view of the data worked best. Basically we had to determine the measure to build from the data.

The department had been reporting this measure for a long time, but only as an average on the 5-point Likert scale. Our leadership wondered what to make of the average grade—how to interpret it. Being problem solvers, they didn't leave the solution to the department—instead they asked for benchmarks to compare the average to. They reasoned if they were better than the "national average" or the average of their competitors, they were doing well. In reality this would only tell them that they were doing better than the average. They could claim to be in the top half. If we were really lucky, we'd find the following:

1. Our peers were using the same questions that we were. The third-party provider had an impressive list of customers, but they did *not* have all of our peers or a monopoly on the service.

2. Our peers were using the same 5-point scale that we were.

3. Our peers were willing to share their average grades.

4. Our peers determined the average the same way—they could discount repeat customers within a short time frame, they could categorize their customers differently, or they could not include certain customers—like internal users of the Service Desk. Another difference could be if they surveyed only a sampling and we surveyed all users.

This magical alignment of stars was unlikely to happen, much less stay in alignment for an extended period of time. So, what we'd have instead as a benchmark would be a sampling of some of our peers. This was my first argument against using benchmarks to try and make the measures meaningful.

My second argument was that even when compared to a valid benchmark, it only showed how well we did versus the standard selected—not how well we were satisfying our customers. We could feasibly be at the "top of our class" and still be well below our customers' expectations. If you bring home a B- average on your Report Card, chances are your parents will not be happy. If you tell them that you are the top student in your class they may be a little more impressed *or* they may decide to change schools. A Report Card should tell you how well you are doing regardless of your position in your graduating class. Once you know how well you are doing (or have done) it is a bonus to know how you rank with your peers.

My third and last argument was based on principles; measures should be meaningful to the organization *before* finding benchmarks. Benchmarks should only be used as an enhancement to the information—not act as the definer of it. The measures had to be meaningful on their own.

Figure 10-12 shows the average grade. Even though I argued against this as being less meaningful than other views, when you add the expectations, even this measure becomes useful.

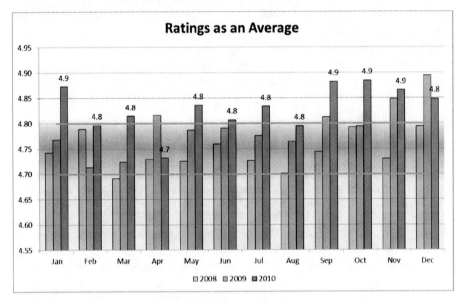

Figure 10-12. Average Customer Satisfaction grade

I still wanted a better representation of the measures. We tried using promoters to detractors, but since the vendor wasn't going to change to a 10-point scale, we had to translate the 5-point scale to the methods Reichheld suggests for determining where a customer fell on the range of support. We ended up making 5s promoters, and 1, 2, or 3s detractors. This was an attempt to match Reichheld's 1s–6s (detractors), 7s and 8s (neutral), and 9s and 10s (promoters). While this was not perfect (or optimum) I believe it was valid and if anything we again were "erring on the side of excellence." But showing this ratio (highly satisfied vs. not satisfied) proved problematic. While it was more meaningful than the average rating, it still was difficult for management to interpret.

The conversation would go something like the following:

> "So, for every 1, 2, or 3 we received, we had twelve 5s?"

> "Yes, your ratio of promoters to detractors was twelve to one."

> "What about the 4s? Why aren't we counting 4s?"

> "Because 4s are being considered neutral. We can't tell how they'll 'talk' about our service. They may say it was good or they may not."

> "I thought 3s were neutral?"

> "Threes are in the middle, neither satisfied nor dissatisfied, and we believe that if someone can't say they were satisfied (4 or 5) then they will definitely talk badly about our service—they will detract from our reputation."

> "Well if we leave out 4s, we're missing data...so it's not a complete picture."

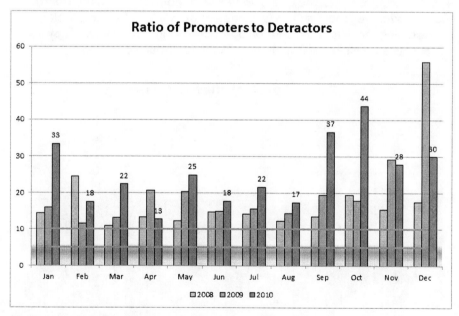

Figure 10-13. Ratio of Promoters to Detractors

Compared to the Average Grade, where we "looked good," this representation (see Figure 10-13) made the Service Desk look incredibly good! And the funny thing was, I believe this was a more accurate representation of just how good they were.

After two years of battling this argument, I acquiesced and found a different way to represent that data. I still believe the promoter-to-detractor story is a good one (and perhaps the best) one to tell. There is an established standard of what is good that can be used as a starting point. Where Reichheld uses that standard to determine potential for growth, it works fine as a benchmark of high quality. That said, the few departments that could conceptualize the promoter-to-detractor measure invariably raised that benchmark way above this standard. One client I worked with wanted a 90 to 1 ratio. As a provider of fitness classes, they felt highly satisfying their customer was their paramount duty and they expected that out of one hundred students, they receive 90 promoters, 9 neutral, and only one detractor (they changed their 5-point scale to a 10-point scale happily).

We ended up with a new measure—a new way of interpreting the data. We showed the percentage "satisfied" (Figure 10-14). This was the number of 4s and 5s compared to the total number of respondents. Definitely better than the average. The third-party vendor of the surveys had no problem representing the data (ours and for our industry) in this manner. They actually produced their reports in numerous forms, including this one.

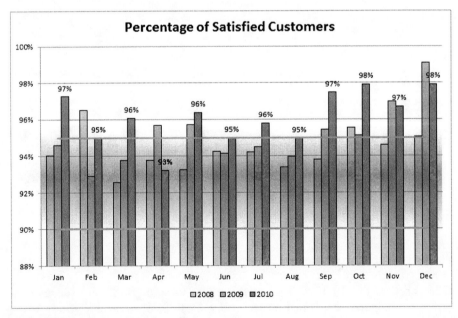

Figure 10-14. Percentage of satisfied customers

At the time of this writing, our organization is testing this view of the data. It still takes some acceptance, and I'm sure I'll hear arguments that all of the data isn't showing (4s and 5s are lumped together, and 1s, 2s, and 3s aren't actually shown at all). Interestingly enough, I think this is more a resistance-to-change issue than it is a fault in any of the representations of the data. Most of those who didn't like the promoter-to-detractor ratio (and those I anticipate arguing against percentage satisfied) didn't complain that the average did not have granularity. In each of these newer views, more data is provided than was given in the average, as shown in Table 10-7.

Table 10-7. Expectations: Customer Satisfaction Ratings.

Category	Measure	Exceeds	Meets	Opportunity
Customer Satisfaction	% of satisfied customers (each question has the same expectations)	>95%	85%–95%	<85%

Weights and Measures

With a complete set of measures in hand, our next step was to pull them together into a "metric." To be a Report Card, we needed to roll the data up as well as provide a deeper dive into the anomalies. So far our methodology afforded some rigor and some flexibility. Let's look at each in this light.

Rigor

- Each metric used triangulation; each was made up of at least three categories of information (Delivery, Usage, and Customer Satisfaction)
- Information was built from as many measures as the service provider saw fit
- Each measure was qualified as exceeding, meeting, or failing to meet expectations
- Each measure was from the customers' points of view and fit under the rules for Service/Product Health

Flexibility

- Each measure was selected by the service provider (our Service Desk department)

- Each data set was built into a measure per the service provider's choice
- Expectations, while representative of the customers' wants and needs, were defined by the service provider and could be adjusted to reflect what the service provider wanted the customers' perception to be. For example, if the customer was happy with an abandoned rate lower than what the Service Desk thought was adequate, the expectations could be higher.

Another important area of flexibility for the service provider was the use of weights to apportion importance to the measures. This was first used in the Delivery category. Since Delivery, one of the three Effectiveness areas of measure, was made up of multiple measures—Availability, Speed, and Accuracy—the service provider could weight these sub-categories differently.

With an organization just beginning to use metrics, weighing these factors was not a trivial task. We made it easier by offering a recommendation. For support services we suggested that speed was the most important to the customer, and for non-support services availability reigned supreme. So for the Service Desk we offered the following weights:

- Availability: 35%
- Speed: 50%
- Accuracy: 15%

These weights could be changed in any manner the service provider chose. The key to this (and the entire Report Card) was the ownership of the metric. Since the service provider "owned" the data, measures, information, and the metric—if they chased the data they would be "lying to themselves." Many of the admonitions I offered preceding this chapter was to help you understand the need for accuracy, but more so for the need of honesty. As David Allen, the author of *Getting Things Done* (Viking, 2001), has said, "You can lie to everyone else, but you can't fool yourself." If the service provider is to use the metrics for the right reasons and the right way, leadership can never abuse or misuse them.

Even though I had the greatest trust in this department, I still stressed the importance of "telling it like it is." The department had to not only be "willing" to hear bad news; they had to *want* to hear it, if it was the way the story unfolded.

Weighing the factors can be an easy way to chase the data and make the measures tell the story you hoped for rather than what it is. One thing we do to make this less tempting is to determine the weights before looking at the data. Then, if we need to change them after seeing the results, it's much easier to self-regulate the temptation to change the weights simply to look better.

This is another great use of the annual survey. We can ask the customer what factors of measure are the most important. Simply ask if Time to Resolve is more important than Time to Respond. You find out whether getting put on hold for 30 seconds is more troublesome than if they have to call back more than once to fix the same problem (accuracy).

Of course, you can weight these factors equally.

Along with weighting the components of Delivery, we can weight the three categories—Delivery, Usage, and Customer Satisfaction. Weights should be clearly communicated to those viewing the Report Card.

Let's look at how we roll up the performance measures into a Report Card.

Rolling Up Data into a Grade

It's time to take the components we've discussed—the Answer Key categories for effectiveness, triangulation, expectations, and the translation grid—to create a final "grade." This includes a means for communicating quickly and clearly the customer's view of your performance, for the staff, managers, and leadership.

You'll need the translation grid (see Figure 10-15) as before but with neutral coloring so that it is less enticing to consider "exceeds" as inherently good.

10	Exceeds Expectations (E)	10
9		
8		
7	Meets Expectations (M)	5
6		
5		
4	Opportunity for Improvement (O)	0
3		
2		
1		

Figure 10-15. Translation Grid

The values I'm using do not reflect the information shared earlier. I wanted to make sure it was clear how to roll up grades and aggregate the measures. Table 10-8 shows all of the measures, their expectations, their actual values and the translation of that value into a "letter grade." These can be programmed into a spreadsheet so that you can have it calculate the grade for you.

Table 10-8, Measures with their final grades.

Category	Measure	Exceeds	Meets	Opportunity	Result
Availability	% of Abandoned calls	<10%	10%–15%	>15%	7% E
	% of Abandoned calls <30 seconds	>95%	85%–95%	< 85%	92.56% M
Speed: Time to Respond	Responds in less than 5 seconds	>50%	25%–50%	<25%	24% O
	Responds in 5 to 30 seconds	>75%	50%–75%	<50%	74% M
	Responds in greater than 30 seconds	<10%	10%–25%	>25%	2% E
Speed: Time to Resolve	Resolved in one hour or less	>85%	65%–85%	<65%	82% M
	Resolved in 24 hours or less	>95%	85%–95%	<85%	90% M
	Resolved in five days or less	>97.5%	95%–97.5%	<95%	93% O
Accuracy	% of Rework	<1%	1%–5%	>5%	1.3% M
Usage	First time callers three-month rolling	>50%	20%–50%	< 20%	32% M
	Preferred provider rating: % who picked Service Desk as first choice	>=60%	25%–59%	<25%	42% M
	Repeat customers on three-month rolling cycle	10%	5%–10%	<5%	5.3% M

Category	Measure	Exceeds	Meets	Opportunity	Result
Customer Satisfaction	Courtesy % satisfied	>95%	85%–95%	<85%	98% E
	Skills/knowledge % satisfied	>95%	85%–95%	<85%	97% E
	Timeliness % satisfied	>95%	85%–95%	<85%	95% M
	Overall satisfaction % satisfied	>95%	85%–95%	<85%	98% E

In Table 10-8, the "grade" (shown in the Result column) has already been translated to a letter value—if the actual measure exceeded expectations, it earned an E, if it met expectations an M, and if it failed to meet expectations an O.

Within each item (information level), the total grade would be a result of an average using the translation grid. As mentioned, you can even use weights within the category. For example, abandoned calls that were less than 30 seconds could be given a weight of 85 percent, while the total number of abandoned calls could be weighted 15 percent. Another example is overall Customer Satisfaction can be given equal weight (50 percent) to the other three satisfaction question combined (16.6 percent each). For this example we'll go with those two weighting choices and all others will be of equal weight within their own information category. Table 10-9 shows the next step in the process of rolling the grades up toward a final Report Card. Note: a double asterisk beside the grade denotes an O grade at a lower level.

Table 10-9. First roll-up of grades.

Category	Measure	Grade	First-Level Roll Up
Availability	% of Abandoned calls	E = 10	(10*15%) + (5 * 85%) = 5.75 M**
	% of Abandoned calls < 30 seconds	M = 5	
Speed: Time to Respond	Responds in less than 5 seconds	O = 0	(0 + 5 + 10)/3 = 5 M**
	Responds in 6 to 30 seconds	M = 5	
	Responds in greater than 30 seconds	E = 10	

Category	Measure	Grade	First-Level Roll Up
Speed: Time to Resolve	Resolved in one hour or less	M = 5	(5 + 5 + 0) / 3 = 3.33 O
	Resolved in 24 hours or less	M = 5	
	Resolved in five days or less	O = 0	
Accuracy	% of Rework	M = 5	5 M
Usage	First time callers three-month rolling	M = 5	(5 + 5 +5)/ 3 = 5 M
	Preferred provider rating: % who picked Service Desk as first choice	M = 5	
	Repeat customers on three-month rolling cycle	M = 5	
Customer Satisfaction	Courtesy % satisfied	E = 10	((10 + 10 + 5)/3)* 50% + 10 *50%) = 9.1 E
	Skills/knowledge % satisfied	E = 10	
	Timeliness % satisfied	M = 5	
	Overall satisfaction % satisfied	E = 10	

** There is an O (opportunity for improvement) grade in a lower level of this roll up grade.

Let's look at the two weighted measures. If the Availability measures were of equal weight the total grade would simply be the average of the two grades, 10 and 5, giving a grade of 7.5. If we rounded up, then this would make it an E. But, since we always choose to err on the side of excellence, we don't round up. You have to fully achieve the grade to get credit for the letter grade. If the weighting were switched (Abandoned Total = 85% and Calls Abandoned in Less Than 30 Seconds was worth 15 percent of the grade), you'd have an overall E since the 10 for abandoneds would give you an 8.5 before you even looked at the abandoned calls in less than 30 seconds.

In the satisfaction ratings, we find that the grade is an E even though there is an M. If, instead of weighing overall satisfaction at 50 percent, we gave all three questions equal weight, the grade would simply be the average of the four grades, giving us an 8.75. Still an E, but a lower grade.

Notice that the Speed: Time to Respond came out as an M, Meets Expectations, but I added the asterisk to signify there was an O hidden beneath. The same is done for the Availability total grade because of the E hidden beneath. It helps the viewer of the Report Card quickly note if she should look deeper into the information. Buried Es and Os are anomalies that need to be identified.

Let's continue with these results. If we go with the weighting offered for Delivery (Speed at 50%, Availability at 35%, and Accuracy at 15%), we get the next level of grades for delivery, as shown in Table 10-10.

Table 10-10. Second and third level grade roll up.

Category	Measure	Grade	First- Level Roll Up	Second-Level Roll Up	Third-Level Roll Up
Availability	% of Abandoned calls	E = 10	(10*.15) + (5 * .85) = 5.75 M**	M* = 5 5 *.35 = 1.75	1.75 + 0 + .75 = 2.5 O
	% of Abandoned calls < 30 seconds	M = 5			
Speed: Time to Respond	Responds in less than 5 seconds	O = 0	(0 + 5 + 10)/3 = 5 M**	(5 + 0) / 2 = 2.5 O =0 0 * .5 = 0	
	Responds in 6 to 30 seconds	M = 5			
	Responds in greater than 30 seconds	E = 10			
Speed: Time to Resolve	Resolved in one hour or less	M = 5	(5 + 5 + 0) / 3 = 3.33 O		
	Resolved in 24 hours or less	M = 5			
	Resolved in five days or less	O = 0			
Accuracy	% of Rework	M = 5	5 M	M = 5 5 * .15 = .75	

** There is an O (opportunity for improvement) grade in a lower level of this roll up grade.

Let's continue on in this manner in Table 10-11.

Table 10-11. Summary of rolled up grades.

Category	Measure	Grade	Roll Up
Delivery	Availability (35%)	M** = 5	O
	Speed (50%)	O = 0	
	Accuracy (15%)	M = 5	
Usage	3 Measures	M = 5	M
Customer Satisfaction	4 Questions with Weighing	E = 10	E

** There is an O (opportunity for improvement) grade in a lower level of this roll up grade.

We again have decisions to make. Are Delivery, Usage, and Customer Satisfaction of equal value? This is only necessary because we are attempting to roll up the grades to a single grade. In my organization, we stopped at this level, choosing to keep these three key information categories separate, even across different services. So if we were to roll up three support services (Service Desk, second- and third-level support) we'd show a roll up in the Delivery overall, Usage overall, and finally Customer Satisfaction overall. We found the view of a service using this basic triangulation as far as we needed to go. If you want to roll it into a final grade (GPA), the only question left is the weighting. For the purposes of this example, we'll keep it simple and make their values of equal weight.

Table 10-12. Final roll up into a single grade for a service.

Category	Measure	Grade	Next-Level Roll Up	Overall Grade
Delivery	Availability (35%)	M** = 5	O = 0	(0 + 5 + 10)/3 = 5 M**
	Speed (50%)	O = 0		
	Accuracy (15%)	M = 5		
Usage	3 measures	M = 5	M = 5	
Customer Satisfaction	4 questions with weighting	E = 10	E = 10	

** There is an O (opportunity for improvement) grade in a lower level of this roll up grade.

So the final Report Card for the Service Desk, based on the weights for each category of information, resulted In an overall grade of M*. This can be interpreted easily to mean that the service is meeting expectations overall with some anomalies that should be investigated.

If you looked at the grades as my organization does, not rolling up the major categories, into a single grade, but looking at each major "subject" area separately, you would get the following:

- *Delivery*: O is an **O**pportunity for Improvement. Time here should be spent investigating the causes for the anomalies.
- *Usage*: M means that we **M**eet Expectations. No investigation required in this area.
- *Customer Satisfaction*: E means that we **E**xceed Expectations. Time here should be spent investigating the causes for the anomalies.

The final summary Report Card would look like Figure 10-16.

		Delivery	Usage	Customer Satisfaction				
	Service Desk	O	M	E				
		Expectations		actual	score	category score	Overall	
	Measure	meets	exceeds					
Availability	% of Abandoned calls	15%	10%	7.0%	E	M**		
	% Abandoned calls < 30 seconds	85%	95%	92.6%	M			
Speed (time to respond)	Responds in less < 5 seconds	25%	50%	24.0%	O			
	Responds in 5 to 30 seconds	50%	75%	74.0%	M			
	Responds in > 30 seconds	25%	10%	2.0%	E	O	O	
Speed (time to resolve)	Resolved in one hour or less	65%	85%	82.0%	M			
	Resolved in 24 hours or less	85%	95%	90.0%	M			
	Resolved in five days or less	95%	97.5%	93.0%	O			
Accuracy	% of Rework	5%	1%	1.3%	M	M		
Usage	First time callers	20%	50%	32.0%	M			
	Preferred provider rating	25%	60%	42.0%	M	M	M	
	Repeat customers	5%	10%	5.3%	M			
Customer Satisfaction (% satisfied customers)	Courtesy	85%	95%	98.0%	E			
	Skills/knowledge	85%	95%	97.0%	E	E	E	
	Timeliness	85%	95%	95.0%	E			
	Overall satisfaction	85%	95%	98.0%	E			

Figure 10-16. Report Card

With each, prose should be included once the investigation has concluded. This prose communicates to the leadership what the service provider has determined to be the cause for the anomaly and any suggested actions to mitigate, avoid, rectify, or replicate the causes. These changes are to processes (not people) and should be designed to control future results.

If we learn from our past mistakes, we should not continue to repeat them.

Likewise, if we learn from our past successes we should find ways to make the anomaly into the common place (if it is deemed an equitable choice).

Recap

The Report Card allows us to aggregate grades at each level of our metric. You can decide at what level to stop compiling to a final grade. You do *not* have to end with a single grade. This chapter has been a step-by-step example of how the concepts presented to this point can be (and have been) applied to create a service-level metric.

I have reviewed in this way working from data to measures to information and finally a metric. From measures onward, I showed how you will apply expectations to each so as to give context and meaning to each. Along with applying expectations, I showed a suggested method of normalizing the information across measurement types and areas. The use of percentages is only one means of consistency. As you use different measures, evaluating various services and products, you will find that this may not remain easy to do. In my experience, the measures used will differ in type.

Another tool of normalization is the scoring method, in which at every turn we seek to err on the side of excellence. This is why an Opportunity for Improvement is treated as a zero and only an Exceeds will balance it out to Meets. Since we don't round up (again to ensure we err on the side of excellence), just one Opportunity for Improvement will keep the total (average) grade from ever being an M unless there is an E included.

What we want are Meets Expectations. Anything else is an anomaly and requires investigation.

Recall some of the following ways that impressions can be skewed:

- Artistic license—color choices, alignment, etc.
- The scale used to represent the measures
- The format used to represent the data (ratio, average, percentage, etc.)

The overall grade gives a "feel" for the health of the subject. Rolling up the grades into a "final grade" is possible, but won't always be desirable. It depends on the audience.

The Report Card shows how to display, compile, and report the results of your metrics. It doesn't go into the tools you may choose to use for gathering the data. The organization I used as an example had multiple automated tools, some human-interactive tools, and fully subjective surveys. Check your organization for existing sources of data. There are usually more places for you to gather data (unobtrusively) than you would expect.

Other tools for gathering data should be found and leveraged. The Higher Education TechQual+ Project is just one example of a (free) survey-based tool that you can use—even if you are not in an IT organization, the concepts of the tool can be applied to your services and products.

"It's not what you look at that matters, it's what you see."

—Henry David Thoreau

Innovation is not coming up with a totally new concept or idea. The greatest innovations come from seeing things that already exist in a new light. It was a great strength of Thomas Edison to see what others missed in their attempts to invent something new.

Conclusion

The Report Card is another mean of creating a scorecard with the added benefit of allowing you to roll up the measures into a single grade if desired. By identifying the anomalies in the measures and information, you can clearly designate which are anomalies and spend your time investigating only those that require the effort. This allows you to:

- Identify the areas needing further investigation
- Spend resources only where needed
- Have an overall "feel" for the health of a service or group of services using a common language for the evaluation

The key isn't in what tools you use to collect, analyze, compile or report the information and metrics you develop. The key is in finding a way of doing this work so that it is easily understood by your audience. Your metrics have to tell the proper story, in the right way, to the correct audience.

Advanced Metrics

You might be thinking, "When should I look at using the other quadrants of the Answer Key?" I've tried my best to keep you from delving into the other quadrants before your organization has had time to work with the Product/Service Health metrics, where you'll get the most benefit initially. This doesn't mean that you can't build metrics to answer specific root questions. But, if you are tasked with developing a metrics program (or are doing the tasking), I'm encouraging you to slowly introduce these concepts and tools into your organization.

Figure 11-1 once again shows the Answer Key, so that we can reference where you've been (effectiveness) and where you're going in this chapter.

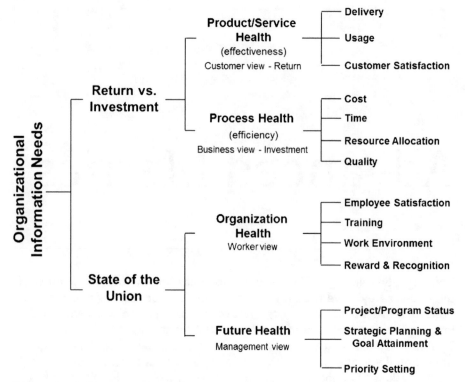

Figure 11-1. The Answer Key Revisited

Dipping Your Toes into the Other Quadrants

So, when should you work on the other three quadrants? It's likely that you'll have opportunities in three areas to test the water in the other quadrants before you embark on full metrics programs in each.

1. As Support for Product/Service Health Efforts

As discussed earlier, when working within the Service/Product Health (effectiveness) quadrant, you are likely to encounter opportunities to develop and use Process Health (efficiency) measures. An example is when one of your effectiveness indicators is awry and you want to improve the situation. Let's say your speed to resolve is showing below expectations. After you do your due diligence (investigate), you find out that the time it's taking to resolve your customers' issues is taking longer than it should, based on your organization's service-level agreements. You may then take it upon yourself to work with the team responsible for the service. You may want to define the process and then institute measures along the way to see if you can improve the process. These measures will more than likely fall under Process Health.

You may recall that I also wrote strongly against delving into efficiency measures before you or your organization is ready. I also warned that management would want to go that route. So, why am I telling you that you might have to go there? Efficiency measures, in this case, will only be used for a specific purpose—to explain the causes of the effectiveness anomalies. This will be a very focused and limited use of efficiency measures. And they will be driven by the effectiveness metrics.

2. To Guide Process Improvement Efforts

Another early opportunity to delve into the other three quadrants may come about when you are doing a process improvement effort. If you are using any of the currently in-vogue improvement methods (like Six Sigma) you will be asked to develop measures—not only to show that your efforts were successful, but also to help determine where improvement is needed. While these measures *can* be from the Service/Product Health quadrant, many times they are from a different area of the Answer Key.

And that's all right.

My admonitions against starting in any of the other three quadrants is based on my reluctance to have you "develop a program" in those quadrants before you're ready. If you are developing metrics to accompany a specific effort, you can definitely use measures from any quadrant.

3. To Accompany Organizational Development Efforts

If and when your organization embarks on organizational development efforts, it should include measures of success. These give clarity to the goals and allow those involved to know how well they are progressing toward the finish line.

As a strategy and planning consultant, I have worked on many organizational development teams. The latest included professional development and employee Integration teams. Each team wanted metrics to show progress and hopefully levels of success.

Say you're asked, "How do we know if we're successful?" Or, "How do we know when we're done?" Your answer will usually will be, "The metrics will tell us."

These measures are dependent on the efforts involved. The efforts will normally determine the quadrant the metrics fall in. If you are doing employee professional development, you will find your metrics in the Organization Health quadrant. If your questions are around achievement of the strategic goals of the organization, you may be in the Future Health quadrant.

Again, the main difference between these and the Product/Service Health metrics I've covered is that these are metrics in response to specific root questions resulting from focused efforts. The scope of these metrics should be well defined. The Product/Service Health metrics I offer are the foundation for a long-term metrics program, not a measure of a specific effort.

These metrics, built around specific efforts, can still be "risky." But, since they come "attached" to the specific effort, the risks of fear, uncertainty and doubt are much easier to mitigate.

Perhaps it would be more correct to consider these "other metrics" rather than advanced metrics. These are not more sophisticated than effectiveness metrics.

The Benefits Metrics Provide an Immature Organization

Before we look at metrics in the other quadrants, let's step back and look at the forest we're in. I've argued that metrics, as an organizational improvement tool, is not suited for an organization suffering from the inability to successfully take on enterprise-wide improvement efforts. (I offered an assessment in *Why Organizations Struggle So Hard to Improve So Little* for determining if your organization suffers from Organizational Immaturity.) I've held this position for a long time because of the dangers inherent in metrics and the risks involved. I've seen the fear rise up and poison an organization. Fear born of poorly defined and poorly implemented metrics.

While I still believe metrics to be one of the most (if not *the* most) risky of tools, I have gained a new appreciation for the value metrics can provide in moving an organization forward.

I'm not referring to changing behaviors through measurement. I find that to be the riskiest of uses for metrics. No, I mean through some little-known byproducts of implementing a metrics program. I have found that metrics, when done well (or at least safely), can be a catalyst to improvement. By measuring, the organization finds out a lot about what it doesn't know.

Let's look at a simple example.

When measuring the speed of a process, the organization learns that it lacks more information than it realized. Many times I've found that the organization doesn't even know the process in question well enough to produce the necessary measures. This lack of understanding becomes apparent because of the attempts to measure it.

Measuring tells you what you didn't know you didn't know.

Every process improvement method I've learned and used begins with defining the process needing improvement. Even in Lean Six Sigma, where your goals are to reduce waste and improve flow, a favorite tool is the value stream map, which requires you to define the process. But, what if you're not doing a process-improvement effort? What if your boss is pushing for measures?

Well, those measures may also require a full understanding of the processes to be measured. You'll need to ask questions like:

> *When does the process start?* Even this simplest of questions is difficult for some organizations to answer. Does it start with the first action a worker takes within the process? Or does it start with the request by the customer? Does it start with the identification of a need?

> *When does the process conclude?* Is it upon delivery? Or is it upon closure of the documentation used to track the progress of the process? Is conclusion dependent on a successful delivery of the service or product? Or does it simply designate the completion of the attempt?

> *Are there subprocesses? Especially ones you don't control?* Within the process there may be many subprocesses—many that are misunderstood or unknown. Who owns those subprocesses? How do

they affect your work? Are they prerequisites to other steps? Are they critical to the successful completion of your process?

By asking for the data, measures, information, and most importantly the root question, you encourage (if not force) the organization to define the thing being measured. In many instances, you will find that you have to improve the thing being measured to make it measurable.

You may need to improve the thing being measured to make it possible to measure it.

By measuring, you gain a better understanding of the things to be measured. This includes processes (if you're doing a process-improvement effort), employee interactions and policies, strategic plans, and how you handle long-term projects. Another improvement area that measuring promotes is in actually changing the way you do things.

Making Your Processes Repeatable

The steps to a process should not just be understood and communicated, but they should be consistent. They should be repeatable. In attempting to measure the process, with the underlying purpose of improving it, you push the organization to have the process defined well enough to measure it. That is why the largest benefit garnered from implementing a metric program may lie in the requirement that the processes be defined and understood well enough to measure.

When you've defined the process, you still will not be able to gain useful measures around it unless it is carried out consistently each time it is used. This consistency allows for corrections and improvements.

As you may have noticed, I like sports analogies. Here's a short one. I am constantly impressed with the ability some people have to throw a basketball from over twenty-five feet through a horizontal cylinder ten feet high. They call it "shooting," as if that makes it more of a skill. But the simple truth is that they are throwing the ball. Many do so in a high arc, allowing the ball to come down through the hoop without touching the metal rim. What I find especially impressive is how many different forms and techniques the players use. The key I've learned is not how you hold your hand, arrange your feet, follow through, or even square your hips to the target. The simple trick is consistency. If you "shoot" the ball the same way every time, you will get better. Not because you repeat the process the same way (or you would continue to miss) but because you can make small corrections. Because you are consistent in your delivery, you can see how each small adjustment changes the results. Eventually, you'll find the right formula, technique, or process that gives you a high percentage of success.

Consistency allows for improvement.

The same is true for process improvement in your organization. You have to understand the process. You have to repeat the process the same way each time. You have to measure the results. You can then make adjustments to improve the results. Your process or methods can be unique, but they have to be repeatable and repeated.

Measuring Helps to Encourage Using Existing Processes

You don't have to try to improve something with measures to affect it positively; simply measuring it has the capability to do so. This is where the adage, "you improve what you measure" comes from. As I've told you, though, measuring can also make the performance deteriorate. There is no assurance that the result of measuring is improvement. The only assurance is that the things you measure will change. The act of measuring acts as a catalyst for change—good or bad.

While that is true for the process being measured, there are other, related processes that are affected as well. For example, in our Service Desk scenario, the speed to resolve a trouble call required the use of the trouble-call tracking system.

When I needed to measure the time to resolve issues for a couple of our offices, it quickly became apparent that the trouble call system was not being used by the technicians. The manager of the departments would have to go through each case history to adjust the close dates and times because the technicians weren't closing them when the process called for them to. They would wait days and even weeks to close cases. It was seen as unimportant documentation and paperwork. I heard more than once that "it's not the real work—the real work is helping the customer." And "filling out that stuff takes time that I could be helping solve more problems."

As with most arguments, there is a fair amount of truth packed into those statements. But as with most things, the paperwork is very important. It's important when the manager is fighting for additional resources. You have to prove not only that you have more work than your staff can handle, but that it is working efficiently and that adding more resources would solve the problem. This is hard to prove if you have no evidence. And if your time to resolve shows up as weeks for simple problems, leadership will rightly assume that you are inefficient.

When we developed the Report Card, these managers got tired of me coming to them each month for a quality check of the data in the trouble call tracking system. It was data that should have been accurate. The metrics I was building wasn't the reason for the data. The metrics only highlighted that the staff was not using the tools properly. People were not following the processes and procedures that were created for them to track trouble calls. The managers *knew* the staff wasn't completing the cases properly, but it was a battle they didn't want to fight. They were actually happy to have a clear reason to push their staff to use the tool in the way it was intended.

Metrics in the Other Quadrants

In Chapter 5, which discussed using the Answer Key, and Chapter 6, which covered effectiveness metrics, I discussed each of the four quadrants. I also suggested that you start with Effectiveness and you end with Efficiency. While you may use efficiency measures (sparingly) to support your Product/ Service Health metrics, you shouldn't embark on a full Process Health program at first.

I recommended that the second area to add to your metrics program would be the employee view, Organization Health. This can yield immense benefits for your organization. By focusing on your "greatest assets" you can help build a stronger, better, faster, happier organization. The measures within the third quadrant will help you do this.

The bonus to developing your organizational health view lies in the same reasoning as to why effectiveness was the safest place to start. There is much less risk that the staff will misunderstand your intentions. Product/ Service Health measures were from the customer's viewpoint. It is easier to convince the workforce that the effectiveness measures won't be used against them since they reflect the customers' view. The biggest benefit, which accompanies the lower risk factor, is that by measuring Product/ Service Health, you can improve your customers' view of your organization and thereby improve your bottom line (even if that bottom line is not financially driven).

By focusing next on Organization Health (Figure 11-2), you still avoid the risks involved, even more easily than effectiveness measures since the metrics are *for* the employees instead of *about* them. It can also help improve your workforce's view of your organization. This should improve morale, loyalty, and dedication. It should also improve productivity—not by measuring, controlling, and manipulating behavior—but by proving to your workforce that when you say they are your greatest asset, you actually mean it.

Organization Health

Figure 11-2. Quadrant 3 of the Answer Key

You don't have to take my word for it. *Fortune* magazine, which produces the "top 500" list of companies, partners with the Great Place to Work Institute to determine the 100 best places to work. Employee satisfaction is a critical factor to a company's success.

In the short term, a company can be highly successful with unhappy and disgruntled employees. A tyrannical approach can work for a leader, in the short term. If you want your company to have longevity in success, the employee view is critical.

The *Fortune* 500 is a good measure of the company's current success. Being one of the 100 best companies to work for may help you determine if a company will succeed in the future. A third available measure is the 100 "most innovative companies" according to *Bloomberg Businessweek*. (Table 11-1 lists the companies that appear on all three rankings, while Table 11-2 lists those that appear on both *Fortune* 500 and Best.)

Table 11-1. Compiled Ranking: Top Companies to Work for

Companies Appearing on All Three Lists in 2011	Ranking on *Fortune* 500	Ranking on Best Companies to Work For	Ranking on Most Innovative Companies
Goldman Sachs	54	23	96
Google	92	4	2
Intel	56	51	17
Microsoft	38	72	5
Starbucks	229	98	9
Whole Foods Market	273	24	36

Sometimes less information is better. Looking at a little less information provides us a different, and perhaps clearer, picture. Picking which data to use is an important part of designing the metric—and a much easier step if you have a clear understanding of the root question you're trying to answer.

Table 11-2. Compiled Ranking: A Clearer View of Top Companies to Work for

Companies Appearing on *Fortune* 500 and Best Companies to Work For in 2011	Ranking on *Fortune* 500	Ranking on Best Companies to Work For
AFLAC	125	57
American Express	91	49
Booz Allen Hamilton	438	85
CarMax	311	81
CH2M HILL	422	90
Chesapeake Energy	263	32
Darden Restaurants	332	97
Devon Energy	231	41
EOG Resources	377	66
General Mills	166	58
Goldman Sachs	54	23

Companies Appearing on *Fortune* 500 and Best Companies to Work For in 2011	Ranking on *Fortune* 500	Ranking on Best Companies to Work For
Google	92	4
Intel	56	51
J. M. Smucker	482	93
Marriott International	210	71
Mattel	392	69
Microsoft	38	72
Nordstrom	254	74
NuStar Energy	497	30
Publix Super Markets	102	86
Qualcomm	222	33
Starbucks	229	98
Stryker	323	68
Whole Foods Market	273	24

Concepts

In doing research for this book, I realized that if I were looking for a job, I'd care more about finding a "best company to work for" than a *Fortune* 500. But you probably aren't looking for metrics for picking your next employer. You are most likely trying to figure out what metrics you need to improve your organization and how to measure progress.

As with getting on many ranked lists, you have to submit information and complete a survey to be evaluated by these companies. To become one of the top 100 companies to work for, you have to take the time and effort to complete the paperwork. And it's not only you or your leadership. Your employees will have to complete an assessment tool.

This is a useful tool—especially from a reward-and-recognition standpoint. But, it's not necessary. What is necessary is for you to obtain your employee's viewpoint and work to develop a solid and healthy organization. This is an example of how an organization (or leader) can get caught up in "chasing data" rather than trying to achieve a goal.

The goal has to be independent of the metrics used to measure attainment of it.

The goal should not be to be in a "top 100 list," but the goal can be to become a top 100 company. It doesn't matter if you are recognized as a top 100 company. What matters is that you have a healthy organization that would qualify. Your goal shouldn't be to obtain a certain internal satisfaction rating on your employee surveys—it should be to have a healthy, happy, loyal employee. You may measure this using a survey, but the nuance is in the details. If you celebrate the survey results, you may miss the boat, and that can be an embarrassing time.

I've seen more than once where a team or person won an award from the organization, based on measures gathered, only to have that same person (or team) readily admit that they didn't "deserve" the award. Someone filled out the paperwork, someone answered the survey, or someone submitted them for the award without knowing the whole story. When a worker receives recognition and rewards he doesn't feel was earned, the reward system loses validity in the eyes of the recipient and others.

If you chase data, you'll miss this and end up believing that:

1. Your program is working well since you are getting a good number of submissions and giving out awards on a regular basis

2. That the organization health is strong since there are so many awards being given out

If the employees believe these awards are given to the wrong people or to undeserving people, the program will take a serious hit. Unfortunately, chances are the administrators of the program (and leadership) may never realize that the program is not viewed as valid.

Don't misunderstand. Workers are very concerned with the company's success. Not just for job security and hoped-for pay increases each year. An employee who loves her job, loves her company, and is loyal to the organization cares about the company's success as much as a college graduate who loved his school cares about the institution's continued success. Your workforce can build a strong attachment for the organization. While the employees care about the company's success, they want leadership to care about them. And employees want their boss to care about them.

The good news is, if leadership and management truly care about the employee and focuses a fair amount of attention on improving the employee's work experience, the company as a whole will benefit.

Employee Satisfaction

If employees are satisfied (happy) with their jobs, they will work harder. They will look for ways to help the organization succeed. They will take pride and ownership in the company's success.

Walking across campus, I habitually pick up stray pieces of trash. I've been asked why I bother. I get arguments about how others are paid to clean up the grounds, how people will just keep throwing trash, and how it should be "beneath" me to pick up other people's trash. I just smile and tell all of them the same thing. "It's my university. Why wouldn't I clean it up?" If there was trash blowing across my yard, I'd pick it up. You should want your employees to feel that the company is theirs, not the CEO's.

Training

Another win-win opportunity is found in training. Employees know you consider them a valuable asset if you put your money where your mouth is. Not necessarily in the form of raises—though I don't know of anyone who is unhappy about getting a raise—but in the form of paying for their education. If you believe the worker to be a valuable asset, you would happily pay to have that asset become even more valuable. You can focus your efforts on trying to manipulate and control the workers' behaviors *or* you can focus on building trust and loyalty. When you train your personnel to be better at their work, they can be more productive. This builds pride. It also lets them know that you care. And, it makes it possible for the workers to be more efficient and effective.

Work Environment

Is your workforce in cramped space? Are your workers living in a cubicle farm? Is the lighting bad? Are the temperature controls adequate? Is it a happy place to work? Is laughter in the halls seen as a sign of a healthy work environment or a sign that the employees don't have enough to do?

Environment matters! Most workers spend more waking hours in the same small office space than they do anywhere else.

If you spend over eight hours, five days a week, in the same environment, it should be an environment that stimulates productive work. It should be an innovative, fun, positive, rewarding place to work. This is not only about the facilities; it is also about the culture of the organization.

Reward and Recognition

People want to be noticed. People want to be rewarded. Actually, all creatures like positive attention. It makes you feel good. This is one of the best ways to improve organization health, but it's also one of the hardest to do right. The problem is that you have to get it right. As described earlier—if you reward the wrong people or for the wrong things, your efforts will backfire. You have to ensure before you hand out rewards that the recipients are the right people and have done the right things. This requires more than putting a "recognition program" in place. It requires more than setting up a system for employees to nominate each other for recognition or rewards. It requires earnest interest in what the workforce is doing and who is really making positive things happen.

There are more ways to mess up than to succeed, as follows:

1. *The Shotgun.* Rewarding everyone in a blanket method doesn't work. "You are all such great workers that I'm giving the entire organization a day off!" There is a problem if *everyone* isn't really doing great work. The workers know who is a good worker and who isn't. The shotgun approach tells the workforce that

   a. You don't know them
   b. You don't care to get to know them

2. *The Elective Process.* If you institute a program where people can submit others for rewards and an administrator sifts through the submissions to determine winners, you are going to create a system that is more of a game than a tool for rewards and recognition. The workers will either ignore the system or see how many rewards you can be made to give to the wrong people. The problems are simple in the workforce's eyes:

   a. Leadership and management should care enough to know when a worker deserves praise
   b. You're asking the employees to do management's job for them
   c. Believe it or not, most deserving workers will feel embarrassed to nominate themselves, so they will feel even more slighted that you are forcing them to do so or get someone else to nominate them—again, it should be management's job to notice.

3. *The Halo and Horns Effect.* Workers already believe that there are "favorites." When you institute a program that continues to reward those believed favorites, even when they haven't done anything

"lately," and continues to ignore the good works someone who hasn't been in the limelight in the past performs—the workforce is reassured that the wealthy become wealthier and the poor become poorer.

Of course, you can attempt to base your rewards and recognition on performance measures, but that has its own set of problems—including encouraging "chasing data." In the end, these issues are only important in as much as they affect the metrics you will develop and use to determine your organization health.

Measuring Organization Health

Understanding the underlying viewpoint of the workforce will help you properly design metrics for this quadrant. When you look at each of the measures, you have to keep the possible issues and missteps in mind.

Employee Satisfaction Measures

No surprises here. You'll have to include the task of asking the employees how they feel. But besides gathering the subjective responses to interview or survey questions, we'll still lean on triangulation to gather other measures. We'll want some objective measures like retention and turnover. We'll want to know the number of types of grievances logged. The rules of creating good metrics haven't changed—just the focus.

Training

Training measures should include skill levels, changes in skill levels, and the amount and quality of training received. You can also have maturity-based questions like:

- Do employees have training plans?
- Is there a professional development program used?
- How often are skill levels assessed?
- Is there a cross-training program in place?

But other simple measures also work, and include the following:

- The number of training hours used
- The number of workers received training
- The number of employees taking advantage of in-house training

- The difference between required skill levels and existing skill levels—and whether it is improving

Training should also include skills. Besides the suggestions already given, you can measure how many of your employees are seen as experts in their field? Do other companies seek them out for advice? Do your peers consider your staff to be experts? Are your workers published? Are they presenting at conferences? Are they encouraged to be recognized as experts?

Work Environment

Again, surveys will work well to determine employee satisfaction levels. But as with employee satisfaction, you should find other means of gathering the measures; hopefully more objective ones. The following are possible measures of the health of the work environment:

- Number of sick days and/or vacation days used (extremes in either direction can be an indicator of an unhealthy work environment)
- Employee turnover
- Laughter in the halls (and if it continues when the boss walks by)
- The number of pictures on employee's walls (do your employees make their workspace pleasant for themselves or does it resemble a jail cell?)
- Early arrivals, late departures

For all of the examples, the question isn't what's good or bad, but whether you're seeing extremes or anomalies. In either case, they are indicators that there may be issues with the health of your work environment. While negative extremes (high absenteeism rates for example) may be worrisome, any extreme (workers not taking their vacation time) can also be an indicator of problems. Besides extremes, you will need to investigate when anomalies (things out of the established norms for your organization) pop up.

Reward and Recognition

It is important that you know if your people feel valued. Besides measuring if the employees are rightly rewarded and recognized internally, you'll also want to measure if they are being recognized and rewarded by outside institutions. Some questions leadership or management may want to consider include the following:

- Are employees doing great things?
- How well do you know your workforce?

- Do you know what your employees' hobbies and pastimes are?
- Do you know if they are winning awards for non-work related efforts?
- Are your workers contributing significantly to the community?

If you want to measure the effectiveness of your "reward and recognition" program, you may want to use the employee satisfaction measures. It will be hard to measure the worth of your program without seeing if the workers believe you are doing so properly. You could measure the program itself, including the following:

- The number of awards distributed
- The number of workers nominated for awards
- The number of unique workers recognized each year

These would be the measures I would suggest for an immature organization. The problem with a reward-and-recognition program is that you *need* one. Funny how we reward and recognize our children without a formal program. Funny how we care enough to pay attention to their successes and failures. Parents know their children's accomplishments because they care about their success. Many times parents feel their children's successes are also theirs.

Too bad managers don't seem to be able to do this, even though there is normally a concerted effort to ensure people don't supervise too many individuals.

For some reason, managers seem unable to pay enough attention to their workers' successes. Conversely, managers seem to know each worker's missteps and mishaps intimately. This may be because errors are elevated to the manager while many times good works go unheralded. I'm not going to try and solve the complexities of trying to implement a reward and recognition program. But I do want to stress that measuring the program will be problematic since you probably don't want to *need* a program. It would be much better if you had a culture of recognition.

That's something worth measuring.

Future Health

The next quadrant I suggest you tackle is Future Health, Quadrant 4, as shown in Figure 11-3.

Figure 11-3. Quadrant 4 of the Answer Key

Concepts

Let's look at Quadrant Four of the Answer Key. When I talk about future health, I'm not referring to the projected financial situation of an organization. You may have noticed that I haven't mentioned the financial stability at all. That's because the metrics I'm presenting in this book are around health in terms of maturity, not finance.

There are many existing measures of financial health (the *Fortune* lists are an example) and for measuring the future potential for financial growth. This area is well trodden and I doubt you are being asked to develop or institute these types of metrics. You should be able to find many resources on measuring a company's financial health—like price-to-earnings ratio, liquidity (how much cash the company has on hand), or leverage (the amount of money a company is borrowing in relation to its capital).

The future health of an organization from a maturity standpoint includes how well the organization can take on and achieve large-scale projects and programs. Implementing a metrics program would actually fit under this umbrella. How well can the organization take these complex tasks on? Is the organization capable of more than just getting the day-to-day operations accomplished?

When I coach others on vision setting, I remind them constantly that they can't afford to get bogged down with the tactical. They have to see things at a strategic level, plan at a strategic level, and stay focused on long-range goals. Immature organizations can't do this. If you find that you're swamped with the daily grind and can't lift your head up long enough or look up high enough to see the long-range goals of the organization, your future health is in question.

At basic levels, the organization must be able to set strong goals for the future, prioritize its work, and be able to complete project- or program-level work. If the organization can't do any of these components, chances are it will never grow. It will be stuck in the present.

Project/Program Status Measures

To measure project and program execution requires that you have policies and procedures for carrying out these larger-scale tasks. Normally, projects require cross-functional involvement and sharing resources across different units within (and possibly outside) the organization. The simplest measures to start with around projects are health metrics of the efforts themselves. These can be built around status updates, which may ask the following:

- How many projects are active?
- How many are in the queue?
- How many are on hold?
- How many have been completed?

You can go further with the project metrics. Our organization has developed a comprehensive set of measures, including:

- How well projects met the schedule
- How much we deliver against what was expected
- How well we deliver to budget
- Quality of the deliverables (how many defects are present)

As with the first and third quadrants, we also want to use triangulation to ensure a rounded set of measures. To that end, you can add in measures of

- Sponsor/project owner satisfaction with the results
- How well the products of the project are used (level of institutionalization)

Many of the measures of Project/Program Status look like the measures you'll use for goal attainment. This is logical since most projects can be described as a concerted effort to achieve a specific goal.

Strategic Planning and Goal Attainment Measures

If you've developed SMART (specific, measurable, attainable, realistic, timebound) goals, the measurements have already been defined. These will be measures of success for the goals. Even in this case, I warn against chasing the data rather than realizing the dream.

Say your goal is to "increase membership by 50 percent over the next six months." That's a pretty clear goal (specific). It's definitely measurable (current membership compared to membership in six months), attainable (let's assume there are enough potential members to make it attainable), realistic (again, assume that it's not beyond reason), and time-bound (six months from now).

So, you may argue that if you achieve the 50 percent increase, why not chase the data? The goal is in the data—to increase membership! And to a degree you would be absolutely correct. The problem is that we are only working with the stated goal and not the reasons for the goal. This is why the measurement area includes strategic planning. If you purely chase the data, you may find ways to increase the membership that wouldn't meet the underlying intent of the goal (long-term or permanent expansion of the membership base). You may change the rules of what constitutes a "member" so that you can achieve the number. You may offer incentives that only result in a temporary increase (meeting the goal but missing the mark).

Besides the stated measures within the goal definition, you may also want to measure the following:

- The cost to achieve
- The time to achieve (showing progress over time)
- Realized benefits of achieving the goal (a tough one that is rarely captured)

Specifically for the Strategic Planning portion, you'll want measures of the effectiveness of your planning. These may include the following:

- Overall goal attainment (as components of the plan)
- How well you met the plans timeline
- How well you met the plans resource plans (costs, time, effort)
- How well the plan was followed
- How often the plan was revised (the more it is adjusted, the more likely it is a living, useful plan vs. shelf-ware)

While measuring the worth of your strategic plan, achievement of your goals, and the effectiveness of your projects and programs, you will realize that to do these well requires a level of prioritization. They can be either formal or informal, but you need a process for setting priorities in either case.

Priority-Setting Measures

The measures for priority setting, is a lot like measuring accuracy. It's a simple set of measures. Are you keeping to the priorities you've established? Or do you allow the latest need to send your priorities spinning? Do you allow the squeakiest wheel to get the attention? Do all of your plans get thrown out as soon as the first crisis occurs?

Of course, if a true emergency hits, you may have to drop everything and solve the crisis. But, do you find that there is *always* a crisis? Do you find that once you've overcome the emergency that your organization doesn't return to the priority list?

If your organization can't set or keep to defined priorities, then it will have a very difficult time growing. Prioritization not only provides direction, it also includes the identification of tasks, goals, and projects that will *not* be done. To truly mature, an organization, like an individual, must realize it can't do everything asked of it. You have to make some hard decisions. If you can't, you may find that you accomplished a lot—more than you expected—but little that you truly wanted to do.

The last quadrant we'll visit is the one most managers want to start with—Process Health, which is shown in Figure 11-4.

Process Health

The last quadrant you should tackle is Process Health, Quadrant 2.

Figure 11-4. Quadrant 2 of the Answer Key

Concepts

So you've stuck it out and are finally going to have an opportunity to play with efficiency measures. Or perhaps you've skipped to this portion because you *must* have them. Process health measures are the most risky because they are the easiest to abuse. It is the equivalent of a coach having statistics on each player's productivity. Like knowing the batting average of your players against each pitcher they will face in the upcoming series of games. You know their performance in night games, day games, even how long it's been since they ate last. Let's make it even more meaningful and say you also have data for how much things cost, how long it takes, how the resources are allocated, and the quality of work, in all situations.

But you might want even more data if you are going to set your lineup based on data. How about how each has performed based on what they ate. What they drank. What time it is. How much sleep they got the night before. The day of the week. And the list can go on forever. And that's a problem.

The point is simple. While data, measures, and information about how well each worker performs in given situations is usable, it's not *truth*. I've already shared this, so I won't belabor it. But understand that you can't avoid the job of the supervisor, manager, or leader by looking at data. No more than a baseball team's manager can look solely at statistics to set his lineup. You have to know your players. You have to talk to them, work *with* them, and put each in a position to be successful.

I use sports analogies a lot. Not because I like sports (although I do), but because sports provide a great example of how a business *can* be run, how an organization *can* function. Table 11-3 shows a comparison of a sports team to a corporate team. You can choose if you identify it better with a professional, college, or high school sports team—just as you can choose to look at the company as either a large, medium, or small (mom and pop) organization.

Table 11-3. Sports Team–Corporate Team Comparisons

SPORTS TEAM	CORPORATE TEAM
General Manager	CEO
Coach	Manager
Assistant/Position Coach	Supervisor
Players	Workers
Star Players	Star Workers
Competition—other teams	Competition—other companies
Successful Coaches—help players achieve potential	Successful Managers—help workers achieve potential
Successful Players—produce at a high level (recognized stars at their positions)	Successful Workers—produce at a high level (recognized experts in their field)
General managers, coaches, and assistant coaches coach; they don't get to play	CEOs, managers, and supervisors *should* lead; they *shouldn't* do the work

SPORTS TEAM	CORPORATE TEAM
There are exceptions—player coaches	There are exceptions—supervisors who share the workload
Success is measured by the team's results	Success *should* be measured by the team's results
There are exceptions—but it's usually not good when a player's success is put above the team's	There are exceptions—but it's usually not good when a worker's success is put above the team's
The best coaches *know* their players; not only what the players can do on the court/field, but *who* they are. The best coaches care about the whole person, not just the athlete.	The best managers *should* know their workers; not only what their workers do on the job, but *who* they are as people. The best managers care about the whole person, not just the worker.

The analogy truly has no bounds. You can take it as far as you like. You can apply it to any aspect of your business. Sports teams—college and professional both—are great examples of how work teams function.

If your work team were a sports team, how successful would they be?

When a sports manager looks at statistics for individuals and the team, she uses these to improve each. Her intent is to find ways to make the team as successful as possible. She *can* use the data as a starting point for conversations about the player's performance. And if she finds the player not performing up to the needs of the position, she will most likely try to develop the player's talents. The team has already invested money in the player. But in the end, if she can't get the player to perform at the needed levels, she may let him go and have to recruit new players. (I even like that fact that players are recruited and drafted—not "hired.")

A good manager will do the same with performance measures. He won't use the measures to manipulate the workers into changing behaviors. He will use the information to work with the employee to improve her abilities, developing her as best he can. If, like the sports manager, he fails, he may have to let her go and hire new workers.

Remember, if the workforce is your organization's greatest asset, then the manager's job is to develop those assets to their highest potential. Sports teams know the greatest assets—and they are paid accordingly.

The manager's job is to develop the workforce to their highest potential.

Process Health Measures

You may want to measure the cost of everything. You may want to know how much each person is paid per hour (even if salaried) so you can determine how much laughter in the halls is costing the company. You may want to be able to show how much it costs the company for the annual picnic. Or the costs of equipment, facilities, and furniture. These measures are *not* the ones you need.

Process health measures are about the process, not the people. How much does it cost to perform a given process in the way it's done today? It's all about process improvement. If you can find ways to improve a process, one of the measures of success may be less cost to the customer, organization, or society.

So, how much does the process cost? How much does it cost for each of the steps? Feel free to include the hourly rate of the employees but remember why you're measuring it—to improve.

Most process-improvement methods are very good at measuring the right things. Besides cost, you'll find most want you to also measure how long it takes to perform a task or process step. How long does your customer have to wait for the service? How long does it take for you to perform the service?

One example, Lean Six Sigma (a process-improvement methodology) is based on flow and defect removal. Flow is all about how the process moves from point A to Z. Do you incur backlogs, stockpiles of inventory, or lost time? Does it take you days to complete a process that in actual hands-on time takes only hours? How much wait time is there between and within steps? Six Sigma will also want to minimize defects (to a Six Sigma level, 3.4 defects per million opportunities). All methods use measures to determine how well they improve the organization's processes.

These are measures of quality. Errors, rework, defects, issues, and problems are all words that fit under process quality. Your job is to use the quality measures to find improvements to the process to reduce (and hopefully eliminate) them. This may include training or retraining your workers. It doesn't include "pushing" your workers to be more diligent. To be fair, you may need them to pay more attention to detail, to be more focused, and to be more diligent. The difference will be in how you do that. You shouldn't "demand, cajole, force, or manipulate" them. You should develop them.

Resource allocation is another measure you can use in Process Health. Besides the process steps, you may have the wrong mix of resources doing the wrong steps at the wrong times. Beware though. Throwing more resources (money, manpower, or equipment) at a problem rarely fixes it over the long term. You'll need to dissect the problem and find solutions that will stand the test of time.

A simplified set of measures includes the following:

- The number of process steps
- The number of handoffs between departments
- Wait times
- The time to complete (by steps/overall)
- Touch time (how much time is active vs. the wait time)
- The costs in the process

  - Materials
  - Shipping
  - Storage
  - Production

- Resources allocated (by steps/overall)
- The number of defects per opportunity
- The types of defects
- Process repeatability

  - Is it documented?
  - Is it done the same way each time?

- Is it tweakable?
- Is the process under control?

The Process Health quadrant, like the others, can be a powerful and meaningful tool for organizational improvement. The risk is that management will use the metrics to improve the worker (rather than develop him) or to influence behavior (rather than improve processes). If you are confident that these measures will be used properly, they can reap great benefits. Process improvement (and therefore Process Health) is at the core of most organizational development efforts.

Recap

Quadrants 2, 3, and 4 of the Answer Key provide important insights into the organization's overall health. Each has its own viewpoint—business, worker, and leadership—and each has benefits and risks. There are other measures you can collect, analyze and use to build metrics. The Answer Key provides a foundation and framework for a comprehensive metrics program.

Besides providing meaningful insights to the organization's health, these advanced metrics also help the organization mature into becoming a data-driven organization. The metamorphosis required to become a metric based organization is not an easy one. It requires patience and unwavering integrity on the part of leadership, management, and service providers.

After Product/Service Health, I recommend moving to Organization Health (Quadrant 3) in which you use measures like Employee Satisfaction, Training, Work Environment, and Reward & Recognition. This is the metric with the lowest risk factor and great potential to build a loyal, dedicated, and happy workforce.

I suggest tackling Future Health (Quadrant 4) next. The only problem may be that your organization isn't ready to look to the future. It may be struggling to maintain its status quo. I fully believe that organizations (and people) can't afford to "strive to survive." To succeed you have to shoot for more than keeping your head above the water. You have to swim to shore. But, not everyone agrees. If your organization isn't concerned with the future, you may have to skip this quadrant. But if you have strategic plans, long-term goals, or have projects in the works—tackle Future Health metrics next.

Finally, I suggest you fully delve into Process Health. It's important to note that if you or your organization is implementing a process improvement effort, you will likely be doing some Process Health measures for those efforts. I'm not in any way trying to deter you from doing so. Any of these metrics and their measures can be used to answer specific root questions. I am suggesting that you don't create a stand-alone metrics program to provide organizational health monitoring in this quadrant until you've built up enough equity in your organization that your workforce trusts your intentions and use of these measures.

Conclusion

Advanced metrics are very useful and can help an organization grow in many ways. They also introduce risks to the organization. To mitigate these risks and get the most benefits from the metrics, I highly recommend you work from root questions for any metrics you want to create. The metrics should only "live" as long as they answer the root question and as long as the question is still in need of answering.

If you must create a metrics program that lives on its own account, without a specific root question, I highly recommend you start with Product/Service Health (effectiveness). Once that is fully implemented and you've built up a level of trust and understanding of the ways to use (and *not* use) metrics, look into incorporating the other three quadrants. Incorporate them in the following order:

- Quadrant 3: Organization Health
- Quadrant 4: Future Health
- Quadrant 2: Process Health (efficiency)

Creating the Service Catalog

How to Enhance the Report Card

One of my biggest challenges when I created the Report Card for my organization was getting the leadership to agree to a list of core or key services. Since I successfully won the battle of using effectiveness measures over efficiency ones, I would need a list of the services (or products) to be evaluated in the Service/Product Health Metrics.

Many organizations are function-centered. You can see this in the organization chart and the way the parts of the organization work with each other. There are sections for marketing, customer relations, project design, and development, test, and implementation. There are areas whose focus is customer support like help desks and second-tier support functions. These units are not focused on a given service or even the concept of services. They are focused on the functions they provide. They are focused on the "task at hand" and the "job."

This is not necessarily a bad thing. But it is in direct contrast to what you get when you structure your organization around services. By focusing on services, your organization can truly embrace continuous improvement and become a more effective team.

Think of it this way: if you are functionally focused, you concentrate on delivering your functions to your customer—internal or external. Once you have completed your part of the process and have finished your tasks, your interest in the process is done. On the other hand, if you are service-centered, there are no "hand offs." Each function understands how their efforts fit into the overall delivery of the service. Being service-oriented encourages teamwork. It encourages a customer-centered viewpoint. It moves an organization away from individualism (including departmental silos) and moves the organization toward maturity.

Besides the benefits to the organization's maturation, being service-oriented helps in the development of meaningful metrics. This is especially true if you are working on the first quadrant of the Answer Key, Product/Service Health. Since the quadrant is focused on the customers' viewpoint and on improving the health of the services and products you provide—having the organization focused on those same services makes the metrics much easier.

Since our organization was primarily service-oriented, the leadership agreed to start our metric program with an assessment of the health of the key or core services. The problem was getting the directors of the different areas within the organization to agree on which services were core.

While I innocently (and naively) thought this should be a simple decision, I soon found out that I was wrong. Where I wanted to know which services should be considered "core" simply to determine which ones to build metrics for, the directors saw this list as a determination of what was important and what wasn't.

I didn't even consider that FUD (fear, uncertainty, and doubt) would be a factor for the directors. I forgot that reactions to metrics are not based on position, paycheck, or power. Fear is a human emotion—and our leaders are just as human as the entry-level staff members.

So, my innocent question about which services were key to the organization created an unexpected firestorm of debate. If the CEO didn't include a service that a director thought was integral for his group, that director feared that the service was expendable. Perhaps when financial cuts had to be made in the future, these non-key services would be at risk. This was especially real at the time, due to the economic woes the United States experienced in the early twenty-first century. So, every director fought to have as many of his services included as possible. Any peer recommendations to exclude a service were seen as an attack against that director's security and that director's group.

My good intentions didn't matter a bit. I even made the mistake of trying to convince these directors that their perception was wrong; that no one was looking to use these metrics to determine how to downsize the organization.

That was a colossal mistake. Where I was consistently careful to mitigate the workers' FUD, I missed the same opportunity with leadership.

Good intentions don't outweigh poor execution.

So, I created an uphill battle for myself that culminated, as you may have guessed, in having to move forward without a list of key services. Instead, I selected seven services that had high customer use and which I felt the directors would agree were among the key services—but not, in any way, a complete list. These services included e-mail, calendaring, the service desk, the network, telephones, printing, and electronic storage services.

In an ideal situation (which requires that the organization be on its way toward maturity), the service catalog would be created easily and as an integral part of the organization's natural definition of itself. If the organization is introspective, it will want to know what services (and products) it provides. Along with the "what," the organization will want to know the who, the how, and especially the why.

Who is the customer? Not the next person or unit in the process, but the final consumer.

When I say "how," you don't have to have the process spelled out (although that would be nice). By "how" I mean you have to know what goes into the service/product. In essence, another "who." Who is involved in providing the service/product? Which units or departments?

The "why" relates to the customer. What is the purpose of the service/product? Why does it have value? Why would your customer "pay" for it?

How to Develop a Service Catalog

While a service catalog is not a requirement for a Service/Product Health metric program, it can definitely help. So, let's take a moment to look at how to create one and then use it.

To create a service catalog, you will need to take each service and run it through a simple analysis. Before you start, take a pre-step to determine what business you are in. Check your mission statement. Why does your organization exist? What is its purpose? If you have a good feel for that, then determine the "types" of services that you provide. One of the by-products of our metric effort has been the identification of service types or categories. Being an IT service organization, we ended up with the following:

- Utilities (including network, telephone, e-mail, and electronic storage)
- Support (general support, like the service desk)
- Academic services (specific support services for the academy)

These categories can help, but are not necessary. If you provide only a few services, like McDonalds, you may not need to break out the services into categories. McDonalds could categorize by meal (breakfast, lunch/dinner), by type of food (entrée, side, desert), or by cost (dollar menu, value meals, individual items). But, the question is, how useful is this? The answer will be in the metrics and what questions you are trying to answer.

Service/Product Health Service Catalog

You will need to take the following steps in order to create the catalog.

Step 1: Identify the service

This can be as simple as writing down the name of the service. What is it known as? How does the customer refer to it?

Step 2: Determine if the service fits within your predefined categories

If the service does not fit within your predefined categories—is it because you missed the inclusion of a particular category? Or is it a service that doesn't fit within your mission? If the service doesn't fit, perhaps you should stop providing it.

Step 3: Identify the service providers

Who within the organization is responsible for the delivery of the service? It may be a cross-unit effort, or it could be part of the definition of the org chart. The ideal situation would require finding the product/service providers meant going across the org chart to identify the different places where contributors exist. Rarely is a service provided by only one person or unit—even in a functionally-focused organization.

Basically, what are the assets involved in the provision of the service or product? What and who goes into satisfying the customers' needs? These insights are some of the benefits a service catalog gives the organization.

Step 4: Identify the customer base

A simple way to look at identifying the customer base is to look at who uses the outputs from the service/product. It really doesn't matter if the final customer is internal or external to the organization. It doesn't matter if the service/product is a "for-profit" or "not-for-profit" endeavor. You need to know who the customers are. Is it a large customer base? Is the customer base a niche market?

Step 5: What is the service environment?

- What is the service's competition? Is it a "monopolized" service? Does the customer have choices in who provides the service?
- Is it a local market?
- Is it a geographic market?
- Is it a national market?

Step 6: What is the service level agreement?

Service level agreements are essentially contracts between the organization and its customers. It clearly defines, for anyone interested, what will be delivered and how it will be delivered. If possible, it should be more than what is agreed to be provided—it should capture the customers' expectations.

If you can't directly ask customers about their expectations, which is the case when you have a large customer base, you need to determine the expectations from existing information. You can glean expectations from sources that explicitly state the requirements. Written agreements, statements of work, or contracts are good sources of information. Many times your own marketing literature will capture the level of service promised or wanted. Sometimes you have to find expectations from implied or suggested inputs like informal promises made by one department for another or requests by the customer.

Another source is the feedback you'll receive in the data collection process when you are measuring the health of the service. Even though you haven't developed your metrics program yet, you very likely have already been using customer satisfaction feedback tools like surveys, comment cards, or unsolicited feedback.

Regardless of where you get the information, the goal is to determine what the customer expects of the service. This will be useful when developing expectations for the metrics.

Step 7: Costs

If it's a fee-based service, what is the cost? Even when you are not a profit center, there may be "costs" to obtaining the service. It could require a membership of some type or that you are a registered purchaser/owner of a product. Some of our services had no other associated costs beyond customers being either a faculty, staff, or student at our institution.

These steps are also logical headers for the catalog. You can organize them using your service categories. You can also organize them using any of the earlier "steps." If you create an electronic (online) version of your catalog, you could allow searches or sorting on any of these steps.

There are other important questions you can ask and answer about your services. One of these crosses the boundaries between a Service/Product Health focused catalog and one built around Process Health. What are the key/core services? This question doesn't answer a customer question, but it can be answered by them. The answer is useful for the Service/Product Health–based catalog, so that you know which services to measure (assuming you don't have the resources to measure them all). From the Process Health-based viewpoint, the key/core services tell you other important information.

Process Health (Efficiency) Service Catalog

If you will use the results of the service catalog for internal process improvement (the second quadrant of the Answer Key specifically), you will need to ask a few additional questions.

Step 8: Key/Core services

The classification of the services and identification of ones considered "key" or "core" to the organization's success can be determined by asking some of the following questions:

- Which services are core to the organization's success?

  - Which are the main income drivers?
  - Which are seen as the customer-generators?

- Which services are of higher priority?

  - Where should *most* of the resources be allocated?
  - Where should the *best* resources be allocated?

- Which services are seen as representative of the organization's brand?

  - Which services have to be done particularly well?
  - Which will help set the customers' view of the organization as a whole?

Step 9: Dependencies

Along with the identification of which services/products are essential to the organization's success, it is also helpful to understand where and how a service is dependent upon another service. This builds toward the clarification of service families. The questions you'll want to ask include the following:

- Are there internal dependencies?

  - What is required to deliver the service?
  - Are other services dependent on this service?

- How does this service fit into the overall service architecture of the organization?

  - Is this a foundational service?
  - Is this service a pillar for other services? For a key service?

When you analyze the services in the service catalog, you will use these two possible viewpoints (effectiveness or efficiency) to determine how you will build your metric. So, it comes down to the root question (again). Is the root question a Service/Product Health–type of question, or is it focused on Process Health? There are, of course, opportunities to use both measures. If your root question is not about a group of services, but about a specific service, you may need information from each type of catalog.

Let's say your root question is "How can I increase the customer base for service X?" This question needs a lot of work. How much of an increase? Why do you want to increase the customer base? What is the actual thing you want to achieve? But, let's use this as our starting point. Perhaps the unit that provides this service needs to increase its customer base by 30 percent in order for the organization to consider it a viable part of the service portfolio. So, the manager of this unit, the service provider, wants simply to know how his unit can survive.

The answers to this very specific question can use information from multiple quadrants. It will be important to have information from the customers' viewpoint. Since your goal is to increase the number of customers (by 30 percent), it should be obvious that you need to see the service from the customers' perspective.

You will also benefit from looking at the efficiency with which you deliver the service. If you can improve the delivery, usage, and or customer satisfaction, you'll have a good chance of gaining more customers. While Effectiveness measures will tell you if you are succeeding (and where to focus your efforts), Efficiency measures will normally tell you "how" to improve. For example, if you determine that you could benefit from delivering the service in a more timely manner (faster), you'll want to look at ways to do it more efficiently—to do the internal processes "faster." Of course, you'll also want to ensure that you are delivering it at a high quality. You can't improve the speed of delivery and have drastic drops in quality. Both of these are internal process viewpoints.

You can even possibly benefit from some Future Health measures. You will likely need to prove the need for additional resources. You will also likely want assurances that if your unit reaches the goal (30 percent increase) that it will be spared the hatchet. This means that you may want items in the strategic plan that include if-then statements. If you succeed, what happens? Of course, if you fail, the consequences can also be captured. Do you have to achieve the goal in a month? A year? Three years? Is incremental improvement over time acceptable?

So, the goal that is driving your efforts may have come from the Future Health quadrant. It may well be a part of the strategic plan. It can also be considered a "project" or part of a program. In any case, the results are obviously future-focused.

So, does the Employee View fit here also? How does the Organizational Health play? First off, it doesn't have to. Note that the Future Health's inclusion wasn't necessary. Effectiveness and Efficiency are critical, but measures of the strategic level or the project/program levels are not as critical. That said, let's see if it fits.

The first question is how will the results of the efforts affect the workers? Will jobs be lost if the service is deleted? Will the workers be laid off or will they be reassigned? If they succeed, are their jobs secured? If so, for how long? How will the situation affect morale? How will the success or failure affect morale of the unit? How will it affect the morale of the rest of the organization? All of these questions are within the Organizational Health quadrant and all are valid concerns.

Granted that the questions for the third and fourth quadrants didn't require the service catalog at all, but I wanted to give you the full picture of how the measures from the different quadrants could be used to answer a specific root question about a particular service. The catalog was helpful especially for questions derived from the Service/Product and Process Health quadrants.

Bonus Material

Service catalogs are essentially a mature behavior, and there are others that work well with a Metrics Program.

In *Why Organizations Struggle So Hard to Improve So Little*, I warned against trying to implement mature behaviors in an organization suffering from immaturity. Metrics was listed as one of the most risky ones to undertake.

Along with metrics, some of the other behaviors that are difficult to implement can actually be positively affected if you just attempt a metric program. Even if you are not fully successful, you can have influence on your organization's adoption of the following:

- Process maps/process definitions
- Process improvement methodologies
- Training plans
- Strategic plans
- Customer feedback tools

These can be encouraged greatly by a metric program. As discussed in Chapter 13 on standards and benchmarks, metrics can drive the organization toward other improvement efforts. When you are trying to develop a process health picture of the organization, you will benefit from having your processes defined (much as the Service/Product Health metrics benefit from a Service/Product catalog). To improve something, you need to understand it. A clear and complete definition of your processes is a necessary starting point for improving those processes.

A good process definition will help you improve the process just through the capture of it.

A metric program can make the need for process definitions obvious to the organization—making its acceptance easier. These process maps are usually the byproduct of a process improvement methodology.

Your organization may have already selected a preferred process improvement methodology. These methods—from Total Quality, to Six Sigma, to Lean, etc.—will help define a lot of the information you will use in your metrics. And your metrics may help define which methods will work best for your organization.

Another tool that will be encouraged by metrics and in turn will support your metric program is a training plan. Positional and personal professional development plans will directly support metrics built around the Employee Viewpoint and Process Health.

Strategic plans are a necessity for the Future Health quadrant and for the future of your organization. The metrics for strategic progress, and the strategic plan, work together to build toward a desired future.

Customer feedback, which comes in a myriad of forms, can also be driven by the Service/Product Health metric. This one is pretty obvious, but by doing metrics, you drive the organization to institute the concept of feedback into the day-to-day operations of the organization, rather than make it only an annual or event-driven activity. The organization will start to seek out, capture, and use customer feedback as a way of doing business.

A metric program will drive more than just analyzing, reporting, and investigating the things being measured. It can have side benefits as a catalyst for other improvement efforts, tools, and byproducts. It is a necessary stepping stone to developing a Product/Service Health–focused metrics program and is a great tool for maturing your organization. It will support or inspire the creation of strategic plans, process improvement efforts, service level agreements, and clear expectations. As with most improvement efforts, if done right, you will gain many side-benefits throughout the journey.

Recap

The service catalog is not a mandatory component of a metrics program. It is a useful tool, especially if your metrics are service-focused, as in a Service/Product Health metric.

Trying to develop a service catalog can lead you into negative, resistance-laden encounters. The same FUD factors that can adversely affect your gathering of data can also negatively affect your creation of a valid catalog. But the risk is well worth it. You will benefit in many ways—from learning more about your organization and customers, to determining what you should and shouldn't be doing. The service catalog and the effort to create it, can be a catalyst for changing your organization's focus from a siloed, "me-first" attitude to one founded on teamwork. Sometimes all it takes to bring a group of people together is a common goal—and the service catalog provides that common focus.

All of the quadrants in the Answer Key can "play" in the service catalog, but it is likely that you will have either an Effectiveness- or an Efficiency-based service catalog. Remember to leverage the indirect benefits (by-products) of the process of creating and maintaining your catalog.

Conclusion

There are many mature behaviors that a metrics program can encourage and work well with. The service catalog may be the most obvious for the Service/Product Health metrics. Others fit the other quadrants of the Answer Key better, as follows:

- *Process Health*: Process maps and definitions
- *Organizational Health*: Professional development plans, employee feedback, and process improvement methods
- *Future Health*: Strategic plans

The service catalog is an excellent tool for an organization seeking to do general improvement efforts. It can help the organization understand what business it's in.

By bouncing the service catalog against the organization's mission (and possibly vision), the organization can determine if it's doing the right things (Effectiveness). The details of the service catalog (who provides, to whom, with what expectations, and at what cost) can provide valuable insights by themselves if the organization is doing things the right way (Efficiency).

Establishing Standards and Benchmarks

Standards and benchmarks, in the realm of metrics, are strongly interconnected. Standards, from the Industrial Age through today, are invaluable for providing a means for interoperability. Standards in the industrial world allow you to use a light bulb that you bought at Walmart in a lamp that you bought at a high-end designer furniture store. Standards allow you to get gas for your car from any station in the United States, without worrying if the gas pump nozzle will fit into your gas tank. From the ingredients label on a can of soup to the technology that allows you to tune your radio, standards give consistency and interoperability for manufacturers, distributors, builders, and customers alike.

Unlike the manufacturing industry, performance measures are more akin to an art than a science. The use of standards for how we measure things for improvement is arguable. What need is there? If our questions are unique, and thus our answers are unique, why do we need standards for our measures?

Since I advocate creating measures to answer your specific questions, I have trouble taking up the other side of the debate. Why indeed?

I would love to have standards for how you develop metrics; as in the use of expectations over targets, for example. Or for the definition of the data owner. But, standards for performance measures as a whole? Why?

Before I answer this question, let's look at benchmarks and why I think the two are interrelated.

Benchmarks: Best Used to Provide Meaningful Comparisons

Benchmarks are best used to provide meaningful comparisons for your metrics. Outside of defining expectations, you usually want to know how well you perform against your peers. If you're ambitious, you'll want to know how well you perform compared to the best—the best in your industry, the best in your country and, perhaps if you're really ambitious, the best in the world.

Benchmarks are a blessing and a curse.

Benchmarks are also useful for drawing a "line in the sand." You can establish a baseline from your own measures so that you can compare your present performance to your past performance. This is critical when your goal is to improve.

Establish Baselines

One of my joys when working with clients on metrics is helping them establish a baseline; mostly because it forces them to put the metrics upfront in their improvement-process thinking. I almost always run into goals to improve effectiveness, improve efficiency, improve productivity, or improve customer satisfaction.

"Improve" is a lousy verb to use in a goal statement. You have to qualify it with more information—as in "how much" of an improvement? By a certain percentage? By a certain number?

My favorite recollection of the poor use of an "improve" goal was in my parish council. I was hoping to bring organizational development expertise to the council. I was teamed with a retired police officer, a successful business owner, a nurse, our priest, and a retired grandmother. The goal? Improve membership in the church. I wasn't perturbed because I had seen this type of goal (increase, decrease, etc.) many times before.

I said, "Improve membership—by how much?"

"What do you mean?" asked the ex-police officer.

"I mean, if it's our goal to improve membership, how will we know that we achieved it?"

The business owner said, "Oh, you're trying to get us to set a goal."

I countered, "I thought that was the intention—to come up with goals for the year?"

"Yes," said the business owner, "but you're trying to set us up for failure. We'll set a number and if we don't reach it, we will have failed."

Now I sat in stunned silence. I may have actually opened and closed my mouth once or twice. "Uh. Well. Would you be happy with just one more family joining?"

"Sure," said the nurse.

"Anything more than that is gravy!" said the ex-police officer.

I turned to the priest, still in shock. "You'll feel we've achieved this goal if we add just one family?"

He shook his head no. As the leader of the team, and our parish, his input carried the equivalent weight of a CEO.

"How many families join each year now?" I asked

"Two or three a year," the priest answered.

"So if we do nothing, we'd achieve this goal?"

He nodded in the affirmative.

We eventually worked out a reasonable and measurable increase over the expected growth without making any changes. The purpose of the goal was to build up the parish. The purpose of the metric was to see if our efforts were successful. We had plans, ideas, and activities scheduled for the purpose of bringing in new members and bringing back parishioners who had fallen away. We needed to (1) set a goal to focus our efforts and ideas; and (2) set measures to tell us what worked and what didn't.

We also needed a benchmark. We could not determine if any of our efforts were producing the desired result if we didn't know the norm. Consider the benchmark in this case a "control group" or value. You have to know what you get if you do nothing different. Then, when you do new things in new ways, you can at least assume that any changes that you made caused the change to the outcome. Even if you implement so many changes that you can't determine what exactly worked or what exactly didn't work, you at least know whether the overall effort(s) worked.

So, benchmarks basically allow you to know where you are and, therefore, where you end up.

A benchmark is the starting line.

Even when a benchmark is used to compare you against your peers, it is essentially a starting line—a baseline to measure your progress against. The purest form of the benchmark is when you set it as an internal baseline (vs. an external comparison). This allows you to measure progress.

Set Benchmarks Responsibly

Benchmarks falter from time to time when leaders want to use the comparison benchmark as the baseline. Most times, it starts with something like, "Can you get our competitors' average availability, response time, or customer satisfaction ratings so that we can compare ourselves to it?"

This requires that the performance of your competitors is a good starting point.

My simple and first argument against chasing this data is: "What if you are already better than your competitors? Does that mean you're doing well enough?"

And usually the leader that sent me after the data, who fully believes that the organization is woefully lagging behind competitors, is not ready for this question. I usually have to ask it twice.

"No, we still need to improve..."

So, while gathering information on another organization's performance can be enlightening, if your goal is to improve, it is not overly useful. If your goal is to be better than your peers, then, of course, this benchmark is essential. Even if your goal is to be better than your competitors, you'll need to know (1) whether your efforts are helping you improve; and (2) how far you are from the performance of your peers (if you're better than your peers, are you done?).

So, if you choose to look only internally at your performance, standards are not necessary. But, if (and when—because eventually you'll want to see how you compare to others) you decide to compare your performance to your peers or competitors, standards will be critical. You can't compare yourself to others when the methods of measurement are different.

Let's say you define the availability of the network as the amount of time without an outage divided by the total amount of time in a given period.

- Availability = 1,440 minutes (number of minutes in one day (or 24 hours)) – 20 minutes (of outage) divided by 1,440 minutes
- Availability = (1,440 – 20) ÷ 1,440 = 98.6%

So far, so good. But, let's say your closest competitor (or peer) has a 100 percent availability rate for the same period. Are you going to step up your game a bit? Are you going to work harder? Is your competitor doing better than you?

Well, without standards, you can't tell if your competitor is doing a better job than you. What if you define an outage as any time span that your customers cannot use the network, but your competitors consider an outage as only those times when the network is unavailable due to unscheduled or unplanned downtime? In other words, let's say that during the same 24-hour period, your competitor had scheduled maintenance for four hours. If you define an outage as any time the service is unavailable (which is likely the way customers will interpret it), then the competitor's availability *should* be reported as follows:

- Competitor Availability: (1,440 – 240) ÷ 1,440 = 83.3%

If you had all of the raw data for your competitor's reports, you could use your personal "standard" and determine how well you perform against your competitor. But this is highly unlikely to happen. What you will get, if you are extremely lucky, is the "score"—and even that can be difficult to get from your peers and competitors.

So, how you define an outage compared to the way your competitor defines an outage is critical to your use of their measures as a benchmark.

Standards Allow Comparison to Others

Standards in performance measurement come down to providing the ability to compare measures between different organizations. Just as manufacturing standards allow you to use your products seamlessly with another organization's products, standards in performance measurement allow you to "use your measures" seamlessly with another organization's measures. If there were standardization of performance measures, you could "borrow" another unit's measures for your own purposes. If you had the same questions, you could trust that that metrics used by Company A could be used to measure the same things in your organization.

Without standards, it is hard to imagine how you could use the metrics of a different organization—even if you had the same exact root questions. And using measures produced by another organization as a benchmark is even more improbable.

Getting Good Data

This problem with benchmarks and standards for performance measurement also creates problems for well-meaning organizations that seek to provide data warehouses of information. This information invariably is intended for your comparison. To make the data warehouse effective, it has to have a clear set of standards for the information provided by the different organizations.

HDI, a third-party survey company, offers benchmarking on customer satisfaction data by controlling data definitions. HDI administers the survey to your customers, collects the responses, and provides you with reports, analysis, and raw data. Since HDI standardizes its questions (the same questions are asked along with the same set of possible replies on a 5-point Likert scale), it is able to offer you comparisons against other organizations, including the following:

- Comparison of your scores (average, percentage satisfied, or other) against all other organizations who have used the HDI service
- Comparison of your scores with others in your industry (self-selected from a list)
- Comparison of your scores to the top nth percentile of others' customer base

This provides you with a higher confidence in the comparability of the information. Of course, there are some drawbacks. Only organizations that use

HDI's service are included in the comparison, and your main competitors or peers may not be among these organizations. Even if you compare your results against the entire customer base, this still may not reflect the pool you want to compare to. Another minor drawback is that you are forced to use one set of questions. No deviations. If you want to use the 10-point scale suggested by Reichheld in *The Ultimate Question*, you could not use HDI's service. And even if you could use the 10-point scale, you could not compare the data to those who used a 5-point scale.

The Goal: Reliable Industry Standards

Industry standards for performance measures would make it possible to truly benchmark, rank, and compare peer organizations. It should be feasible to convince an *industry* (like higher education IT) to standardize performance measures before the chance of adopting *universal* standards. The tighter you can make the pool for standardization, the easier it should be to come to agreement. Higher education information technology is a pretty specific pool. If you started with information technology performance measures—your pool for coming to consensus on the standards is too large. If you narrow it to *education* information technology, you're doing better. *Higher education* tightens it a little more.

Consensus is required for success. Publishing a standard does not make it effective. You must have the majority of organizations (in your industry) using the standard to make it useful. Since you need high participation in the use of the standards, it logically follows that you should involve as many of the target audience in the creation of the standard as possible

I offer that the consortium structure is the best bet for creating standards for performance measures. The consortium creates, evaluates, reviews, and manages standards for an industry. The problem may be that the "industry" in this case is hard to define. Of course, if you do as I suggested and find a tighter definition of the target audience, you can make it happen. But, looking at performance measurement as an industry is obviously too large. So, as a performance measurement expert, you'll have to define your "industry" to build a consortium. If you have some standards for performance measurement to reference, you are ahead of the game.

Recap

Standards are tools that allow for interoperability. In the case of performance measures, standards allow for comparison between organizations.

Benchmarks are either the starting line (baseline) for your improvement efforts or a goal for you to achieve. As a baseline, it helps you determine how far you have to progress to achieve your goals, how well you're getting there, and how far you have come. As a goal, it represents how good you want to become—"as good as Company A" or "better than the average."

To have real external benchmarks, you must have standards that are in agreement among the organizations you choose to compare to.

If you can find or develop standards for your performance measures, and your peers agree to them, you can compare measures.

START YOUR OWN CONSORTIUM

Depending on your industry, there may be little to no standards for performance metrics. If you lack standards, you will also lack the ability to benchmark against your competitors or peers. Creating a consortium for developing, publishing, and using standards for your industry is a feasible answer to this need. I created the Consortium for the Establishment of Information Technology Performance Standards (CEITPS) in 2009 to address the lack of standards for performance measures in Higher Education IT. This effort has been more difficult than I anticipated.

The population I have been working with—metrics analysts in peer institutions—all agree that the ability to compare performance metrics is critical to organizational leaders' acceptance of metrics. They also readily agree that this is nearly impossible without standards for the measures that make up the metrics.

I'm not sure if the difficulty in getting anyone to draft standards is a result of a low priority for measures comparison or a fear of the future environment if standards are created and adopted. In some situations, standards can be "enforced"—especially if there are governing bodies with power to do so. If you are like most us, you'll have to build consensus, communicate the standards, market them, and then hope for adoption. There is a real reason to fear your own success in this endeavor. If you succeed and have standards adopted in your industry, you will then be asked to follow through with allowing comparison of your organization's performance with your peers. No excuses, no subjective "feelings" of how good you really are. You'll have real values to compare against. While most metric analysts won't "fear" this situation, many organizational leaders may.

I've had so little success in getting peer assistance in the development of standards (although the CEITPS has a healthy membership) that I have turned to alternative methods for drafting standards. At the next national conference, where most of these representatives will be present, I plan to lead a set of group sessions to create drafts for key measures. I will start with Effectiveness measures as defined in the Answer Key. My hope is that the consortium will be able to draft a full set of measures for our first standard: service availability based on outages.

Conclusion

Standards and benchmarks are inextricably joined at the hip. Benchmarks are meaningless if there are no standards to ensure that definitions and measurements are consistent across organizations. This is particularly an issue with external benchmarks, where you are attempting to rank yourself against your peers and competitors.

Standards are unnecessary if you are only using internal benchmarks.

Benchmarks are better used for demonstrating progress against a baseline than they are for comparisons against outside organizations.

When are standards and benchmarks required?

- When you are comparing your performance against competitors or peers.

  - External benchmarks are required to determine
    - the average performance of your comparison group
    - the range of performance of your comparison group
    - the top performers in your comparison group
  - Standards are required to ensure you are comparing apples to apples with brand, type, color, and size. In other words, standards are required to ensure that you are comparing specifics.

- When you are determining a realistic goal, tracking progress to a goal, or deciding if you have achieved a goal.

  - Internal benchmarks are required to determine
    - a norm to help set realistic goals for improvement
    - a baseline or starting point to track progress from your current state
    - a means for determining the achievement of a goal (when that goal was defined as achieving a specific level of improvement)

Benchmarks are also useful in determining if your efforts in organizational development or process improvement are having a positive effect on your environment, services, or products. If you anticipate your efforts (especially changes to processes) are going to have an effect on performance, you'll want baselines for any possible areas concerned. If you can also get historical data, it will help to determine if changes are due to your efforts or if they are normal fluctuations.

Respecting the Power of Metrics

The short length of this chapter is intentional in order to help you focus on the power of metrics. You must respect the power of metrics and be careful of the damage they can do to your organization if wielded improperly.

When I was a young Airman in the United States Air Force, I had the privilege to work with a civilian electrician, Tom Lunnen. Tom was a no-nonsense guy and a good friend. He was older than me (still is) and helped me with good advice on more than one occasion. Perhaps the best advice he gave me was to respect the power of electricity because even trained electricians have been badly hurt—or worse—performing electrical work. Electrical injury is the second leading cause of fatalities in the construction industry.

I bring this up because metrics are like electricity. Metrics can be used to do a lot of good. As a tool, they can help us understand our environment. They can help us evaluate how well our efforts are going. They can make communication easier and clearer. But like electricity, metrics must be respected. If you follow the rules, you can use electricity—and metrics—to make life better. But, even if you follow the rules, there remains the potential to cause damage. The risks are high enough that you have to decide in each case whether the benefits make it worth it.

Most of this book discusses how to develop, analyze, report, and most importantly, *use* metrics for improvement. But unlike most organizational improvement tools, like training plans, strategic plans, and employee recognition programs, metrics can do as much harm as good if used improperly. And in most cases, it's because the wielder of the data isn't well-trained or wary enough to understand the powerful but risky nature of metrics.

Metrics have the potential to do more harm than good.

As I've already covered, you have to work hard to get to the *right* root question: develop an abstract picture of the answer, identify the information needed to paint the picture, and then painstakingly set up processes for collecting, analyzing, and reporting the metric. And through all this, you have to double- and triple-check everything from the data to the collection methods to the metric itself, and then, finally, the root question.

Be diligent and rigorous in your efforts because it is extremely easy to make errors. Even when all of your data are verified, you can have errors in interpretation. I once had an interesting debate with a coworker over the concept of facts. He felt that metrics, at least good ones, were facts; and if they weren't facts, we shouldn't use them to demonstrate performance. I had to explain, at least from my view, that metrics are not facts. Metrics are first and foremost indicators. They give us insight, but they are not necessarily the *truth* that is being sought. They are not facts.

Metrics are not facts. They are indicators.

Metrics: Indicators or Facts?

This distinction as to whether metrics are indicators or facts is at the core of proper metrics use. If we treat metrics as facts, we run the real risk of making decisions too hastily.

How about measures or data? Is the speedometer on your car relaying facts about your speed? Is it precisely accurate or does it have a +/- deviation? If your speedometer says your going 55 and the police radar says you're going 58, which is truth?

You may argue that while there are variances in measuring devices, there is obviously a true speed you were traveling at. And, I'd agree. You were definitely traveling at a specific speed at a given moment. But, I have little faith that any device used to capture a particular moment in time is accurate enough to call that measure a "fact."

Let's try subjective measures. Say I ask you to rate your satisfaction with my service on a scale from 1 to 5, with 1 being highly dissatisfied, 2 being dissatisfied, 3 being neutral, 4 being satisfied, and 5 being highly satisfied. I should be able to consider your choice to be a fact, right?

Wrong.

The only fact that I can ascertain on a survey is that the answer I receive is the answer you gave. And even then we may have errors. In customer satisfaction surveys, we often find that respondents get the numbers inverted and give 1s when they meant to give 5s. Barring this type of error, can't we say the results are facts? Again, the only thing we can categorically attest to is that the answer we have is the answer the respondent chose. We cannot know for a fact that the answer given was the true answer.

This uncertainty has been analyzed and researched to the point where I can say with confidence, that most answers are actually *not* true. In *The Ultimate Question* (Harvard Business Press, 2006), Fred Reichheld researched the best customer satisfaction questions to ask to determine potential business growth. His study was based on responses from promoters (those who would recommend a product/service) and detractors (those who would steer people away from a product/service). One by-product of this effort was the realization that people don't answer surveys in a totally truthful manner.

Basically, Reichheld found that on a 10-point-scale question, a "6" is not truly neutral. Most people who felt neutral about the product or service being rated actually gave 7s or 8s, although this range was clearly marked as being more favorable than neutral.

I believe this happens on a 5-point scale also. Most customers don't want to give you a "3" if they feel ambivalent about the product or service. Let's look at a simple translation, shown in Table 14-1, which I propose is much closer to the truth for the majority of respondents of a customer satisfaction survey.

Table 14-1. Customer Satisfaction Survey Translations

Rating	Description	True meaning
1	Highly dissatisfied	Angry
2	Dissatisfied	Very dissatisfied
3	Neither satisfied nor dissatisfied	Dissatisfied
4	Satisfied	Barely satisfied or indifferent
5	Highly satisfied	Satisfied or ecstatic

What I've found is that unless the respondent was actually angry about the service, he won't give it a "1." Therefore, 2s become the choice of the very dissatisfied (those just short of angry). Threes are given by customers who are not satisfied, but not enough to say so. Fours are provided by those who are either barely satisfied or indifferent. And 5s are given by those who are quite satisfied.

If you discounted all 3s as neutral responses, you may be ignoring a large contingent of dissatisfied customers.

So, what metric is fact? Especially in our definition of a metric, which is made up of multiple data, measures, information, and even at times other metrics. There are enough variables at this level to make any answers way short of "fact." How about at the lowest levels, though? How about data? Can't it be trusted to be factual?

No. Scientists keep finding that things they knew to be a scientific fact yesterday are totally wrong today. Automated data collection systems can easily be miscalibrated and provide erroneous data (my bathroom scale is constant proof of this). When we add people to the equation, the possibility of errors increases.

Technology is great; as it advances, the accuracy of data increases. But even when using current technology, it is critical not to treat metrics as facts. When you give metrics more weight or significance than they deserve, you run the risk of making decisions based solely on the data.

Although base information should never be considered to be entirely factual or without fault, it shouldn't deter you from the proper use of metrics. But hopefully this knowledge will guide you to use metrics as they are intended to be used—as *indicators* to help support your decisions.

Metrics should never replace common sense or personal involvement.

Misused Metrics: "Our Customers Hate Us"

Let me provide a real life example of how a manager's well-intentioned use of metrics did more harm than good. A team of hard workers were told that they were hated by their customer base. Or at least that's how they interpreted the story shared with them by their boss.

Every two weeks, the CEO would meet with his department heads. For the first 30 minutes of the meeting, they'd review every customer satisfaction rating of a 1 or 2 (out of 5) across the organization. These ratings were labeled highly dissatisfied and dissatisfied.

In reality, all this exercise showed was the number of respondents who chose a 1 or 2 rating. We don't know much more than that.

The comments with each rating, when given, were also scrutinized. Based on these comments, most customers were clearly unhappy, but occasionally it was obvious that the respondent simply picked the wrong rating.

Looking at each case, it was clear to me that most customers only gave a 1 when they were angry, and they always used the opportunity to give a lengthy comment on why they were upset.

After the department heads reviewed the surveys with 1s and 2s, if time allowed, they would look at 3s since the comments provided normally indicated a level of dissatisfaction and pointed toward areas that could be improved.

This review was well-intentioned. The company leaders were, after all, *listening to the customer's voice*. That's why they administered the surveys and reviewed the negative responses.

For each survey response, the following needed to be explained:

- Why the low rating was given. If a customer's comments weren't clear (or there were no comments) someone on staff should have contacted the customer for clarification.

- What was done to "make it right" with the customer.
- What could have been done to avoid the low rating. (A better way of phrasing this would be, "What could we have done to prevent customer dissatisfaction?" A nuance, but important. If we tie our improvements to the measure rather than the behavior or process, we run the risk of improving the numbers without changing the behavior or process.)

Unfortunately, the last item—how to improve so that the customers are not dissatisfied in the future—received little attention in these meetings. This isn't uncommon, however. I've seen leadership demand explanations of why customers were dissatisfied, but the goal should be to improve processes to eliminate repeat occurrences.

So, the department heads did what you might expect. They reviewed the survey results well ahead of the meeting. They identified which teams were the recipients of the ones, twos, and threes. They tasked those teams (through their managers) to:

1. Contact the customer and determine the nature of the problem.

2. Explain the cause of the poor rating.

3. Explain what they were going to do to keep from getting that rating again (yes—at this point the manager wasn't using the metric properly).

What the workers heard was:

1. Contact the customer and see if you can appease them.

2. Figure out who was to blame.

3. If you couldn't appease them, and you were to blame, what are you going to do about it?

But let's get back to the impact on the team. All they heard from leadership was that the surveys were highly critical of them—the customers obviously hated them. Since leadership only shared the lower-rating surveys, the team assumed that they never received higher customer satisfaction ratings.

The funny thing is that all of the surveys were available to the team, but no one on the team had ever considered reviewing the surveys for himself.

What you say may not be what others hear.

The team believed they were the dregs of the organization due to the following mistakes in handling the customer satisfaction metric:

- The CEO and department heads (innocently) requested explanations for each poor customer satisfaction rating.
- The manager passed on this request to the team, without considering the affect it would have on them.
- The manager never bothered to review the surveys for his team.
- The team never bothered to use the survey reviews for anything other than appeasing the bosses.

Bottom line? The data was only being used by upper management to ensure service quality for the customers. And when the requests for more information came down stream (a good thing in itself), the surveys were taken "out of context" (the team believed they were hated by customers) and no one shared or looked at any of the positive comparison data.

This innocent behavior created stress, low morale, and a misperception of the level of satisfaction the customers had of the team.

After more than a year of this type of interaction, I was tasked with developing a scorecard for the key services in our organization. This team's service was one of our core services, so I visited them to develop their scorecard.

When I offered to include customer satisfaction on the scorecard, I met unexpected resistance. I was not aware of what they'd been going through on a bi-monthly basis.

I knew that customer satisfaction ratings were consistently a strength in the larger organization, and I was sure that this service would be no different. But the team was just as confident that the ratings would be horrendous. They also argued that since each of the customer satisfaction surveys were administered to customers who had had problems (hence the need for the second-level support they provided), the results would be skewed against them.

Again, I tried to assure them that this was not normal for the organization. And again, speaking from their observations and experience, they assured me it was going to be ugly.

One of my best moments working with metrics happened when I presented the full metrics on customer satisfaction to this team. It turned out that the ratio of highly satisfied customers compared to those who gave them lower ratings was far higher than the team realized. In fact, the team's customer satisfaction ratings were consistently ten-to-one in favor of good service!

While the team, their manager, and I were very happy about the outcome, it was enlightening to all of us how such a seemingly logical use of a metric could cause so much harm.

The damage to the team's morale was enough to confirm for me the need to be extremely careful with metrics.

Misuse of Metrics: The Good, the Bad and the Ugly

Respect the power of metrics. This respect should include a healthy fear and awe. By having a small, healthy dose of fear and awe when dealing with metrics, I hope all levels of users will use a little caution in how they let metrics affect their decisions.

Be assured, used improperly, metrics can seriously endanger your organization's health. Not respecting the power of metrics often results in errors in the way we use them. These errors manifest in forms of misuse.

The Good

The following misuses of metrics are classified as "good" not because they are acceptable, but simply because the perpetrator lacks malicious intent, innocently misusing a metric rather than deliberately causing damage. Sometimes this is due to arrogance and other times ignorance. In either case, a healthy dose of respect would solve this problem.

- *Sharing only part of the story.* Remarkably, after spending time and investing effort to develop a complete story, people still mistakenly share only part of the story. This seems counterintuitive. Whenever you selectively share parts of the metric and not the whole story, you distort the message. Don't create misinformation by simply not sharing the whole story.
- *Not sharing the story at all.* Again, why go through the effort to develop a full story only to hoard the results? Not only must you share the metrics with the customers (those who could and should use it), but you should share it with those who are providing you the data. Not all those who use the metric will be a provider of data, but all those who provide data should be users.

    Another way I see this manifested is reluctance to build the metric at all. It happens because of fears of what the metric will show. Most times I hear that the "data is invalid" or "we can't get the data." Basically, these are excuses designed to kill the metric before it is ever created.

- *Sharing only good metrics.* The most common reason for not showing all the metrics is because, in someone's opinion, something in the metrics makes someone else look bad. Of course, if you're using metrics properly, they are indicators for the purpose of improving. If you only have good results, then what do you need to improve? The reluctance to show unfavorable results misses the point of metrics. To improve, you need to know where improvement is needed. To show progress, you need to be able to show improvement. To show only "good results" is to cheat someone of the information needed to help them improve.

- *Sharing only bad metrics.* There are times when only the negative results are shared. Purposely. For example, when a manager wants to "motivate" his staff, perhaps he may choose to make things look a little worse than they are. We won't go into the more sinister abuses of metrics—I'll leave that to your imagination. Suffice it to say, another misuse of data is to reveal only the negative results.

- *Showing the data.* Remember the difference between data, measures, information, and metrics? Showing data (or measures) means that you distract the viewer from the story. It's like showing the used palette instead of the painting. When you show data (instead of the metric) you invite the viewers to do their own analysis and form their own stories.

You may have noticed a theme to these examples of "good" misuses of metrics. Most are born of not showing the complete story. This supports why the use of root questions and the development of a complete story is so important.

The Bad

In contrast to the innocent misuse of metrics, the "bad" describes knowledgeable misuse. You would think this would be the rare case. You would hope that those receiving metrics would not knowingly misuse them. But some don't respect the destructive power of metrics; they wield it haphazardly and end up causing serious damage. These types of misuses are as follows:

- *Using metrics for a personal agenda.* After seeing the metrics, there are those who decide that the metrics can be used to further their own cause. And there are those who may actually task the creation of metrics for the sole purpose of fulfilling a personal agenda. These people are easy to spot. They refuse to work with you to determine the root question, either out of embarrassment over a transparent desire of a specific answer or from reluctance to share before they can prove their case. These people offer numerous excuses to avoid getting to the root. If you're trying to do metrics right, you'll be extremely frustrated by this abuser.

- *Using metrics to control people.* There is group of professionals who make a living developing, analyzing, and reporting "performance metrics" specifically designed to measure how well people perform. You can also use performance metrics to evaluate processes, systems, and even hardware. From the discussions in online community sites, it is a widely held belief that performance metrics are a good tool for manipulating people's behavior. This is unacceptable. The words "control" or "manipulate" may not be expressly used, but by saying "you can and should drive performance using metrics," this is what is meant.

- *Using metrics to make decisions.* I understand that management wants metrics (they call it data) to base their decisions on so that they are making "informed" decisions. I am not saying this is bad. It only becomes bad when leadership believes that the metrics are facts. It becomes an issue when decisions are made as a result of the metric. Metrics can be used to inform decisions, but only after they've been investigated and validated. It's not enough to know the *what* (the metric), if you're going to make decisions based on them; you have to also get to the *why*.

  When my gas gauge shows near empty, I make the decision to get gas right away or wait a little while. This decision isn't a critical to anyone. If the gauge shows near empty, it shouldn't hurt if I don't get gas immediately. I know the gas gauge is an indicator and not a fact (depending if I'm going up or down hill, the reading changes). I also know it can potentially be incorrect; if it shows empty when I've just filled the tank, there is something else wrong. Bottom line? I use data, measures, information, and metrics to *inform* my decisions, not to make them.

- *Using metrics to win an argument or sway opinion.* This is probably the most common misuse of metrics. We see it in politics. We see it in debates. We see it in funding battles across the conference room table. The problem isn't that you use metrics to prove your point, it's that you only use the data that helps your case—and ignore the rest. This is a grievous misuse.

You may have noticed that most of these "bad" misuses are based on "how" they are used—the intention behind the report. If your intentions are bad (selfish, manipulative, controlling, or lazy), you will end up misusing the information. Negative intentions drive you to misuse metrics in the worst ways.

The Ugly

If the good is a result of non-malicious intention, then the "ugly" is a direct result of malicious intent. I won't spend a lot of time on this, because those who have the intent to misuse metrics probably aren't reading this book.

The reason I'm discussing this at all is just to remind you that there are those who would intentionally use metrics to cause harm.

So, you have to respect the power of metrics. Not only must you ensure you are careful with how you use them, but you have to protect others from the dangers. This is part of the trust you need to build with those who provide the data. Just because you would never purposefully use metrics to hurt others, it doesn't mean others won't. When you take on the responsibility of collecting, analyzing, and reporting metrics, you also have to protect others.

Constant diligence is required to ensure metrics are used properly.

The Art of the Unintended Consequence

Besides the danger of telling the wrong story and all the unintended consequences of that (wrong decisions, improving the wrong things, not improving things that need to be improved, etc.), misuses lead to other dangerous consequences.

We've already discussed the damage to morale caused by showing only the bad metrics. Besides demoralization of the workforce, you also run the risk of creating, continuing, or increasing the following:

- Fear of metrics being abused
- Anger over misuse and abuse
- Uncertainty of what to do or what will be done
- Doubt of the validity of the metrics
- Mistrust of those collecting, analyzing, and reporting the metrics

- Avoidance of activities which could positively or negatively affect a metric
- Reluctance to participate in future improvement efforts

Each of these are worthy of discussion, but first it is important to realize who we're talking about—those who are providing the data and those who feel the data is about them. Note that I said data. It doesn't matter if the metric is an aggregate or tells a bigger story. Those who provide the data won't care about your plans for the metric if they believe the data may be misused or abused. These reactions to the metrics are warranted. Fear, uncertainty, doubt, anger, mistrust, and avoidance are emotions that can't be dismissed or debated.

Emotional reactions to the misuse of data cannot be dismissed.

Let's go into more depth.

- *Fear of metrics and their abuse.* Metrics are dangerous and can cause more harm than good. Employees may fear the misuse and abuse of metrics before you collect the first data point. Even if you do everything right—show how the data will be used (to tell a complete story, which in turn will be used to improve processes) and how it won't be used (to punish or control staff)—fear may still exist. Fear that you will not live up to your promises or will change your mind about how you use the metrics. Fear that others will get access to the data and then misuse or abuse them. This fear is real and warranted. Your mission is to find ways to build enough trust to overcome it. In short, you'll build trust by explaining how you will and won't use the metrics and keeping those promises.
- *Uncertainty of what to do or what will be done.* When those providing the information for your metrics are uncertain about how it will be used (or if they will be used at all), they may hesitate to provide you data. Uncertainty leads to many other potential problems, such as eventual doubts about the accuracy of your information.
- *Doubt of the validity of the metrics.* Rather than truly doubting the validity of the metrics, some people decide to call the validity of the data into question so that they won't have to deal with the metrics. If the metrics are invalid, then they can ignore them. If the metrics are proven to be invalid or inaccurate, the power that metrics should yield is lost.

- *Anger over misuse and abuse.* This, in my opinion, is a better response to misuse than fear or uncertainty. Anger shows a level of concern and involvement, which is a good foundation toward improvement. Anger, however, also usually creates a defensive reaction and has the ability to bring out the worst in others. Leadership may want to punish those who show anger, or label them as "disgruntled" or a non-team player or "disruptive." Rather than simply condemn those who react with anger, their passion should at least be appreciated. Passion, involvement, and self-motivation cannot be taught or instilled.
- *Mistrust of those collecting, analyzing, and reporting the metrics.* When we find mistrust, it is a deeper problem than anger. Mistrust requires a deep effort to overcome. Mistrust as a whole can't be fixed easily, but mistrust about the use of the metrics can be addressed. If you can build trust in this effort, then perhaps you can use it as a foundation for improving overall trust. To build trust requires steadfast dedication to the principles—use the metrics only in the ways you offered and never use them in the ways you said that you would not.
- *Avoidance of activities that could positively or negatively affect a metric.* Fear, uncertainty, doubt, anger, and/or mistrust can lead to passive resistance toward your metric efforts. The simplest form of resistance is to avoid anything to do with the metrics—avoiding involvement in the identification, collection, analysis, or reporting of the metric. This avoidance may not even be noticed unless you need involvement. Again, you will have to proactively deal with this. If you want to have a successful program, it is just as critical to deal with passive resistance as the more overt behaviors.
- *Reluctance to participate in future improvement efforts.* This consequence is often overlooked when dealing with metrics or any organizational improvement effort. When you misuse the power afforded to you, the simplest retort available is to resist future improvement efforts. Even when it was not intentional, it is hard to support another improvement effort or technique if the previous one was mishandled.

These unintended consequences don't have to happen—if you're careful and respect the power of metrics.

Recap

Metrics are a powerful tool—and like most powerful tools, they can do some serious damage. You have to take precautions, use the proper safety equipment, and finally you *have* to respect that power.

The rules of thumb are as follows:

- Metrics can do more harm than good.
- Metrics should never replace common sense or personal involvement.
- Metrics are not facts, they are indicators.
- What you say may not be what others hear.
- Damage from misuse of metrics hurts everyone in the organization.
- Constant diligence is required to ensure metrics are used properly.

We covered the following:

- *The Power of Metrics.* Even innocent misuse of metrics can cause damage, such as low team morale. If word spreads through your organization about the misuse or abuse of metrics, irreparable damage will be done.
- *Misuse of Metrics: The Good, the Bad, and the Ugly.* These include:
    - Sharing only part of the story
    - Not sharing the story at all
    - Sharing only the good metrics
    - Sharing only the bad metrics
    - Showing the raw data
    - Using metrics for a personal agenda
    - Using metrics to control people
    - Using metrics to make decisions
    - Using metrics to win an argument or sway opinion
- *The Art of the Unintended Consequence.* The major types of consequences you can expect from misusing metrics, are as follows:
    - Fear of metrics and their abuse
    - Uncertainty of what to do or what will be done
    - Doubt of the validity of the metrics
    - Anger over misuse and abuse
    - Mistrust of those reporting, analyzing, and reporting the metrics
    - Avoidance of activities, which could positively or negatively affect a metric

Conclusion

Respecting the power of metrics essentially means being cautious and a little fearful of the harm that can be caused by metrics. This fear shouldn't paralyze you; it should instead energize you to handle the metrics with care. Put on your safety gear, take precautions, and ensure that others are kept out of harm's way.

Avoiding the Research Trap

Let's start with my take on research. By research I don't mean the focused, directed investigation I suggest you do to determine root needs. Nor do I mean the further investigation we perform once we've identified anomalies in our data. I also don't mean the deeper dive you should perform when finding the data, measures, information, standards, or benchmarks for the specific metrics you've designed.

By research, I am referring to the non-directed exploration of information.

This type of research can be broken into many different categories. They include scientific and historical methods; qualitative and quantitative views; exploratory, constructive, and empirical research; primary and secondary research; and many others. All of these types of research have the following commonalities:

- High expense
- Long length of time to conduct
- Considerable effort to conduct
- Unknown applicability

The government and other research supporters find it useful to fund research in many areas, expecting that a certain percentage of the analysis garnered will result in breakthroughs. Many times resulting innovations or insights are made in areas totally unrelated from the original intent. Velcro and micro-wave ovens are examples. Many of our new technologies resulted from military research that ended up in uses other than combat-related activities. Research is an excellent means to give us new ways to see old problems and sometimes research uncovers new problems which would have gone unnoticed. Research is an essential part of humankind's progress and future.

Research can also be a great tool for businesses seeking information to help improve. In *First Break All the Rules* by Marcus Buckingham and Curt Coffman (Simon & Schuster, 1999) and *Good to Great* by Jim Collins (HarperCollins, 2001), the authors conducted some serious research on business performance improvement. Collins had a team of researchers sort through the performance histories of nearly 1,500 companies and Buckingham and Coffman used more than 80,000 interview results from 25 years of research done by the Gallup Organization. The authors used their results to come up with concepts and theories for organizational development. Their ideas were born from their research and many businesses benefitted from it.

But this halo effect causes some to believe that they should partake in research or at least follow the principles used in research. Just because there has been very good use of research, it doesn't mean that a business should try to replicate these efforts, especially not for practical application.

It's important not to ignore or forget all of the failed attempts at innovation, all of the research that proved not to be useful, and all of the results that led researchers down the wrong paths.

Many leaders use examples of others' success to push them to try a new idea. They cherish books like *In Search of Excellence* by Tom Peters and Robert Waterman (Warner Books, 1982), where success stories fill the pages.

Most leaders want to see metrics that others are using. They don't want to undertake a venture without proven success from similar organizations or competitors—to some degree ensuring that they are never in the lead or on the cutting edge. This aversion to risk-taking was addressed in more detail in chapter 13 on benchmarking.

Research can be a very good thing. But most organizations really can't afford to conduct non-directed research (that is, any research not directly related to product development). It is not that research is bad—it's simply too costly in terms of time and expense.

Can you afford to perform non-directed research?

The Cost of Research

Research involves gathering data using interviews, surveys, observations, experimentation, documentation and instrumentation. Research involves a lot of time to gather the data; not only the researcher's time, but the time of those providing the information. Experiments take time, especially when you consider the need for control groups and double-blind techniques.

You can't afford to create metrics without a purpose. You can't afford to gather data, create measures, and compile information without a direction for it. You can't afford to build a structure and hope that later someone will come to fill it or use it.

So you may be thinking, "But I never wanted to do research and I doubt that my company will ever want to do research!"

Although you may not want to do it, I assure you that you'll end up doing research.

If you are collecting analyzing, and reporting data without a root question, you're performing non-directed research.

Research in Disguise

A common task assigned to a metrics analyst by well-meaning management is to come up with some "interesting" data. Basically, the leader is admitting he doesn't know what he wants, but he is willing for you to take the time and effort to try and come up with something he likes. Like Justice Potter Stewart's assertion regarding pornography, he'd know it when he saw it.

Management wrongly believes that the right metrics, the metrics they want, will be revealed through just a bit of trial and error. If you simply collect enough information, management will be able to separate the wheat from the chaff.

To satisfy a request to go out and find some useful, interesting measures, you can:

- Examine existing products
- Read books on your industry and the processes involved
- Ask a lot of industry experts about their opinions and experiences

- Study how processes are carried out
- Choose from any one of the many research tools available (online databases, search engines, indexes, and publications)

That's right, you are conducting research. So while I'll agree that none of us go into our daily tasks wanting (or expecting) to conduct research, we all end up doing so anyway.

It is essential to drive to a root need. When you are presented with the ambiguous request for conducting research in disguise, you have to push back. You may need to push back in a manner appropriate for your organization, but you must push back nonetheless. The best means of this is to carefully use the five whys. Rather than seek the elusive answers to questions you haven't identified, spend that energy "researching" the root question.

Most organizations (including all of the ones I've worked for) can't afford to conduct wide-ranging research and then process and utilize enormous amounts of data. It's just not cost effective. Most of us don't have the time or resources to engage in non-directed research.

Even when we try to use results of research conducted by outside sources, many times it doesn't end well. It is rare that I've found research data that fits the specific root questions my organization was working with.

Are You Already Trapped?

If you find yourself seeking answers to unknown questions, you're probably trapped. You may find yourself blocking-out four or more hours a day for a few months so you can gather information. You then find yourself determining what data is available. You start mining data from numerous sources.

One of the benefits and problems with technology is the proliferation of data. When you know what you're looking for, it's great to have it all "at your fingertips." When you don't know what you're looking for, the mountains of data can bury you.

When you're firmly in the trap and you've gathered a lot of data, you'll be confronted with the daunting task of analyzing that data. You'll have to figure out how to pull them together—which measures have relationships with others and which don't.

When you share the results of your hard work, your boss may tell you that you've missed the mark (the mark which he himself couldn't describe, point out, or identify). You won't know if the data was the wrong data or if your analysis of that data was off. Even if you get past that, you run the real risk of inspiring your boss. He may think of other "interesting" data you could collect. This will require more searching. If you can't locate any secondary data that's already been published, you will probably have to find other ways to get the data. This may include conducting surveys, focus groups, observation, or the creation of automated tools for collecting. This in itself can be extremely expensive due to the cost to buy, and learn to use or develop tools. You realize that this path is an expensive one—with ever-diminishing returns.

The best advice I can give is, if you find yourself in a hole, stop digging. Instead, try to climb out of the hole—preferably by asking for a little help from your manager. I usually start by asking him to stop shoveling dirt on my head. Then I ask for a hand in climbing out. This help should be a willingness to work on the root needs. The problem is that you have to convince your boss that you need his help. You need him to give you some of his time and effort.

Ask your boss for help out of the hole (after you get him to stop shoveling dirt on your head).

Stop Digging

"We need three key metrics." My boss had called me to his office to give me a strong motivational speech.

"Three?" It amazed me how many organizational development things came in threes. Three goals. Three process improvement ideas. Three metrics.

"Yes. But, if you come up with four or five, that's all right."

"Uh huh."

"It shouldn't be too hard. We have a contract with a consulting organization that has a lot of data on IT services." I knew of this arrangement, but I hadn't seen much useful data, measures, or information in their databases.

"What information do you want exactly?" I tried not to get frustrated.

"I'm open to whatever you come up with. Just use their existing data as a benchmark..."

"And find three, right?"

"Right!" I could tell he was happy with his clear direction.

I did as asked (I wanted to keep my job). I looked at the consulting firm's data, without any specific question in mind, trying to find three we could use as a benchmark. Unfortunately the data they had didn't relate to our problem areas. We had specific areas we were trying to improve. These were not unique problems, but they weren't issues that the consulting firm had previously researched. They had researched the general areas of interest, but these weren't the areas we were having trouble with. The three I found to use—the availability of servers, abandoned call rates, and customer satisfaction ratios—were defined differently than we would have defined them.

For example, they defined availability on a 24 hours a day, 7-days-a-week basis—while we had scheduled downtimes during low-usage timeframes (our customers did not expect 24/7 availability).

Abandoned calls did not take into account the time before the caller hung up. We always had a message you had to listen to before a technician would pick up. This message was updated daily (at a minimum) and informed the caller of any current issues. For example, if we had a current problem with e-mail, the message may say, "We are experiencing e-mail connectivity issues; we hope to have it resolved by 1:00 p.m." If the purpose of the call was to let us know about this issue, the caller could hang up, confident that we already knew about the issue and were working it. This call, in our opinion, shouldn't be counted as abandoned. The research didn't differentiate the amount of time spent on the line before the caller disconnected, so it didn't actually match our information.

It was easy to see the disconnect in the customer satisfaction measures. The consultant's research had a four-point scale; we had used a five-point scale for the last three years. Their questions were also not an exact match. Finally, they gave a value of "1" for "very satisfied" and a "4" for "very dissatisfied." We used the scale in the other direction.

In a forced effort to have comparison data, my boss made me use the data anyway, comparing it although it wasn't an exact match. He would say, "It may not be Macintosh to Macintosh, but it's still apples to apples."

Finding a cache of data can mislead you into force-fitting your questions to align with the available answers.

To stop the madness, you'll need to admit to your boss that you can't do what he's asked. You can't perform the research because you don't have the time, skills, or energy to chase the unknown. Instead, you need his help. You need his help to direct your efforts and allow you to be more efficient and effective. You need his help to ensure you're productive.

What's Wrong with Research?

You should have already formed your questions first and then sought out the answers via existing research or standards. Of course, if you're struggling with the questions, reviewing existing research data may help you, or then again, it may lead you deeper into the woods. The chief risk is that you may settle for what is available rather than what you actually need. The following are a few precautions to consider when using others' research:

1. Research data may not match your needs exactly. As my boss said, you may have apples-to-apples, but yours might be a Red Delicious while mine is a Granny Smith. While you may use others' data to compare, you have to note where it doesn't match your situation.

2. It's too easy to skip the question identification phase when you have reams of data to choose from. You end up just building pictures from what's available instead of determining the proper questions.

3. Worse than skipping the question altogether, when you have research results, you may be driven to creating questions to fit the answers in the metrics. This makes it nearly impossible to convince management to re-evaluate their needs.

4. Research data are still merely indicators; they are not truth. What happened to similar institutions doesn't mean the same will happen to your organization. (I was watching the NBA playoffs and the announcers were discussing one of the many statistics culled from researchers. "Teams that have lost the first two games of a best-of-seven playoff series have lost the series over 80% of the time." While this may be accurate, it doesn't mean that this particular team with two losses stands an 80% chance of losing this series.)

5. Research is not cheap. While technology makes the collection of data much easier than in the past, it's still costly. The monitoring software and hardware may be expensive. The use of manpower to analyze and report the data is always expensive.

While I strongly advise against conducting exploratory research, I fully support your taking every advantage of those who have the time, resources, and will to do so.

Recap

Here are some points worth highlighting:

- Don't neglect defining your questions because someone can provide you with ready-made answers. Don't let existing research cloud your issues and keep you from asking the right questions. It's tempting to use others' research and not do the upfront work of determining your needs.
- Don't let existing research push you in a direction that allows comparison at the expense of having meaningful data for your situation.
- Don't let others dictate your metrics with the ambiguous "interesting." Learn to say "no" to the "I think it would be interesting..." requests.
- Don't rely on others to provide your questions—only you truly know your needs.
- Don't give more weight to aggregate data than to your own metrics.

You may have noticed that the admonitions above all stem from the core methodology for developing metrics—first identify the root question. The biggest issue with non-directed research may be the lack of a meaningful question. If the research is being conducted by an independent entity, the question is usually generic, and therefore, meaningless for most.

An example would be research done on the high-school graduation rate for children from one-parent families. This "interesting" measure can garnish a decent grant from our government, but how useful is the information to your local high school? Besides the ability to say that high school X has a better graduation rate for their single-parented population than high school Y, how useful is this data? If the data shows that fewer children from single-parent homes graduate than those from two-parent homes, will the schools focus differently on those children because they are more at risk? It may be useful data for debates against single-parent child-rearing or for more support for these families. The bottom line is that while the research is interesting and may be worthy of funding, it is not highly useful for the local school. It has uses, but not for where the "rubber meets the road" in education.

At least the example given involves research for a purpose, albeit a vague one. The other type of research, which your organization is more likely to engage in, is much more problematic. The research conducted by your organization not only falls prey to the same lack of a meaningful question (usually it's conducted without forethought or planning but simply because someone thought it would be interesting), but wastes *your* resources! So, unless you have limitless resources (including time), I highly recommend against collecting, analyzing, or reporting any data that does not answer a specific and meaningful question.

Conclusion

Research has great potential for helping us find answers. The trick is to remember that the research conducted by third parties will rarely provide the direct (or full) answer to your questions. You definitely should leverage the work of others, but only after you've clearly defined your question.

The other key point to remember is that you likely don't have the resources to conduct non-directed research (leave it to those who receive grants for such things or are in the business of research). This may seem easy, but you may find yourself falling into the research trap when you are tasked to find "interesting" data. Beware these veiled research assignments.

You may also find yourself unwittingly but voluntarily conducting non-directed research. Go back to the beginning (my favorite place to start) and identify the root need. With the root question in hand, design your metric with the end in mind. Avoid the research trap and use your time wisely.

Embracing Your Organization's Uniqueness

The prince didn't know how else to explain it. It was love at first sight. She had captivated his whole being. And then she slipped away, leaving behind only her glass shoe.

"I must find her," said the prince. "She is the one. With her by my side I can do anything, be anyone."

"But sire," responded the chancellor, "She's just a commoner. How can she alone make you more than you are?"

"I can't explain it, but I know it will happen. She will make me better."

So, the prince sent the king's chancellor to scour the countryside for the mystery girl who stole his heart. The chancellor went from house to house and had each female of marrying age try on the glass shoe.

And it fit every girl's foot.

The chancellor was lost at what to do. So, he did what his father always told him, "When in doubt, follow orders." He brought each and every maiden back to the castle.

"Sire," he said, "I've brought you the women who fit the shoe."

"Women?" The prince looked at him with widened eyes.

"Yes, sire."

"How many?"

"All of them."

"Very humorous," said the prince. "How many are all of them?"

"No, sire. I don't jest. I brought all of them. All the eligible maidens in the kingdom fit into the shoe."

"How is that possible?"

The chancellor chose his words carefully. "I believe it's called a one-size-fits-all."

"How is it of any use, then?" wondered the prince.

"Well, it's the only type of shoe that we have."

"True," said the prince.

So the Prince became depressed and eventually banned all one-size-fits-all apparel in the kingdom. This made the tailors in the kingdom quite happy, but the manufacturing unions organized a revolution. They re-tooled shoes, socks, and T-shirts to make weapons. They easily overthrew the monarchy and established a free and open market.

While the prince learned that a one-size-fits-all tool for measuring something may not be meaningful, there are still many who seek this out. They want the one-size-fits-all metric. If you've followed along up to this point, you should realize that the only way someone else's metric will be meaningful to you is if you both have the same root question. Even then, for the data, measures, or information to be meaningful, you need to have defined the components the same way.

The only way someone else's metrics will work for you is if you have the same root question.

There is nothing wrong with your organization being unique. Organizations, like people, should embrace their uniqueness instead of trying to make everything a one-size-fits-all endeavor. This penchant for finding a single so-lution for problems actually causes more issues than it resolves. If you are designing a product like a new energy-saving lightbulb, you may well want it to fit most (if not all) lamps. But an organization is a complex living organism, and the problems it needs answered will be as unique as the problems each of us face in our lives.

Forcing a "one-size-fits-all" solution to your problems actually causes more issues than it resolves.

You may argue that we actually aren't unique and that we are alike in more ways than we are different. You may argue that people, and therefore organizations, which are made up of people, have problems that are more alike than different. While there are enough variables to ensure our issues are not identical, the root causes, and the root questions, are very common.

And I'd have to agree.

Unfortunately, this commonality doesn't help. It actually causes us to head off in wrong directions.

When you start a metrics program, you will be challenged by many to "not re-create the wheel." You'll be encouraged to visit other organizations like your own, research information on the web, and find existing successful examples to follow. You will be expected to leverage the work of others. You will be expected to produce quickly since you won't have to start from scratch.

This causes problems because this expectation—that you can use other organizations' metrics—makes finding your organization's root questions much more difficult. It makes sense. If there were actually one-size-fits-all metrics, or at least existing metrics that you could just "borrow," then

- You could use someone else's root questions and
  - You wouldn't need to elicit requirements or gather inputs
    - No focus groups
    - No interviews
    - No questionnaires
  - You wouldn't need to break the root question down into its components to ensure understanding and that you've reached a true root need
    - No "five whys"

- No facilitation
- No consulting

- You could use existing metric development plans. Actually, you wouldn't need a development plan because you wouldn't have to develop any metrics. You would just use ones already created and documented by someone else.
- You wouldn't need to bother leadership, management, or the workforce to develop your metrics program.

Of course, you *will* need to have the same collection, analysis, and reporting tools. You will also have to have the same (exact) processes and procedures. You will also have to provide/deliver the same services and products. You will have to have the same environmental factors affecting your organization. This would be, of course, virtually impossible.

Your organization *is* unique. *You are unique.* You have to embrace your uniqueness to be successful.

You have to embrace your uniqueness to be successful.

I don't mean that you can't benefit from the work of others. But when leadership tasks you to find "benchmarks" and to research what your peers/competitors are doing—it's not to become wiser. It's to save time and money. It's to avoid the hard work required to develop a metrics program.

There are no shortcuts—that work.

There are tons of ways to get things done much faster. You can find many shortcuts. You can skip many of the steps I've offered. You can (and likely will) fall off that narrow ledge you've been crawling on because of the shortcut.

In the center (socially, if not geographically) of the university where I work, there is a student center with four different eateries. It would be ludicrous for the managers of these to ignore what makes each unique. The reason four different food providers can thrive in the same building (go to your nearest mall) is mostly because of their differences, not the things they have in common.

Your organization has the chance to be exceptional because of the things that make it unique, not the things that it has in common with others.

These unique factors are critical to your success. They can be strengths or weaknesses. The first step is to embrace these unique factors. They will not only affect your success, but they will also be a major player in your metrics program.

Questions Simplified

When looking at a metrics program (besides using the tools I offered in the development plan), you must answer five simple questions: Why, What, When, Who, and How.

Why

Why are you doing metrics? Why are you doing a specific metric?

"Why" leads us to the root question. Your whys might be, and should be, unique. Others won't have the same needs you do. Unless another organization is in the same business, in the same market, and battling the same challenges, chances are, while your whys may be similar, they won't be the same.

What

What are you doing? What are your goals? What are you measuring?

If you are lucky enough to actually find another organization that has the same "whys," you may still decide to handle them differently. If you and a peer have the same problems, how will you decide to solve those issues? Will you wait and do whatever your peer does? Or will you want to create your own solutions? Even looking at two businesses that are very much alike—McDonalds and Burger King—chances are you will find more differences than you could imagine. And I don't mean in their recipes. They will have different values, processes, procedures, and policies. They have different solutions for problems, even if they share the same issues.

When

When are you going to implement the change? When are you hoping to achieve the goal?

When are you going to measure? The first of the month? The first workday of the week? In the morning, afternoon, or evening?

At what frequency will you collect, analyze, and report your metrics? Daily? Weekly? Monthly? Quarterly? Are you on a fiscal, annual, or academic calendar?

"When" is more than a way to define the scope of your efforts. It helps you determine deadlines and focus your efforts. It also gives you insights to how the workload and processes will change when you implement a program.

Who

Who will lead the effort? Who will assist? Who will be involved? Who will collect the data? Who will compile the measures? Who will analyze the information? Who will create the metric? Who will report the metric and to whom? Who will explain the anomalies? Who will get the credit? Who will take the blame? Who owns the program? Who will have access and who won't? Who is going to pay for the work?

"Who ..." is a critical question to ask if you actually want to get anything done. You have to know who the customer is, who the providers are, and who will use the metrics.

How

How will you implement the program? How will you use the metrics? How won't you use them? How will you improve the organization? How will you communicate your needs? How will you share the results? How will you determine the usefulness of your metrics? How will you kill metrics that are no longer needed?

The "how" can be as simple as a checklist or as complex as an operational manual. The documentation you choose will determine the size of the how. The way you choose to capture and share the how will drive changes in your organization.

These are many of the questions I've asked you to consider during the development of your metrics program. I bring them back to your attention to point out that the answers to these questions are very likely to be unique to you and your organization. Metrics designed to help you improve your organization mean that you will be dealing with your organization's strengths and weaknesses. It is unlikely that these will exist in the same shape and form in other organizations. You'd have to get inputs from thousands of organizations to find matches for all of your unique needs. That assumes, of course, that there are thousands of organizations like yours, already doing metrics, doing them properly, and willing to share with you.

What If Your Boss Doesn't Agree?

What do you do if your boss insists on you finding others to follow? What if you can't convince him to embrace the organization's uniqueness? I offer the following list of steps you can follow to embrace your uniqueness, understanding that you will have to pick and choose which will work for you.

Don't Be Caught Off Guard

Don't be caught off guard. Expect leadership to send you on the goose chase.

Don't resist (resistance is futile) the tasking. Instead, attempt to explain that you still need root questions to ensure that you find good examples or benchmarks. Let's say you run into the extremely stubborn leader who argues, "Why create your own root questions if you can use someone else's?" You can attempt to explain why using someone else's requirements instead of determining your own is a bad idea. Or you can give him a copy of this book. Or you can get to work on the research and get it over with.

You'll need to get as much defined for your organization *before* comparing or seeking out examples. This includes root questions, metrics, and all of the components you will need. Get as much done as you can so that you clearly differentiate what you want from what your peers/competitors need. It will also give you something to barter with if your contemporaries are willing to share on a quid pro quo basis.

Do the Research

Be ready to do the research. You can even have a positive (hopeful) attitude! You never know, you may be the one organization that proves everything I've said wrong. You may be the exception to the rule.

The first thing to research is to identify your peers and competitors and find out if they have any metrics. You'll want to make sure the metrics they have (if any) are related to what you need (if you've been allowed to do any groundwork). Identify the areas you want examples for. If you succeeded in building as much of your development plan as possible, you will be able to better identify what you'd like to compare.

Deal with Failure

Don't be surprised if you find that you *are* unique. Or that the organizations you believe are your perfect match either have no metrics or are unwilling to share what they do have. You may very well be ahead of the curve. Your needs may be unique. If so, you have to tell your leadership that you have failed.

Of course, you did not actually fail. You were tasked to find examples. A legitimate result of research has to be that the hypothesis that you are addressing may be proven false.

Realize that your leadership may consider you to have failed. While they asked you to find out if any metrics already exist, what they really wanted was for you to find a match so...

- They wouldn't have to trust you to know what you were doing
- They'd have a warm fuzzy because someone else was already using them
- It would mean less work on everyone's part (including you); less cost, less time, and less effort

Deal with Success

I expect you won't find an exact match, and suggest that you should be surprised if you do. It's rare. Be thankful if you also get that organization to freely share what they have and how to replicate it. Be even more thankful if they are willing to participate with you in a benchmarking effort so that you both can benefit from the metrics. Even if this miracle occurs, realize it won't be for every metric.

Expect that even if you find some viable comparisons

- That they won't be for every root question
- The other organization may not be willing to share
- The other organization may not have any of the rigors I've recommended to accompany its information (no documentation or development plan)

Your exact match may not have the same definitions surrounding the data, measures, information, or metric. This means that you will need the raw data used to build the metric. Unfortunately, this increases the likelihood that the other organization will not want to share.

The other organizations will want something in return—even if it's just to see *your* raw data. Your leadership may not be willing to share.

Expect that your leadership's reactions to your research will not make you feel successful. Chances are they will decide that the examples you found are not a good match or simply not good enough (this may be a good thing

—but after the joy you'll feel in finding them, you may forget that I wanted you to embrace your uniqueness).

Your leadership may feel you failed, especially if you have nothing to show for the effort. If that were the end of the tasking, you could count your blessings. Most likely though, your leadership will want you to try again. They may even provide you with their peers' contact information.

Another possibility is they may decide to bring in outside help, because they are convinced that you didn't look in the right places, didn't ask the right people, or just didn't understand what they wanted.

Is It Really That Bleak?

Yes, I painted a pretty bleak picture. And I could tell you that from my experience that I was actually being very realistic, but I could have perhaps let you down with a little more compassion.

I don't agree.

In the case of embracing your organization's uniqueness I again feel it necessary to give you "tough love" rather than give you the flowery picture. You have to know what you may encounter so you can be prepared for it and react properly.

The martial arts teach that we should be like water. This means that you react exactly proportional to the stimulus, not more not less, and then return to a steady, calm state. When you drop a pebble into a pool of still water, ripples fan out from the center and dissipate until the surface returns to the calm that preceded the change. Hopefully this calm, steady state is one of happiness; if not, you may need to find a new job. I've found that you can only react appropriately if you are either a Zen master or if you can anticipate the size of the pebble hitting your pool.

So, I try to give you what I've found to be the most likely response, not to depress or scare you, but to make it easier for you to be like water and react appropriately if my prediction comes true.

Why Embracing Your Uniqueness Is Healthy

It doesn't require a lot of research to realize that the most successful companies and people are those who have embraced their unique strengths. I recently put together a presentation on visionaries, and each has two things in common.

First, they all have a compelling, life-changing, positive vision (I avoided those megalomaniacs with visions to take over the world).

Second, they all embraced their unique qualities and made them strengths. From creators and inventors like Albert Einstein, Dr. Marie Curie, Henry Ford, Leonardo da Vinci, Granville Woods, Bill Gates, and Steve Jobs, we learn that uniqueness in inventiveness isn't enough. You need to embrace those unique ideas and trust in them. You have to have faith in yourself and your ideas. A good example would be Herbert Kelleher, who took Southwest Airlines to new heights by embracing its uniqueness. He built a successful passenger airline that continues to withstand downturns in the industry. The company does it with a unique style and sense of humor. Southwest Airlines definitely side-stepped the "norm" the other airlines wallowed in, and embraced its uniqueness. Your organization may have unique ways of doing business, like those brought out by Herb Kelleher.

The ability to maintain faith in your convictions, principles, and values requires that you believe in yourself or your organization. Almost all innovators have to weather the storm of ridicule from their peers, many of whom would rather say something can't be done than to watch it happen.

Colonel Billy Mitchell (father of the US Air Force), Father Edward Sorin (founder of the University of Notre Dame), W. Edwards Deming (father of Total Quality Management), Jimmy Wales (founder of Wikipedia), and Bruce Lee (founder of Jeet Kune Do) all had to withstand the slings and arrows of naysayers. In most cases, their biggest opponents were their friends, family, and countrymen. What makes their ideas live on successfully today is a result of their dedication to their ideas. But that dedication wasn't easy. Their ideas were seen as non-status quo. Against the establishment. Ideas that would require a drastic change in the way things had always been done. Your organization may have unique, innovative ideas about how things should be. You have to embrace that uniqueness and make it the strength of your organization.

OK, so your organization may not have a vision that will change the world. You may not be moving mountains and changing lives. Perhaps you're just trying to provide needed services. Perhaps you're just trying to make a living.

But should you? Should you be doing more? Should your organization have a bigger purpose? A vision?

Why not?

If you do or not, if you organization does or not, you still should embrace your uniqueness. You should not conform to what others are doing just because "that's what's always been done" or "because that's what everyone else is doing."

Here's a more concrete example (in case the previous was too abstract). Let's say your company is concerned about where it stands in relation to its competitors. Let's say it looks at the metrics published by its top competitor and your leadership decides to change so that it matches this competitor.

Let's say both organizations are relatively successful, but in some ways they are unique. For example, Organization 1 has a ratio of one IT support person for every ten people supported. Organization 2 has a drastically different ratio—one IT support person for every fifty people. Organization 1 is entirely US-based while Organization 2 outsources support to a country overseas.

So, after research and metrics gathering, Organization 2 decides that it will change its support model to be more like Organization 1. It believes it will have the success that Organization 1 has. Organization 2 wants the positive press that having a US-based support unit brings and the leadership believes the smaller support-to-customer ratio will build better relationships with customers and improve customer satisfaction.

So Organization 2 spends a lot of resources to change its support model and move its operations back to the United States. It also hires more IT support staff to meet the example of Organization 1. The changes take 18 months to complete.

And Organization 2 sees gains from the change and is happy with it.

At about the same time, Organization 1 announces that it has moved its IT support function overseas. The leadership of Organization 1 had looked carefully at its closest competitor (Organization 2) and decided it wanted the economy of scale that the other company had. By supporting more customers with fewer workers and moving support services overseas, Organization 1 expected to see cost savings that it could return to its customers. It hoped this would generate higher levels of customer satisfaction. It also hoped more customers would try its services since they would be able to offer a more competitive price (like Organization 2—before it changed its model).

Organization 1 is also happy with the change.

Far-fetched? Not really. Sports teams do it, companies do it, institutions of higher education do it. But the ones that can weather the storms are the ones who embrace their uniqueness and believe in themselves.

Rather than look for benchmarks to determine what is good, you have to be able to determine what is good based on your organization's values, principles, and purpose. If you independently determine what good is, then you can find others who meet your criteria. This will allow you to learn from others; not copy or use their root questions and their metrics. But it will allow you to leverage their experiences.

To be truly successful, you have to define success for yourself. You have to embrace your uniqueness.

Recap

It's OK to be unique. While it would be nice if we could find our exact match, our organizational twin, it is unlikely to happen. And if it does, chances are our mirror image will not have all of our metrics questions answered.

We have to embrace our uniqueness and create metrics that fit our specific and special needs. We can and should leverage any existing metrics we can find—but we have to do it with the purpose of using them as a guide rather than a set of ready-made answers.

If we can focus on our unique strengths and weaknesses, we will create metrics that have meaning in our environment.

Conclusion

Organizations are complex living organisms. If your metric program is intended to help your organization improve, you will have to embrace your organization's uniqueness. It is your organization's uniqueness that will give it the opportunity to excel.

Tools and Resources

Tools can be (and often are) confused with resources. I'll use a simple delineation between the two. Tools are items that can be used to *do*—to actually design, create, analyze, and publish metrics. An example is Microsoft Excel.

On the other hand, resources are reference in nature and provide information that provides guidance or knowledge used for designing, creating, analyzing, and publishing metrics. Rather than an analysis tool (like Minitab), resources include textbooks on how to use software or perform statistical analysis, how-to videos, articles, blogs, books, and discussion groups (such as those found on networking sites like LinkedIn). There are also organizations (new and established) that you can join and participate in to learn more about metrics.

In this appendix, I'll share some of my favorite tools and some that come highly recommended by colleagues and friends. Please don't buy any of these tools on the basis of their inclusion here; instead, if something sounds good to you, research it further. Just as with metrics themselves—you'll need to marry the possibilities to your specific requirements. Based on your root questions, your environment, and the programs you develop—different tools and resources may be called for.

Tools

Some tools play multiple roles, but most specialize in a primary function and have other functions as a supplement. Most trouble-ticket tracking tools work this way. They are designed (and do a good job at) capturing and tracking trouble tickets, and may also provide basic graphing tools. They don't provide much in analysis; and provide nothing toward being a complete metric tool. But trouble-tracking tools are good at what they are supposed to do. The key is not to try to make a specific tool do more than it is designed to do.

The really good news is that a meaningful and useful metrics program doesn't require a ton of statistical analysis or complicated charting. Always keep in mind that the purpose of a metrics program is to provide insights that can support decisions, direct investigations, and expose areas of concern.

Tools simply provide different ways of looking at the information you've gathered. Depending on your root question and what you are trying to learn from your metric, you can use many different forms of analysis. The tools I cover in this appendix are the few that I find useful and simple. They are simple for me to produce/use and simple for my audience to understand. Always remember your audience when displaying your metrics. Even if you use more complex analysis to get to your answers, you may need to find ways to display them in more simplistic terms.

Microsoft Excel

I've found Excel to be much more than spreadsheet software. I guess it was originally created to assist with accounting or bookkeeping. Ages ago, I used to explain that spreadsheet programs were good for working on numbers. If you wanted to perform math on your data, spreadsheets were the way to go. Today, Microsoft Excel has grown to be much more than a glorified calculator. I use it for much of my metrics work. Like most current software applications, Excel has more capabilities than most users realize or will ever use. Besides the breadth of functionality, Excel also provides a lot of flexible power, as in macros (mini programs) and add-ins like PowerPivot. I collect, analyze, and produce graphs for most of my work in Excel. With Excel add-ins, I can also perform more complex analysis inside the spreadsheets. With Excel 2010, I can handle as many records as I need. I use Excel as the foundation for my work.

Excel has a statistical add-in that comes with the full version, but you have to "turn it on." It doesn't come with this functionality preset. Turning it on will give you some basic statistical tools like histograms and regression tests.

SigmaXL

SigmaXL is a tool that can be accessed through Excel. It creates a more intuitive set of menu items in its own tab than the statistical add-in that comes with Excel. I was especially happy to find that it had a BoxPlot tool (graph), which I was unable to find in any other add-in. I am truly impressed with the SigmaXL capabilities.

Minitab

While working on my Green Belt in Six Sigma, I fell in love with SigmaXL. Before the honeymoon was over, my instructors told me about Minitab. They described it as better, smarter, easier to use, and more comprehensive than SigmaXL. The biggest problem with statistics is they're just too hard to deal with, especially for the benefits gained. SigmaXL makes it worth the effort; and *if* Minitab is better (I haven't used it yet), I want a copy.

Visualization Tools

Visualization tools are primarily (if not solely) designed to provide access to your data—in the form of dashboards, scorecards, or other visualizations. These can be used for metrics per my definition.

Theoris Vision Software

Theoris Vision Software provides a dashboard and reporting solution that includes charts, graphs, scorecards, maps, and ad-hoc reports. Everything is driven from the dashboards. I like that I can create my own visual and reporting content pretty easily. From what I've seen, the real power of this application lies in the unique ability it has to map to various data sources and files, instead of the traditional approach of pulling everything together into a spreadsheet or database.

Vision is not a metric design tool per se, but it is a powerful tool for visualizing your measures. It also allows others (stakeholders) to access your metrics on their own. I especially like the ability to set up hierarchies in the data, which in turn allows viewers to drill down into their data further. This capability is further expanded to allow the creation of ad-hoc reports at different levels of information. This can be a bad thing—depending on the level of maturity of your audience—but for the most part, it's pretty slick. Overall, this is really an impressive tool for displaying metrics and starting those critical conversations. Currently, Vision is mostly focused on the health in-dustry, but the competition had better watch out as Vision branches into other industries. A really nice tool which I've added to my wish list.

iDashboards

iDashboards is exactly what you'd imagine by its name: an excellent tool for creating and displaying dashboards—or compilations of Key Process Indica-tors (what I'd call measures). With iDashboards, you could use your meas-ures to create a view of your metric for a given question.

I like both Vision and iDashboards for this purpose. The question for me then becomes cost and ease of use. If you are thinking of obtaining a tool for displaying your data in this manner, I'd encourage you to spend time demo-ing both products. This one is also on my wish list—and I'll be happy with either as a surprise for Christmas.

Tableau

Tableau is not an add-in, but it works well with Excel. You can easily import data into Tableau from Excel or other common tools. Tableau's power is in the ability to quickly and easily try different graphical representations (visu-alizations) of your data. I know some people who love it and use it before they do any thorough analysis. I haven't found it works for me, but I do see the potential value (I have a copy, but haven't been able to put it to a lot of use).

Survey Tools

The following three survey tools each offer different benefits. In order, the first provides some useful analysis of what's important to your customers as well as how well you provide those services. The second is a third-party service (not really a tool in the true sense) and makes the survey work easy. The last is a favorite of mine as it allows you to create what you need, cus-tomizing your surveys to fit your requirements (and the cost is attractive).

TechQual+

TechQual+ (www.techqual.org) is a good example of a survey tool; it was created by my friend Timothy Chester, the CIO at the University of Georgia.

Most of the questions are preset in TechQual+, causing some limitations; but these are also its strengths. Since the questions are standardized, you can compare your results to others who chose to use this tool. There are other third-party survey organizations (HDI, for example), but a large benefit of TechQual+ is that it is free.

HDI

The HDI Customer Satisfaction Index is a survey service. HDI does everything for you: they survey your customers, tabulate your results, and provide you with reports in multiple formats. They also provide comparisons to others (for example, by industry or all other customers). HDI is only one example; there are other third-party survey services that offer this service. I suggest you price shop *and* look for ones that already have a large customer base in *your* industry. Customer satisfaction surveying is an interesting business niche.

SurveyMonkey

I confess—I like SurveyMonkey; partly because it's free (if you use it sparingly; though, if you want to use it on a larger scale, the costs are very reasonable), but mostly because of its simplicity. With SurveyMonkey, you build the survey; then you provide a link to the survey to your customers. SurveyMonkey also offers simple analysis tools, but I usually download the results into Excel and do my own analysis.

IT Solutions/Business Intelligence Tools

Many "IT solution" companies now include dashboards and scorecards in their service packages. This is a clear indicator of the need for metrics and the power of software to help deliver them. IT solutions packages may include the metrics tools as an add-in to the suite of services—pulling the data byproducts from key offerings (process control, management, architectural design, etc.).

The major difference I've found between these tools and the stand-alone tools is in the scope. If you don't need (or can't afford) a large-scale solution set, you can get a lot out of the tools specifically designed for metrics. If you're looking at purchasing (or already own) a large-scale IT solution, you may want to look into its capabilities to also provide metrics assistance.

ASE 10

An example of a data-centric toolset for organizational improvement using scorecards, dashboards, and measurements is ASE 10, from ActiveStrategy (activestrategy.com). It's a bit complex, but offers pricing based on company size. ASE 10 is heavily based on predefined methodologies, but seems to have enough flexibility to work with the metrics that you design. I haven't used this tool, but it has been recommended by a colleague whose opinion I trust.

The issue for most larger-scale tools is that they may offer too much. Ignoring the cost, these tools offer more capability than most people need—especially if you are just starting on your metrics journey.

Other Tools

Other tools may not fit the definition of a metric tool at all, but be very helpful to your metric efforts. The two examples I offer are at different ends of a scope/size spectrum. QPR is a larger scale process improvement tool which has useful applications to a metrics effort. Powerpivot is a tool which works with (and "in") Excel.

QPR

QPR (QPR.com) is an example of a business-driven solution. Its scope is so large that I can't tell you about it all. QPR is used mostly by companies outside of the United States; but I believe it will make a big splash on our shores soon. Rather than a simple, lower cost, limited-use tool, QPR's solution is a mid-range, enterprise-level solution.

QPR's web-based solutions can be selected based upon your need. If you need to build an understanding of your processes, one of its tools, "Process Analyzer," assists in developing business process diagrams using a logging file input structure. If you need to share your database of business processes, "ProcessDesigner" provides that solution. Most metric-centered reporting requirements can be satisfied with the "Metrics" solution. If you need to integrate business process reporting and metrics, a combination of these solutions provide you with an integrated management reporting system.

The cost will reflect its expansive power. I include it as an example of a high-end tool, and because it does so much more (process analysis, process management, etc.) than metrics, the higher costs are no surprise. I especially like that such a nice enterprise-level solution includes specific tools for metrics.

PowerPivot

Unlike most of the tools, PowerPivot isn't an analytical tool at all. It allows you to use Excel to be more like its brother, Microsoft Access—a database tool. Although most metrics are number-based efforts, there are many times when it would be useful to have a relational view of the data. A relational database would be the perfect tool *if* it had the ability to do mathematical and statistical analysis on the data. PowerPivot promises to give you the best of both worlds—a number-based program you can treat as a relational database. I've been working with its first release and I am looking forward to the release of the improved 2.0 version.

Resources

Whereas I told you to research before you buy any tools (tools are high-cost compared to a book or a membership in an organization), in this section, I recommend you try the resource. If you don't want to buy the book, check it out from your local library. For the most part, to determine the usefulness of a resource, you'll need to have complete access. Most of the resources I offer are either free or low-cost (less than $50).

When you search for resources, depending on your industry, you will find many to choose from. In the information technology arena, I've been hearing a lot about the COBIT framework, ISO/IEC 20000 (international standard for IT service management), and the Information Technology Infrastructure Library (ITIL).

Rather than provide you a list of web sites, I will share some ways to perform a search. Search engines offer results in different formats: video, web, images, blogs, shopping, etc. Most useful will be web, video, and blogs. The web classification is where you'll find everything from articles in e-zines, books, and encyclopedic definitions, to how-to guides for developing metrics.

If you search "metrics" you will find too many results on the metric system of measurement. You'll want to narrow your search. "Performance Metrics" will bring you a lot closer to what you're looking for. Even then, you may want to narrow your search depending on your particular needs and industry. For example, you can search on "IT metrics" or "IT performance metrics" if you are in the information technology arena. You can also search on "business intelligence" (the newest catch phrase for data-based decision making) or "IT solutions."

Depending on your industry, you may find a healthy store of standards, benchmarks, and predefined data, measures, and information for your metrics. The financial industry is one example of a robust metric environment. Another is the manufacturing industry. If you are reading this book, you are not likely in an industry that has an established metrics framework. Chances are you are in need of meaningful metrics for your organization and your processes. Even so, you can learn from other industries and their metrics. You may be able to leverage some existing works for your own metrics efforts.

A simple search via your favorite web-based search engine returns a long list of measurement, statistical analysis, and metrics tools. I won't provide you with a list that you can visit on your own. Instead I offer insights and a short list of resources and references.

While I built the list from tools and references that I've personally used, I highly recommend that you do what I've preached from the beginning——investigate for yourself. I have found some books to be "on target" and others to have views that I would argue strongly against. Every book, blog, and article I've read has been useful in developing my overall view and concepts about metrics. Even the ones I've found outlandishly off-target have proven to be beneficial to the overall concept I offer in this book.

Don't discard the entire work because you find some portions to be "wrong," in your viewpoint. You can learn much from those who disagree with you. One of my colleagues who helped in the writing of this book disagreed with me more often than we agreed; it was one of the reasons that I asked him to be the technical reviewer for the book. I trusted him to provide an honest view, even if it were a totally dissenting one. While I believe in the concepts and tools I've presented, I'm open to other opinions. I welcome them as they should help to make my understanding of how to make metrics work better.

I want you to look at the resources and references listed here, and any others you investigate later, in the same way. There are no silver bullets, there is no holy grail. There is no one right way to do organizational development or process improvement. There is no one way to do metrics. Stay open to new ideas and different opinions. And always make sure what you use works for you. Don't use it because I or anyone else say to, use it because you've tried it and it works for you.

So, let's look at some of the resources and references I've found useful in my metric journey.

Web Sites

The following are web sites that I've found useful.

XPC Palladium Group

XPC (http://community.thepalladiumgroup.com) is primarily a community for discussing Balanced Scorecard methods, but I have found it a good place to converse on metrics in general. Most of the participants on the site are disciples of Kaplan and Norton and believe in using measurement in ways I disagree with. The good news is they are open to other opinions. It is a well-run web site. Just recently I have heard that they are going to charge for membership—and as you may have ascertained from my opinions on tools, I don't believe in paying for the opportunity to network. As with all of my recommendations, check it out (especially if you have to pay) before you buy.

LinkedIn

I like networking; especially networking for professionals. In addition to the LISTSERVs I participate in through different organizations, I enjoy LinkedIn (www.linkedin.com). LinkedIn groups allow for conversations and discussions on pretty much any topic you want—and you can simply create a new group/topic if it doesn't exist. I belong to more than one group concerned with metrics (Performance Measurement, IT Performance Measurement, and IT Metrics–CEITPS) and have found them to be very useful. And membership is free.

The Consortium for the Establishment of Information Technology Performance Measures (CEITPS)

CEITPS (www.ceitps.org) is a nonprofit organization that I founded for the sole purpose of developing standards for IT performance measures. It is a very young organization. All standards created by this organization will be made available free to the public via the web site. Membership has a minimal fee and the biggest benefit you get for your money is that you are given the opportunity to help in creating and voting on the standards. The membership income is used to pay for the web presence only.

smartKPIs

smartKPIs.com is a repository of **K**ey **P**rocess **I**ndicators (measures). Since it offers free access to a good portion of its KPIs, I think it is worthy of mention. I can't recommend paying for any of their offerings (only premium subscribers have access to calculation, references, and PDF export and filtering functionalities) as it goes against my beliefs toward benchmarks and canned metrics. But, if you want to see what others have come up with, the free catalog of examples is a good place to start.

I won't repeat all of the cautions I've offered in the book—but I will suggest that if you use this (or other comparable references) that you do so with a grain of salt *and* also ask around. Your industry peers should be great sources, and by asking them you'll build your relationships and your professional network.

Books

You might guess which books I'll list here; they're ones I've referenced throughout the book.

How to Measure Anything

How to Measure Anything: Finding the Value of Intangibles in Business by Douglas W. Hubbard (John Wiley & Sons, 2007). I love Hubbard's positive, can-do attitude when it comes to finding ways to measure literally anything. I especially enjoyed his work on calibrating your ability to estimate accurately. Some of it was a little too deep for me, but I found almost all of it useful and an easy read. All in all, it is a nice text on how to measure and estimate—untethered to any specific improvement methodology. I recommend this book, but suggest you may find yourself picking and choosing chapters to read or reference.

Transforming Performance Measurement

Transforming Performance Measurement: Rethinking the Way We Measure and Drive Organizational Success by Dr. Dean R. Spitzer (American Management Association, 2007) is another favorite. I found it easy to read (with minor exceptions). I consider Dean a kindred spirit. Most of my disagreements come in how to deal with the fear, uncertainty, and doubt that surround metrics. I find that we are on the same wavelength, however, when it comes to the problems and hurdles you have to overcome to make metrics work. I believe we go to the "same church, different pew." Definitely worth the read.

The Intelligent Company

The Intelligent Company by Bernard Marr (John Wiley & Sons, 2010) is yet another favorite. I came upon it well into the writing of this book and knew that I had found another member of the metrics family. As with Dr. Spitzer's book, I found a fair amount to argue against in Marr's book. But I find this book more useful than one with too much jargon or technical speak. I learn a lot (more) from viewpoints different than my own. Overall there is more that I agree with than I disagree with *and* it's an "easy" read. I recommend this book for your library.

Measuring What Matters

Measuring What Matters: Simplified Tools for Aligning Teams and Their Stakeholders, by Rod Napier & Rich McDaniel (Davies-Black Publishing, 2006). I found this book to be less a guide for developing metrics and more a manual for the American Society for Quality (ASQ). That's not a bad thing, but it wasn't as much help with developing metrics as I would have liked, especially based on the title. I like it much more as a general organizational development book than a metrics book. It's worth a perusal.

Why Organizations Struggle So Hard to Improve So Little

If you're interested in organizational development, I humbly include *Why Organizations Struggle So Hard to Improve So Little: Overcoming Organizational Immaturity*, by Michael Langthorne, Donald Padgett, and me. I've actually read it twice since it was published in 2010 by Greenwood. It is a very easy read with important insights to why you may be struggling to improve or change your organization. The chapter on metrics makes a good introduction to this book. If you're looking at implementing organizational change, I recommend you read it.

Other Books

There are books that I wouldn't recommend for the purpose of developing a metrics program, but are useful in performing analysis; and if you have room on your library shelves, it wouldn't hurt to include them. One that I like in particular is *IT Measurement: Practical Advice from the Experts* (Addison-Wesley, 2002) a compilation by the International Function Point Users Group. I have a special place in my metrics heart for this group since my first metrics mentor, Errol Shim, was a past president of the national group. The 43-chapter book was written by a variety of experts. Some definite gems can be mined here—and hopefully I've given you the tools necessary to find the gems that fit your needs.

Recap

Tools are useful for performing the work—designing, creating, analyzing, and publishing metrics. Resources are references that make doing the work easier or better. Unfortunately, tools can be expensive. The good news is that the methods I've offered for developing a metrics program don't require any particular tools. You can do quite well with whatever tools you have already available. But as you become proficient at metrics development, you may want more out of your toolset, so I offered some tools to consider or explore. Remember, it's only a starting point—find what will work best to meet your requirements and your budget.

Resources, on the other hand, should be investigated as early as possible. I'd be flattered if you only used this book: dog-eared it, highlighted the best passages, wrote in the margins, and used it to help you develop your metrics program. But, chances are you won't agree with everything I've offered. Or you may want confirmation through other works. Or you may feel that I left some gaps in your comprehension of the material. I encourage you to read other books, articles, and papers on the topic.

I have faith in what I've been teaching on metrics and I welcome arguments to the contrary. If the concepts within this book are correct, then they will stand up to thorough scrutiny. To that end, feel free to contact me and offer your opinions—be they in agreement or disagreement. Join me on LinkedIn discussion groups, send me an e-mail, or post your thoughts, questions, or arguments on my web site. The bottom line is simple: do something! Learn more, try more, do more. Share your opinions, try the suggestions I've offered, create a meaningful metric and see how it goes.

Conclusion

I consider one of my first mentors in metrics, Erroll Shim, a giant of a man. I consider him a giant in his field, function point analysis and metric analysis. He taught me a great deal and he helped set me on the path that led to the development of much of what you've read here. His expertise was very impressive—he would accurately predict the complexity of a software change and estimated correctly the effort and time required (which were normally very different than our unit had estimated).

But, the problem was that his abilities were his own. They weren't transferrable. It was borne of years of experience. I wanted to develop a simplified method to provide the types of insights he produced independently, to anyone who needed it. These insights were at once more general in nature (they deal with metrics across the business spectrum) and specific in the methodology—building from a root question, using data, measures, information, and other metrics to tell a complete story.

I want you to develop meaningful metrics. I want you to be able to do so without obtaining a certificate in statistics, buying expensive tools, or spending months in training. I hope that this book has provided what you need to be productive in the development and implementation of metrics for your organization.

Index

A

Advanced metrics
  consistency, 249
  immature organization benefits
    goals, 247
    long-term projects
      handling, 248
    measurement, 247
    organizational improvement
      tool, 246
    risky tools, 246
    root question, 248
  improvement process, 249
  measuring, resolving time, 249
  measuring,catalyst, 249
  organizational development
    efforts, 245–246
  process improvement efforts, 245
  product/service health
    efforts, 244
  program implementing, 248
  resources, 250

Answer Key, 97, 243, 244
  balanced and dashboard
    scorecard, 98
  bonus material, 113
    answers, categorization
      exercise, 116
    business viewpoint, 115
    categorizing root
      questions, 114
    performance measures, 113
  definition, 97
  fifth tier, 111–112
  first tier, 99
  four tier, 105
    future health,110–111
    information, 105
    organizational health. See
      Organizational health
    process health /efficiency. See
      Process health efficiency
    product/service
      health/effectiveness, 106
  fourth tier, 104
  measures type, 112–113
  metrics shortcut, 98
  second tier, 99
    return vs. investment, 100–101
    state of the union, 101
  third tier, 102
    company effectiveness, 104
    deliver, 103
    future health organization, 103
    human resources concern, 103
    organization views, 102
    return vs. investment, 103
    service/product, 103
    tiers, 102
  tool, 97

B

Benchmarks
  baseline establishment, 284–286
  competitor performance, 286
  competitor's availability, 287
  consortium, 290
  customer satisfaction data, 288
  goal, 289
  metrics, 284
  network availability, 287

C

Common language, 1
  clarification chain, 23
  data, 6–7, 22
  data-metric paradox, 17–18, 22
    comprehensive metric, 19
    metric design, 18, 20
    metric redesign, 19
    mid-course correction, 19
  information, 9–10
  measures, 7–8
  metrics, 11, 12, 20–21
  plain English, 1
  root questions
    analogy, 13
    collectable components, 15
    customer service desk, 15–17
    data collection, 14
    direction determination
      map, 13
    focus and direction, 14
    metric definition, 13
  Three Little Pigs, 1–6
  vocabulary, 1

D

Data collection, 42–44, 53
  automated data, 45–46
  human provision, 47–48
  rules of thumb, 44
  software and hardware, 46
  surveys, 46

Development plan, 37, 40, 75,
    181, 209
  analysis phase, 70–72
  analysis schedule, 69
  automated system, 63
  automated tools, 76
  byproducts process, 79
  collection process, 70
  collection schedule, 69
  consistency, guidance and
      direction, 66
  customers, 67
  data analysis, 77
  data collection, 63
  data owners, 183
  data storage, 78
  design and creation, 75
  documented agreements, 67
  emotional tension, 65
  fear factor, 63
  game plan, 58
  human interaction, 76
  information analysis, 184
  information request, 68
  information sharing, 67
  long-term success, 75
  metric
    customer, 183
    designing, 64
    picture, 72
  narrative description, 73–74
  non-threatening tool, 39
  personal data, 62
  personal information, 65
  process repeatability, 77
  productivity, 38
  public domain, 67
  purpose statement, 59–62, 183
  raw data accuracy, 76
  reporting schedule, 69
  root question, 62, 63
  rule of thumb, 76
  staffing, 65
  templates, 79
  timetables, 58

timing, 68, 69
version control, 79
visual depiction, 72
workload division metric, 37–38
zero defects, 77

E

Effectiveness
answer key, 119, 120, 134
customers viewpoint, 129, 131
efficiency measures, 131
efficiency metrics, 131
employee view, 250
future health, 120–122
    company financial health, 260
    maturity, 260
    priority setting
        measurement, 262
    project and program
        execution, 261
    project metrics, measures, 261
    quadrant 4, answer key, 260
    strategic planning and goal,
        261–262
health process
    cost measure, 266
    lean Six Sigma, 266
    measures, 263, 267
    performance measures, 265
    quadrant 2, answer key, 263
    quality measures, 267
    resource allocation, 267
    sports, business example, 264
    sports–corporate team
        comparisons, 264
organization health, 122–124, 251
    data, 254
    employee satisfaction, 255
    Fortune 500, 251, 252
    goal, 254
    measurement, 257–259
    organizational
        improvement, 253
    quadrant 3, answer key, 251
    ranking list, top companies, 252

reward and recognition, 254,
    256–257
tool, 253
training, 255
work environment, 255process
    health, 125–126
product/service health, 126
    airbags, quality-check, 129
    cars airbags, quality-check, 129
    customers identity, 127, 128
    habitat for humanity, 129
    measures, 127, 250
    personal level customer, 128
    quadrant 1, answer key, 127real
        life example, 131–132
return *vs.* investment, 124, 134
state of the union, 134
tiers and quadrants, 134
trust culture, 133

M

Metrics, 11, 12, 155, 293
    components, 20–21
    designing, 25, 56
    data, 50–51
    data collection. *See* Data
        collection
    information decision, 49
    information, measures and
        data identification, 40–42
    measures, 50
    metrics development. *See*
        Metrics development
    root question. *See* Root
        question
    spaghetti code, 26
    web/teleconferencing value, 49
discovering expectations
    benefits, 167
    customers expectations, 165
    frequency chart, 168, 169
    histogram, 168
    performance norm, 167
    sample data, 165
    statistical analysis, 168
    two-year sample, 166

Metrics (*continued*)
  expectations, 159
    adding expectations, 162
    customer issue, 161
    customers expectations, 162
    customers point of view,
      159–160
    efficiency measures, 164
    help-desk cases, 161
    meeting expectations, 162
    neutrally colored
      expectations, 164
    nuance differentiating
      targets, 163
    service center, 160
    service/product health metrics
      program, 163
    technician conversation, 160
  goal measures, 157
  incentive programs, 159
  indicators/facts, 294–297
  stretch goals, 156
  targets and thresholds, 158–159
  tool, 293
  unintended consequence, 303
    fear and abuse, 304
    mistrust, 305
    misuse and abuse, anger, 305
    positive/negative affect, 305
    reluctance to participate, 305
    validity doubt, 304
    what to do/what will be
      done, 304

Misused metrics, 297
  bad, 301–303
  CEO meet, 297
  customer satisfaction metric, 299
  good, 300–301
  rating, 297
  scorecard, 299
  survey response, 297–298
  survey results, 298
  ugly, 303

O

Organizational health
  employee satisfaction, 109
  measures, 109
  quadrant 3, 108
  reward and recognition, 110
  skills and training, 109
  work environment, 109
  workers viewpoint, 108

Organizational uniqueness, 319
  compelling, life-changing, positive
    vision, 328
  development plans, metrics, 322
  exact processes and
    procedures, 322
  one-size-fits-all metrics, 321–322
  organizations root questions, 321
  qualities, 328
  questionaries, 323–324
  research and metrics
    gathering, 329
  research information, 321
  resources, 329
  steps,embrace
    bleak picture, 327
    deal with failure, 325
    deal with success, 326–327
    dont be caught, 325
    research, 325
  strengths, 327–328
  tool,one-size-fits-all, 320

P

Process health efficiency, 104
  components, 107
  cost, 107
  organizations processes and
    procedures, 108
  quadrant 2, 106
  quality, 108
  time, 107

Product/service health–focused
  metrics program, 280

R

Reichheld method, 228

Reichheld's "Promoter to Detractor" ratio, 197

Report card, 239

   abandoned call, 184–187, 208

   accuracy

      expectations, 220

      permutations, 220

      rework percentage, 218, 219

      service desk, 218

   anomalies, 181

   availability

      abandoned rate, 215

      anomalies, 213, 214

      charts, 215

      customer expectations, 214

      expectations, 212

      grade, 213

      grades, 213

      translation Grid, 215

   calendaring, 178

   core service template, 176–178

   customer, 175

   customer expectations, 208–209

   customer patterns of usage, 181

   customer satisfaction, 180, 205, 206

      annual customer satisfaction survey, 201

      average grade, 227–228

      benchmarks, 227

      classic customer satisfaction survey, 196

      detractors and promoters, 228, 229

      development Plan collection and analysis, 201

      expectation, 207

      expectations, 231

      graduating class, 227

      leadership, 227

      Likert Scale, 198

      monopoly, 227

      neutral scores, 200

      organization reputation damage, 202

      percentage, 200, 230

      potential customer base, 202

      rating score, 199

      Reichheld method, 228

      Reichheld's "Promoter to Detractor" ratio, 197–198

      service desk, 229

      TechQual+ Project, 203–205

      third-party agency, 196

      third-party vendor, 230

      trouble-resolution surveys, 201

   data owners, 172

   delivery measures, 175

   e-mail, 178

   final roll up grade, 238

   first grade roll-up, 235–236

   grade, 173–174, 234–235

   Internet and telephones, usage frequency measurement, 178

   management chain, 211

   metric program, 181

   metrics development plan. See Metrics development plan

   organization's health, 172

   overall rolled up grades, 238

   rework, 191–193

   satisfaction ratings, 236

   scorecard methodology, 172

   second and third level grade roll up, 237

   service catalog, 175

   service desk, 178

      development plan collection and analysis, 182

      internal service provider, 180

      manager's attitude, 179

      measures, 179

      trouble call tracking system, 179

   service providers assessment, 205

   SLA, 206

   speed, 216–218

      automated call system, 187

      customers perception, 187

      data accuracy, 187

      scheduled resolution time, 188

Report card (*continued*)
   speed (*continued*)
      stop clock switch, 188
      Time to Resolve, 189
      Time to Respond, 190
      trouble call tracking
         system, 187
   subject area category, 239
   third-party survey company, 181
   translation grid, 233–235
   trouble call tracking system, 176
   usage
      advantage, 194
      annual customer satisfaction
         survey, 194
      assistance, first choice, 195
      automated call system, 196
      customer base, 226
      definition, 221
      development plan collection
         and analysis, 195
      expectations, 221, 222, 225
      first time callers cumulative
         over time, 221, 222
      first time callers three-month
         running total, 224
      potential customer base, 193
      service desk, 225, 226
      unique customers, 193, 194
   weights and measures, 231–233
Research trap, 309
   abandoned calls, 314
   benefits and problems, 312
   businesses tool, 310
   commonalities, 309
   customer satisfaction measures, 314
   data comparison, 314
   data gathering, 311
   disguise, 311–312
   halo effect, 310
   metrics, 310
   organizational development,
      goals, 313
   precautions, 315
   servers availability, 314
   types, 309

Root question, 33, 53
   data collection and measures, 26
   decent metric, 26
   documented strategic plan, 29
   Emerald City Services, 27
   Five Whys tool, 27
   full-blown metric, 29
   itinerary runs, 30–32
   metrics design, 33–34
   post-it pads, 30
   strategic plans, 28
   testing, 35–36
   trouble call system, 28

S

Scorecard methodology, 172
Service catalog creation
   catalog, 273
   customer feedback, 279, 280
   customer support, 271
   departmental silos, 272
   fear, uncertainty, and doubt
      factor, 272
   mission statement, 273
   process health service catalog
      efficiency, 277, 278
      key/core services, 276–277
      organizational health
         quadrant, 279
      root question, 277
      strategic plan, 278
   process improvement
      methodologies, 279
   process maps, 279, 280
   product/service health–focused
      metrics program, 280
   service type/categories
      identification, 274
   service/product health metrics, 271
      costs, 276
      customer base
         identification, 275
      predefined categories, 274
      service environment, 275

service level agreement,
275–276
service provider
identification, 274
strategic plans, 279, 280
support functions, 271
training plans, 279, 280
Service level agreements (SLA), 206
Service/product health metrics, 271
Spaghetti code, 26
Standards
consortium, 290
customer satisfaction data, 288
data warehouse, 288
goal, 289
interoperability, 289
performance measures, 288

T

Triangulation
collection method and sources,
143
accuracy, 146
availability, 145
create effective metrics, 144

customer satisfaction,
143–145
delivery, 143
speed, 146
usage, 143
conflict, 151
high *vs.* low result, 148
interpretation, 149–150
debated and challenge, 140
demography, 147, 148
historical perspective, 139–140
measures, 140
answer key, 140, 141
customer feedback, 142
customer satisfaction
surveys, 142
customers viewpoint, 142
metrics, 141
product/service health
quadrant, 141
product/service health
quadrant, 152
trouble-tracking and reporting
tools, 142
perspectives, 146, 147
practical application, 140
types, 139

CPSIA information can be obtained at www.ICGtesting.com
Printed in the USA
LVOW071043111211

258872LV00001B/2/P